The Italians before Italy: Conflict and Competition in the Mediterranean

Part I

Professor Kenneth R. Bartlett

THE TEACHING COMPANY ®

PUBLISHED BY:

THE TEACHING COMPANY
4151 Lafayette Center Drive, Suite 100
Chantilly, Virginia 20151-1232
1-800-TEACH-12
Fax—703-378-3819
www.teach12.com

ISBN 978-1-59803-349-6

Kenneth R. Bartlett, Ph.D.
Professor of History and Renaissance Studies, University of Toronto

Kenneth Bartlett, Professor of History and Renaissance Studies at the University of Toronto, received his Ph.D. from the University of Toronto in 1978. He served as editor of the journal *Renaissance and Reformation/Renaissance et Réforme* and president of the Canadian Society for Renaissance Studies. He was founding director of the University of Toronto Art Centre and first Director of the Office of Teaching Advancement.

Much of Dr. Bartlett's career has been devoted to bringing Italian Renaissance culture into the undergraduate and graduate classroom. He has taught regularly in the University of Toronto Program in Siena, Italy, as well as in the Oxford Program. In 2002, he was appointed the first director of the Office of Teaching Advancement for the University of Toronto, and he has been the recipient of numerous teaching awards, most notably, the 3M Teaching Fellowship, awarded by the Canadian Society for Teaching and Learning in Higher Education, and the inaugural President's Teaching Award for the University of Toronto. In 2007, Dr. Bartlett was one of the 10 finalists in TVOntario's Best Lecturer competition, which pits students' favorite instructors against one another in a battle of charisma, clarity, passion, and conviction; that same year he was recognized by an inaugural Leadership in Faculty Teaching award by the government of Ontario.

Professor Bartlett is the author of *The English in Italy, 1525–1558: A Study in Culture and Politics* (1991), *The Civilization of the Italian Renaissance* (1992), and *Humanism and the Northern Renaissance* (with M. McGlynn, 2000); co-editor or translator of four other books; and author of more than 35 articles and chapters on Renaissance history and culture. In 2003, he was co-curator of the exhibition *Gods, Saints and Heroes: Italian Renaissance Maiolica from the Metropolitan Museum of Art* at the Gardiner Museum of Ceramic Art. In addition, Dr. Bartlett has been the academic consultant on the Illuminated Filmworks videos about the Vatican Library, *The Halls of Virtuous Learning*, *The Galleries of Sixtus V*, and *Pages of Light*, as well as for the international exhibitions *Raphael and His Circle: Drawings from the Royal Collection at Windsor* and *Angels From the Vatican* at the Art Gallery of Ontario.

Professor Bartlett lives in Toronto, Ontario, with his wife, Gillian.

Table of Contents
The Italians before Italy:
Conflict and Competition in the Mediterranean
Part I

The Italians before Italy:
Conflict and Competition in the Mediterranean

Scope:

This course discusses the political, economic, and social worlds of the Italian city-states in the period from the Middle Ages to the loss of their autonomy in the later 16th century. The course includes some references to the status of certain Italian cities in antiquity and brief mention of their subsequent development from 1559 until the *Risorgimento*, the movement of Italian national unification in the 19th century. The focus is on the development of the institutions and structures that gave each independent state its essential character. Thus, Florence will be discussed in the context of the rise of the bourgeois republic and its concomitant mercantile economy, until the hegemony of the Medici family gradually transformed the commune into a monarchy in the 16th century. Siena, that other great Tuscan republic, which once rivaled Florence, will be shown to have declined over this period as a consequence of factional and class division, until it was incorporated into the Medici duchy of Florence in 1557.

Venice will be investigated not only as a state that managed to sustain republican patrician rule until its extinction at the end of the 18th century but also as a city-state that built, over time, a great empire on Italian soil and in the Mediterranean. Genoa and Pisa were also great mercantile republics but wracked by internal dissention and external threats. These cities once rivaled Venice for control of the luxury trade routes to the East and established maritime empires of their own until they were eclipsed by the Venetians. The complex history of Rome will emerge as the seat of an imperial papacy, building on ancient memories and responding to contemporary challenges, such as the Reformation, to create a state whose power rested more on confessional allegiance and artistic grandeur than on military force. Milan, despite suffering from many incompetent rulers, had the resources to create the most powerful state in the north, one that came close to uniting the peninsula while creating a vibrant courtly culture. The principalities of Mantua, Urbino, and Ferrara reflect simultaneously the exquisite culture and the brutal military power of their rulers, many of whom financed their states by serving as *condottieri*, that is, mercenary captains. Naples, that feudal kingdom to the south of the Italian peninsula, must be seen as a world apart from the republics and petty principalities to the north.

The introductory lectures in the course bring together the common threads of a history shared by the independent states of Italy. Various attempts were conceived to unite the peninsula, beginning with Dante's hope that the Holy Roman Emperor would impose his rule and reduce the power of the pope. This Ghibelline vision remained strong, despite the continued authority of Rome and the papacy on the peninsula to sustain the Guelf cause. These almost ideological calls for unity accompanied the real ambitions of such princes as Giangaleazzo Visconti of Milan to assemble the vast wealth and military power of his state to build a single kingdom from the mosaic of independent states. Equally, the Holy See attempted to use the authority of the Church to cement the allegiance of the entire Italian nation, both through faith and through force of arms. Cesare Borgia's campaigns on behalf of his father, Pope Alexander VI, came close to success at the turn of the 16th century; and Pope Julius II's campaigns restored papal rule in the states of the Church after the disintegration of Borgia power.

Finally, this course argues that the richness of the culture of Italy resulted from its lack of political unity. The various constitutional, cultural, and economic experiments among the patchwork of states, together with their competition with one another and their jealousy and ambition, all made such an efflorescence of culture possible.

Lecture One
Italy—A Geographical Expression

Scope:

Italy as an idea has ancient origins, but Italy was not in reality a united country until 1860. To discuss Renaissance Italy, then, is to discuss a collection of independent states, each with its own constitutional structure, economy, and ambitions. We start this course with a discussion of the general circumstances of the peninsula before turning to the Crusades and analyzing how this European adventure added enormously to the wealth and power of the peninsula, particularly in the maritime republics, such as Venice, Genoa, and Pisa. Competition in the Mediterranean over trade resulted in constant warfare amongst these states, only to be superseded by the desperate struggle of Christians against the Turks. Rome, as the capital of Christendom, was the hinge on which Italian affairs turned in our period. To the south, the feudal dynastic monarchy of Naples was a fief of the Church, ruled by foreign dynasties and prey to the factionalism of its magnate families. Dynastic difficulties also threatened the signorial regimes of Milan, Mantua, and Ferrara, as well tiny Urbino. Equally volatile, but for different reasons, were the independent republics in Tuscany. Eventually, that territory would be stabilized and united through the imperial ambitions of the Medici of Florence. Altogether, the mosaic of the peninsula and the tense competition among its states resulted in the Renaissance explosion of imagination and creativity, and even today continues to provide rich and diverse local cultures in modern, united Italy.

Outline

I. Before the Italian city-states were united under Victor Emmanuel II of the House of Savoy in 1861, Italy was, as Prince Clemens von Metternich said to Lord Palmerston, "merely a geographical expression."

    A. After the collapse of the Roman Empire in 476, Italy was a fragmented collection of independent states.

B. Some of these states can be grouped in clusters, such as the maritime republics of Venice, Genoa, and Pisa. These states reaped economic advantage from the Crusades and from the geographical position of the Italian Peninsula as the natural point of contact between East and West.

C. There were other Italian states, as well.

1. Rome was the center of Christendom, defined by both its imperial memory and its Christian present.

2. Naples was a great feudal kingdom. Because of the chaos surrounding its various dynasties, almost all of which were foreign, it became the battleground of Italy and the point of entry for invaders who would bring about the end of Italian independence.

3. The principalities of north-central Italy were characterized by the dynasties that ruled them. The rule of these families involved not just the extension of political and military might but also the creation of culture as an element of policy.

4. The republics of Siena and Florence were the petri dishes of politics. Here, new forms of social, political, and economic organization could be tested, but the independence of these states would be severely compromised by events of the 16th century.

D. When Charles VIII of France crossed the Alps in 1494 to claim the kingdom of Naples, the result would be not only the loss of Italian liberty, but the transformation of Italy into the battleground of Europe, where the struggle between the French royal House of Valois and the imperial/Spanish House of Habsburg would ultimately be determined.

E. The Treaty of Cateau-Cambrésis in 1559, to a large extent, ended this struggle by establishing spheres of influence in the continent, but it also recognized the loss of Italian freedom, turning the peninsula over to the House of Habsburg, which would rule much of it until the period of Italian unification in the 19th century.

F. This course focuses on the years before the middle of the 16th century, when the Italians were managing their own affairs to a large degree, creating their own culture, and defining what it was to be not just Italian but Genoese, Florentine, Roman, or Neapolitan.

G. The *Risorgimento*, the movement that ultimately brought the peninsula together under the rule of the House of Savoy and King Victor Emmanuel II, saw Italy not only as a place of history but as a nation of people who spoke the same language, shared elements of the same culture, and shared the same religion. We will look at the complexities of the peninsula before that time, beginning in the Middle Ages.

II. The celebrated phrase "It's not impossible to rule the Italians, merely pointless," has been attributed both to Giovanni Giolitti (the long-serving prime minister of Italy in the late 19th and early 20th centuries) and to Benito Mussolini. It's a commonly held belief, in fact, that the Italian Peninsula is particularly intractable to centralized control and government.

A. There seem to be forces at work that deflect the desire to turn the peninsula into a single entity. It is, in fact, a democratic challenge to rule Italy, as the number of Italian governments that emerged since World War II can attest.

B. But Italy's long, complex history of opposition can help us understand how this curious circumstance was brought about. The particularism, the geographical separation, the sense of localism versus a sense of national patriotism—all of these things are the result of history.

C. We should also remember that for the 400 years before unification, Italy's history was a tale of foreign oppression. During this period, to pay one's taxes willingly, to cooperate with the government, or to recognize the ruler as legitimate was a form of collaboration.

D. These deep-seated attitudes toward government were very much a part of the Italian experience and Italian history. Such attitudes were defined by social and economic issues in the various regions of the country, as well as by larger issues: interdependence versus independence of Italian states, the sense of competition versus cooperation, the union of self-identification as an Italian versus the fragmentation of identification as a Genoese, a Florentine, a Venetian, or a Neapolitan.

III. The fragmentation of the Italian Peninsula began even during the Roman Empire.

    A. In fact, the idea of Italy being united under Rome is something of a myth. The Romans had a veneer of unity that covered a great deal of fragmented local allegiances, traditions, and cultures that continued even during the most powerful years of the empire.

    B. Rome did provide some elements of unity that were particularly significant, such as a single law, a single coinage, and the vehicle for contact and communication through roads and harbors.

    C. Other elements, however, were always on the periphery. Sicily, for example, the breadbasket of the Roman Empire, maintained the memory of the Greeks that had settled that island during the period of colonization in the ancient world. Such elements contributed to the explosion of culture and imagination seen among the Italian people.

IV. As we look at the political, social, and economic development of the cities in Italy and the states they represented, the element of culture is always present, and indeed, we still see this element today.

    A. One of the most exciting and rewarding experiences of a tour of the peninsula is the observation of how the world changes by traveling just a few kilometers down the road. Visitors note the difference in wine and cheese, language, politics, architecture, and fashion from one city to the next. The identification between people and place in Italy is profound and part of the national collective unconscious.

    B. The Mediterranean is, in fact, the place that defined European culture and politics for a long period of recorded history. The Mediterranean is the *Media Terra*, the "center of the Earth," where culture and civilization developed.

        1. During the period of Italian fragmentation, the Mediterranean became a source of threat. This was the time when the Turks, representing Islam, and the Christians, representing the Latin West, fought for supremacy of that inland sea.

2. This wasn't only a battle of religions but also a struggle for the economic authority that came with controlling the sea routes between East and West. It came about as a result of the expansion of Islam into the Mediterranean and into Europe itself.

C. The Italian Peninsula grew rich because of its geographical position and its ability to control the luxury trade routes that moved from the East to the West. The peninsula also found itself the vanguard of Latin Europe once the challenge of the Turks was made visible, and up until the 1560s, that challenge seemed to be insurmountable.

V. The issue of sovereignty and power has also loomed large in the history of Italy.

A. With the collapse of the Roman Empire in 476 and the fragmentation of imperial authority, who would control the destinies of the people who had lived under Roman rule? Occasionally, individuals simply assumed power on their own, enforcing obedience and providing some measure of protection and administration. Thus, local power based on the exercise of force became extremely important.

B. Ultimately, two sovereign powers were recognized on the peninsula, one that resulted from the religious circumstances of the empire and one from the political memory of imperial authority.

1. The Romans had imposed a single rule and a religion over most of the known world. This religion was closely identified with the cult of the empire and the emperor. Thus, the combination of paganism and political power was part of the Roman mentality and was built into the structure of their rule.

2. In 313, however, the emperor Constantine the Great, with the Edict of Milan, adopted Christianity as the official religion of the empire, and Christianity played a completely different role.

3. The emperor now represented secular power, and the bishop of Rome—the pope—represented ecclesiastical power, although both claimed to be acting for God. The result was two sources of authority and an issue that would divide all of Italy.

4. The supporters of the papacy and ecclesiastical sovereignty would be known as Guelfs. The supporters of imperial sovereignty were Ghibellines. This division between Guelf and Ghibelline would become one of the dynamics that helped characterize the Italian state system itself.

5. The idea of separation between Guelf and Ghibelline was not merely abstract; it was also a reflection of differences of social class, geography, and circumstance.

VI. The role of words in Italian culture has always been fundamental.

A. We associate with Dante (d. 1321) the creation of a single language that would glue the peninsula together. Despite his own objections, the Tuscan dialect used by Dante became the literary language of Italy. Further, we associate the creation of an Italian people with the Three Crowns of literature: Dante, Petrarch (d. 1374), and Giovanni Boccaccio (d. 1375).

B. We find other literary references pervading the culture of Italy. The idea of *gattopardismo*, for example, is a literary allusion, a reference to a novel written by Prince Giuseppe Tommasi di Lampedusa in the 1950s called *Il Gattopardo*, or *The Leopard*.

1. The character Don Fabrizio remarks that for everything to remain the same, everything will have to change.

2. Of course, this comment seems to reflect the nature of Italian politics since World War II, which was, until recently, characterized by revolving-door administrations but consisting of the same politicians.

3. The situation was something like a game of musical chairs on the political stage. The theater of democratic action seemed to be at work, but the reality was that a relatively small number of people exercised power for their own political and personal advantage.

C. Italy, then, is the distillation of all these elements. It is the result of imaginative myth-making, the definition of a world that exists perfectly in art or literature, or architecture, or even political theory, when in fact, other things going on beneath the level of mythology are much more closely related to the reality of political action.

VII. As we will see, Italy must be understood locally in order to be understood generally. We will learn how Italy functions as a unity by seeing how its parts operated together and interrelated with one another. To begin, we must start with the collapse of the Roman Empire and the rise of the city-states.

Essential Reading:

J. Larner, *Italy in the Age of Dante and Petrarch, 1216–1380.*

Supplementary Reading:

L. Martines, *Power and Imagination: City-States in Renaissance Italy.*

Questions to Consider:

1. Are the factors discussed to explain the diversity of Italian political and cultural life applicable to other places at other times?

2. Consider what constitutes the local culture and the political and social traditions of the region in which you live. How do these differ from other parts of your country and why?

Lecture One—Transcript
Italy—A Geographical Expression

Hello, my name is Ken Bartlett, and I'm a Professor of History and Renaissance Studies at Victoria College in the University of Toronto. This course is on the states of Italy, the states of Italy before the unification of the kingdom in 1861, the states of Italy really between that period, between the collapse of the Roman Empire in the 5th century and the loss of Italian independence in the middle of the 16th century. But there will be other elements as well that will introduce us to the idea of Italy and why the states of the Peninsula are so varied in character, say something about their history and their culture, and bring these together so that we can have a view of the Italian mosaic and understand why the Italy we see today is as complex a place as it is.

Before the Italian city-states were united under Victor Emmanuel II of the House of Savoy in 1861, Italy was, as Prince Clemens von Metternich said to Lord Palmerston, "merely a geographical expression." With the collapse of the Roman Empire in 476, with the deposition of the last Roman-born emperor, Italy was really just a memory. It was an expression; it was a collection of memories, of myths, of historical vignettes that tried to put a kind of union, or glue together a group of independent states that had grown out of a complex and chaotic situation that resulted from the disintegration of the Roman imperial system. The reality of Italy, then, was a fragmented place. Italy was a mosaic; it was a collection of independent states that resulted from the events of history.

Some of these states can be grouped in clusters. For example, there were the maritime states of Venice, Genoa, and Pisa—states that reaped huge economic advantage from the adventures of the Crusade and from the geographical position of the Italian Peninsula itself, sticking as it did into the Mediterranean and being the natural place of contact, of intermediacy, between East and West; the East where commerce continued and where urban life thrived, and the West, where—as a result of the collapse of that Roman imperial system—urban life declined and commerce became much more local.

There were other states as well, with different characters. Rome, the center of Christendom, was defined by both its imperial memory and also its Christian present. The anomalous kingdom of Naples to the south of Rome—Naples was a great feudal kingdom, almost in a northern European model. And because of the chaos surrounding its various dynasties, almost all of which were foreign, it became the battleground of Italy, and ultimately the Trojan horse through which the invaders would enter and bring about the end of Italian independence. There were the principalities of north-central Italy that were characterized by the dynasties that ruled them; the personalities of the various *condottiere* princes and the families that saw their rule as not just the extension of political and military might, but also the creation of culture as an element of policy; the commission of art, and music, and architecture that would ensure these petty despotisms would survive in the collective unconscious of the Italian, and indeed European, people to provide one of the great monuments of Western culture.

There were the republics—like Siena, and particularly Florence. These were the petri dishes of politics. These were the experimental areas in which new forms of social, political, and economic organization could be tried because of the ability of the government to be changed, of social mobility, of the introduction of new men with new ideas into an environment that was prepared to receive them. The independence of these various states was to be severely compromised by events of the 16th century. This was the time when the great territorial dynastic monarchies of northern Europe that had just recently coalesced into powerful territorial states crossed the Alps in order to assert dynastic claims on the Italian states, particularly Naples and Milan.

When Charles VIII of France crossed the Alps in 1494 to claim the kingdom of Naples, there would be, then, not only the loss of Italian liberty, but the turning of Italy into the battleground of Europe—the place where the struggle between the French Royal Valois and the Imperial/Spanish House of Habsburg would ultimately be determined. Their competing claims would become almost the metaphor, the metonymy, of the struggle for European power; and Italy, of course, would suffer. The Treaty of Cateau-Cambrésis in 1559, to a large extent, ended this struggle by providing spheres of influence within the continent, but also recognized the loss of Italian freedom, turning the Peninsula, to some extent, over to the House of Habsburg, which would rule much of it until the period of Italian unification in the 19th century.

The Italian states continued, but they continued in really only a half-life. So the focus of this course is really going to be on those years before the middle of the 16th century, during that time when the Italians were managing their own affairs to a large degree, creating their own culture, and defining what it was not just to be Italian, but to be Genoese, or Florentine, or Roman, or Neapolitan. The *Risorgimento*, that romantic movement of Italian unification that ultimately brought the Peninsula together under the rule of the House of Savoy and King Victor Emmanuel II, saw Italy as a place not only of history, but as a nation comprised of people who spoke the same language, people who shared elements of the same culture, and who shared the same religion. It was only then that we could properly speak of Italy. And what we need to do is to look at the complexities of the Peninsula before that.

In fact, in order to understand this complexity, we really have to go back to the period of the Middle Ages when much of the Italian state system was being formed—created out of the barbarian kingdoms, traditional tribal areas, episcopal sees, and petty despotisms that emerged as Rome began to disintegrate and decline. It also helps us understand not just early Italian politics, but contemporary Italian politics. The celebrated phrase that's been attributed both to Giovanni Giolitti—the late 19th- and early 20th-century long-serving Prime Minister of Italy—and to Benito Mussolini, that "It's not impossible to rule the Italians, merely pointless," says much about the nature of Italian political life. It's a commonly held belief, in fact, that the Italian Peninsula is particularly intractable to some form of centralized control and some form of central government.

What we do know is that there are forces at work that try to deflect that centralizing tendency that all governments recognize; try to deflect that desire to turn the Peninsula into a single entity. It is, in fact, a democratic challenge to rule Italy, as the number of Italian governments that emerged since the Second World War can testify to. But this long complex history of opposition, the things that we're going to be talking about here, will really help us understand what it is that brought about this curious circumstance. The particularism, the geographical separation, the sense of localism versus a sense of national patriotism; all of these things are the result of history. And we have to also remember that this history, for the 400 years before unification, was a history of foreign oppression. During this period, to pay your taxes willingly, to cooperate with the government, was a form of collaboration. To recognize your ruler as someone who ruled legitimately was, in fact, a form of collaboration.

So, these deep-seated attitudes towards government were very, very much a part of the Italian experience and Italian history. These were elements that were defined not just by the particular history of individual places that characterized the class, the geographical area, the economic conditions, and the social structure of the various regions of the country, but they're also the result of the bigger issues—the issues of the interdependence of Italian states as well as their independence; the sense of competition as well as a sense of cooperation; that union of what it is to be Italian versus the fragmentation of what it is to be a Genoese, or a Florentine, or a Venetian, or a Neapolitan. In other words, to understand Italy, we must understand these various states. We have to look at the conditions that created Italy, and to do that we have to see how the states developed in their own context—to look at them individually and severally, to talk about them as they grew and developed, and ultimately to talk about them as they began their decline into the loss of liberty that characterized the period of the 17th and 18th centuries, and the first years of the 19th century.

In reality, the fragmentation of the Italian Peninsula began even during the Roman Empire. In fact, the idea of Italy being united under Rome is something of a mythological structure. When you look at the nature of Italy under Rome, we have to remember that the Romans had a veneer of unity that simply covered a great deal of fragmented local allegiance, and traditions and cultures, and indeed a sense of otherness that continued even during the most powerful years of the empire. The north of Italy wasn't even identified as Italian; it was seen as Hither Gaul, Gallia Cisalpine—that part of the Gaelic world that had been settled by those Gaelic invaders that, in the early years of the Republic, had even captured and sacked Rome itself.

There were the Etruscans with their independent states linked together in a federation—the Etruscans with their sophisticated economic structures and long-distance trade, and their very, very powerful culture. The Etruscans and their culture lasted well into the Roman Empire, well into the time of Augustus. These Etruscans still identified themselves as being not Romans—as being subject to

Rome, but not Romans themselves. So the historical memory, even of Italy during the period of Roman unification, was in fact something of a historical myth. There were, in fact, elements of reality, and those elements of reality were particularly powerful. Rome did provide a veneer of unity. Rome did provide the vocabulary that allowed Italians to talk about the Peninsula in a singular way. They did provide a single law, a single coinage. They provided the means of communication of roads and harbors that permitted the peoples of the Peninsula to come into constant contact, both with one another and with the great capital in the city of Rome itself.

But then there were the other elements that always were on the edge and the periphery. Sicily, for example, the breadbasket of the Roman Empire, maintains—and maintained until very recently—the memory of the Greeks that had settled that island during the period of colonization in the ancient world. There were those descendants who then sustained an element of culture that allowed for Rome to, in some ways, be greatly enriched by this dynamic, this dialogue of historical experience—and what I will argue as this course progresses is that it's one of the great elements of Italy. It's one of the explanations for the explosion of culture and imagination that we see among the Italian people and in the Italian Peninsula; that this dialogue, this dynamic, continued for such a long period of time, creating a world in which new ideas, through competition and through argument, and through occasionally warfare, could not only develop, but in fact be seen to be the instruments by which Italians could define themselves and others.

Culture, then, was part of the Italian sense of self. It was an element of policy. It was an element of aggrandizement. It was an element of economic investment and of social mobility. It also was, to some extent, the definition of Italianness. So when we think of Italy, we will think of culture, and when we look at the political, social, and economic development of these cities and of the states that they represented, this element of culture will always be there. We can see it today. One of the exciting and most rewarding elements of a tour of the Peninsula is how the world changes just traveling a few kilometers down the road. We see the difference in wine, and cheese, and bread. If you know the language, you can see the difference in dialect, in vocabulary—occasionally even grammatical structures—from one town to the next.

We can see that there are fundamental differences in political allegiances. We can see in the graffiti on the sides of buildings the venom with which your opponents, whether political or the soccer team of the next town, will be reviled. You can also see the sense of identification with your own town, which attendance at one of those soccer games or political rallies will make abundantly clear. You can also see it in the shape of the cities and of the states that these cities represent as well. You can see when you go into a particular city that there are wide-open spaces. There are large piazze surrounded by public buildings. You will see large private dwellings throughout the entire town or city.

You'll go into others, and you'll see that the town is dominated by a fortified palace or castle, moated for protection. Here you will see very few large piazze, usually just in front of this castle, or more usually in front of the cathedral. Otherwise, there is a sense very much of being enclosed, of being both protected and watched. This difference in architectural personality and character reflects the difference in the political, social, and economic structure of these various places. So to understand the reality of Italian life today, we have to understand how that life developed from the circumstances of Italian history and Italian politics.

When you go into the cities, particularly of the North, a city like Milan, you see that the inhabitants are dressed in the latest fashion. They're dressed in the most elegant European style. If you go into other particularly small towns, particularly in the South again, you'll see that there is a maintenance of traditional dress, that there is still a sense of modesty and a sense of being enclosed. This, too, is a historical burden that the people of Italy carry, where they see themselves differently, and their relationship between not only themselves and their fellow Italians, but between Italy and the rest of Europe—and to some extent, the world—in different ways. So, there are these elements that we have to always take into account. We have to remember that there is this identification between people and place in Italy that is profound and part of the national collective unconscious.

We see it in the desire of individuals to return to the place where they and their fathers and grandfathers were born. Occasionally, they spent their entire lives working abroad in the United States, or Australia, or Argentina, or Canada, but they want to go back to the village of their birth in order to retire and to connect once more with the ancestors that produced them, buried in the local churchyard, so that they can be part of that continuum—that vertical sense of history that is part of the Italian mentality. These critical forces, then, are things that really characterize the complexity of Italian life. The idea that there are forces at work that go beyond the political and define what it is to be Italian must be identified and must be researched and analyzed in a bit more detail because there are other forces as well. There are those great power issues in which all nations participate and participated—those great power issues that, during our period, are focused really on the Mediterranean.

The Mediterranean is, in fact, a place that defined European culture and European politics for a good period of recorded history. The Mediterranean is the *Media Terra*; it's the center of the earth. It's the place around which culture and civilization developed. During the period of Italian fragmentation, the Mediterranean became not only the source of great opportunity, but also became a source of great threat. It was a time when the Turks representing Islam, and the Christians representing the Latin West, fought for supremacy of that inland sea. It wasn't just the battle of religions; it wasn't just a clash of civilizations. It was for the economic authority that came with controlling the sea routes between East and West. It came as a result of the expansion of Islam not only into the Mediterranean with the conquest of the Balkans and the conquest of Greece and the islands of the Aegean, but also the movement into Europe itself, moving north, resulting under Suleiman the Magnificent the defeat of the Christian army at Moháchs in 1526—that slaughter of the Christians that allowed the Turks then to move north and to besiege Vienna itself in 1529.

Italy was the vanguard of this struggle. Italy was the place where East and West came into conflict, and Italy previously had been the place where East and West had come into contact economically and culturally—so there is a continuum. The Italian Peninsula grew rich because of its geographical position, its ability to trade with the East and to control the luxury trade routes for the spices, and silks, and slaves that moved from the East to the West. The Italian Peninsula also, then, found that it was the vanguard of Latin Europe once the challenge of the Turks was made visible, and up until the 1560s, that challenge seemed to be insurmountable because the Turks seemed to be invincible.

There was also the issue of sovereignty and power. With the collapse of the Roman Empire in 476, and the fragmentation of imperial authority, who would control the destinies of the people who lived under what had been Roman rule? Whom should you obey? Under whose authority did your local powerful individual act? Occasionally, they simply assumed power on their own; they simply took power because they were able to exercise it, and they had the force to ensure that it would be obeyed. Usually, because they had force, they could also protect you and provide some measure of law and administration. So, local power becomes extremely important—local power based on the exercise of force. But that's not sufficient because if you want to ensure that your coinage is accepted broadly, that your laws are respected by more than just the exercise of force, but because they have some actual functional use and ability to deliver in your own lives, then in fact you need an idea of sovereign power.

There were two sovereign powers in Italy—two sovereign powers that resulted from the complexity of the history of the Peninsula: a sovereign power that resulted from the religious circumstance of the empire, and a sovereign power that resulted from the political memory of imperial authority. The Romans, after all, had imposed a single rule over most of the known world. They also imposed a religion—a religion that was closely identified with the cult of the empire and the cult of the emperor. Paganism, that religion of many gods, included usually the emperor himself. One of the perks of being emperor is, in fact, to be admitted to the Pantheon—to be able to climb Olympus and become a god himself. In fact, the Emperor Claudius's last words were, "It seems as though I'm about to become a god."

This idea of the union of paganism and religion in political power, then, was part of the Roman mentality, was part of the Roman political and religious system, and it was built right into the structure of their rule. In 313, though, the Emperor Constantine the Great, with the Edict of Milan, adopted Christianity as the official religion of the empire. Christianity played a completely different role. Christianity did not recognize the divinity of the emperor, although the idea of the emperor functioning as God's minister was something that was implicit in the Christian message, particularly during the days of Rome. The idea, then, that the Christian world was associated with the Roman imperial world was, in fact, particularly important.

The emperor, though, represented secular power. With the emperor, there was the bishop of Rome, the pope. The pope represented ecclesiastical power, religious power, and indeed both of them claimed to be acting for God; where the pope was the successor of St. Peter, the Vicar of Christ on earth—Christ's charge to Peter that as he binds on Earth, he will bind in heaven. All of this seems to give the bishop of Rome and the papacy the ability and the authority to function as a source of sovereignty. The emperor, though, still had not only the real power to exercise as Emperor of Rome, but also he had the sovereign power that came from that role, and from that continuum of secular rule that goes back to the foundation of the Republic.

Consequently, we have two sources of authority, and that issue would divide all of Italy—become, in fact, the great ideological divide between the two of them. The supporters of the papacy and papal or ecclesiastical sovereignty would be known as Guelfs. The supporters of imperial sovereignty or secular sovereignty would be Ghibellines. This division between Guelf and Ghibelline would become one of the dynamics that helped characterize the Italian state system itself. Whether you supported the authority of the Church, or whether you supported the authority of the empire, largely determined exactly what it is that you would do and what it is that you would be.

The idea of Guelf and Ghibelline, this idea of separation, was more than just an abstract idea. It also was a real reflection of differences of social class, of geography, of circumstance—so history determined it. If your state had been traditionally Guelf or Ghibelline, well, that was one of the glues that kept your state together, and it was dangerous to change it. If the ruling family you overthrew had been Ghibelline, and you then needed a power base with which to replace that family, it would be wise to become Guelf. If the papacy seemed to be in ascendancy, being a Guelf would be reasonable. If the emperor seemed to be victorious, or if you needed that sovereignty that he could provide, then it would be wise again to choose that allegiance. So, in other words, what we see, then, is that Italy is being defined by forces larger than the political issues in each one of its states, but there are meta issues as well. There are ideological operations at work, things that are determined both in the history and also in the religious and political structure of the Peninsula.

The other thing about the Italy of myth is that it's a place of words. The role of words in Italian culture has always been fundamental. The idea of theater, of acting out myth, of turning history into theatrical moments to allow either politicians or princes to behave in particular ways; the idea of *la bella figura*—the idea that you in fact can create something by simply acting it or saying it—is very much a part of the Italian character. In fact, what do we see when we look at the creation of a place that's recognizably Italy functioning in a language that is recognizably Italian; the creation of a single language that would glue the Peninsula together? We associate this with Dante, with a poet who died in 1321, who created—despite his own objections to doing so—a dialect, Tuscan, that became the literary language of the entire Peninsula and provided one of those glues of unity. So when we think of the creation of an Italian people, we think of it done through literature: the Three Crowns of Dante; of Petrarch, who died in 1374; and Giovanni Boccaccio, who died in 1375.

There also are other references to the idea of Italy as almost a theatrical or literary convention. What other nation could talk openly about *gattopardismo*, which is their reference to a novel written by Prince Giuseppe Tommasi di Lampedusa in the 1950s called *Il Gattopardo*, or *The Leopard*. The character, Don Fabrizio, who is based on the prince's own great-grandfather during the period of Italian unification, remarks that for everything to remain the same, everything will have to change. Of course, this is something that seems to reflect the nature of Italian politics since the Second World War, where you had—until recently—revolving-door administrations, but if you looked carefully, the administrations consisted of the same men. It was a musical chairs game on the political stage—the same people exercising power, representing the same parties with the same intent. So the theater of change was there. The theater of democratic action was always at work. The reality was that it was a relatively small number of people who truly were exercising power in the interests of their political and personal advantage. So, *gattopardismo*, this idea of everything seeming to change for everything to remain the same, becomes extraordinarily important.

Italy, then, is the distillation of all of these things. It becomes, in fact, the sum of its myths, the sum of its history; and it becomes greater, though, than the sum of these parts. Italy takes on an existence that's over and above that, and even more significant and greater. It's the result of this imaginative myth-making, defining a world that existed perfectly in art or literature, or architecture, or even political theory, when in reality there are other things going on beneath this level of mythology that is much more closely related to the reality of political action and political theory. What we see, then, is that Italy must be understood locally in order to understand it generally. We have to see how Italy is going to function as a unity by seeing how its parts operated together and interrelated with one another.

To begin this, we have to really start with that collapse of the Roman Empire. We have to see what happened when Rome disintegrated in 476 to see the rise of those city-states, the rise of those larger territorial political organizations that eventually gave character to the Middle Ages and produced the culture of the Renaissance. So, when we see the Gonzaga, the Este, and the Medici creating culture, creating politics, making war, we see them both on the level of the theater of national and international life, and we see them simultaneously creating something very real: a wonderful culture with great art, something that reflects both the history and the myth of the Italian people, and also the energy and the dynamic that would create a united kingdom under the House of Savoy in 1861.

Lecture Two
The Question of Sovereignty

Scope:

The collapse of the Roman Empire in the 5th century A.D. left the Italian Peninsula at the mercy of competing interests. It was invaded by various barbarian tribes, some of whom stayed to establish kingdoms. At the same time, the Byzantine emperors attempted to recover parts of the old empire in the west by establishing political and military bases, as well as by offering protection to local cities, such as Venice. For its part, the papacy managed to sustain enough authority to control considerable territory around Rome and central Italy, an ecclesiastical state that was enlarged by gifts from pious rulers. Finally, the Germanic kings, after the coronation of Charlemagne in Rome, claimed to inherit the sovereignty of Roman rule. They made regular incursions into Italy to seek tribute, initiating the Guelf-Ghibelline struggle that was to dominate Italian politics for centuries to come. The consequence of this complex and chaotic environment was the emergence of a great many independent states, simultaneously jealous of their territorial integrity and ambitious to expand.

Outline

I. With the collapse of the Roman imperial system and the deposition of the last Roman emperor in 476 A.D., the issue of sovereignty became central in Italy.

   A. Some of the barbarian invaders that came into the Italian Peninsula were heavily Romanized and Christian. Others, such as Huns, were nomadic, had no connection with either the religion or the traditions of Rome, and had little desire to sustain anything of the imperial system. Consequently, the peninsula experienced a sense of collapse.

   B. This unhappy situation was made more complex by the attempts of Byzantine emperors to reconquer bits of the peninsula.

1. These incursions of the Byzantines destabilized some of the barbarian kingdoms, including some of those that were the most Romanized and deeply established.

2. The Byzantine incursions also had positive outcomes, such as the development of Venice close to the exarchate at Ravenna, thereby forming a new state—the Venetian Republic.

C. There was no central government on the peninsula to control the coinage, establish a single law, or maintain communications. Thus, power was assumed by those who could do so. For example, on the vast estates, the *latifundia*, landlords used their peasants as private armies to ensure some order and protection.

D. However, Italy, unlike the rest of Europe, didn't suffer from the collapse of urban life. The cities in Italy continued and, in many cases, thrived, partly because the episcopal sees were located in cities. Cities also had the advantage of being centers of trade and markets.

E. With no central government in place, local government assumed new importance. The world of Italy was defined locally, in economic terms according to the locality that it served and in political terms by those who could assume authority and provide the basic organization of life.

II. At the same time, the principle of universal sovereignty was sustained by the Roman Church.

A. The bishop of Rome was recognized throughout Christendom as the leader of the Latin Church in the West. The connections with St. Peter and the empire under Constantine gave Rome a particular authority. Further, as the memory of the empire was sustained, the memory of the Church was sustained with it.

1. The Edict of Milan (313), which made Christianity the official religion of the empire, reinforced powerfully the position of the bishop of Rome.

2. Pilgrims from across Europe, looking for the place of martyrdom of the apostles Peter and Paul, saw Rome not just as a political or even an ecclesiastical unit but as a

place of sanctity. This view also gave luster to the authority and power of the pope.

B. The pope, though, was more than a spiritual leader; he also was a prince. He ruled a state that was associated increasingly with the exercise of political and secular, as well as ecclesiastical, power.

C. The territory of the pope grew as a result of gifts and expansion, and the popes used their territory as a power base. They could offer the ability to rule to others, who would rule in the name of the pope and take the sovereignty of the Church as their legitimization. In this way, the states of the Church began to send tentacles beyond Rome, into parts of central Italy.

D. The Papal States were not, however, particularly stable. These territories varied dramatically in size and in central government according to the personality of the pope and the circumstances in which he ruled. Events both within and outside of Italy could have an effect on the amount of power the pope could exercise.

E. The papacy had no secure sources of income. At times, the pope was able to impose taxes and use the income for secular purposes, but that ability, too, depended on events elsewhere.

F. Papal policy, then, tended to be somewhat erratic and depended heavily on the personality of the pope and the circumstances in Italy and Europe.

G. Finally, the pope wasn't able to impose order on those who had the power to withstand him. The Orsini, the Colonna, and other families ruled largely independently until the 16th century.

III. Another element to be factored into the political dynamic on the peninsula was the Holy Roman Empire and the memory of secular sovereignty.

A. The Frankish King Charlemagne, following the policies of his father, wanted to protect the independence of the Church from the forces that sought to bring it into secular control.

1. In order to do this, Charlemagne used the great empire that he assembled north of the Alps as an instrument to legitimize the rule of the pope, protect the Church, and add to his own authority.

2. Thus, to some extent, Charlemagne was recognized by the pope as the secular extension of the religious power of the Church. For this reason, on Christmas day in the year 800, in the Basilica of St. Peter, Pope Leo crowned Charlemagne Holy Roman Emperor.

3. In so doing, Leo recognize Charlemagne's authority and created another jurisdiction, another source of sovereignty that revived the idea of imperial rule.

B. These two ideological elements—the sovereignty of the secular rule of the empire and the sovereignty of the spiritual authority of the papacy—characterized Italy in the Middle Ages.

C. The result of this dual authority would become the fundamental divide between Guelf and Ghibelline—between those who supported the pope and those who supported the empire. This dispute divided the peninsula and, to some extent, became part of the relief of European life. In Italy, it became the basic factor that characterized politics.

IV. Charlemagne's successors made regular incursions into Italy to attack and plunder. The Germanic emperors had only a small power base in their own territories, and they saw the rich cities of Italy as sources for ready cash.

A. Moreover, these emperors disrupted the social, political, and economic structures that were beginning to develop indigenously.

1. The emperor might, for example, establish Italian rulers as imperial vicars to act in his name, thereby giving authority to one faction to the exclusion of another.

2. In north-central Italy, in particular, imperial vicariates developed that reflected the values and feudal structure of northern Europe, including the political element that saw sovereignty as residing in the power of the Holy Roman Emperor.

B. In this situation, the contest between emperor and pope was, to some extent, inevitable.

    1. In general, the supporters of the Ghibellines were feudal magnates, often rural-based, usually of the knightly class, and closely associated with the exercise of military authority.

    2. The Guelf supporters tended to be urban and closely associated with mercantile wealth; they saw the papacy as a much more irenic role and viewed papal values as hostile to, or at least in contravention of, the principles that characterized feudal life in the countryside.

C. The initial winner in the first round of struggle between empire and papacy was Pope Gregory VII, known as Hildebrand, who humiliated the Emperor Henry IV at Canossa in 1077. Henry, having been excommunicated, had to go as a penitent to the castle of Matilda of Tuscany and stand barefoot in the snow for days until, ultimately, Gregory gave him absolution.

D. The struggle between the two sources of sovereignty didn't end with the humiliation of Henry IV at the hands of Gregory VII. Various rulers acting in the name of either the emperor or the pope engaged in proxy wars of these two elements of sovereignty on a local level.

    1. Sovereign rights were always accessible if one was willing to support one ideological faction over the other, and the emperor and pope used this strategy effectively to gain small advantages.

    2. Such allegiances, though, created two exclusive factions in the Italian Peninsula—the Guelfs and the Ghibellines—each of which saw themselves as representatives of true power and each of which recognized the danger inherent in not suppressing or completely destroying the other.

    3. The term *Guelf*, in fact, comes from one of the imperial families that sought the authority of the papacy to challenge imperial rule. Similarly, *Ghibelline* is the Italianization of Waiblingen, the battle cry and the name of the castle of the House of Hohenstaufen.

E. By the time the Italian communes (independent states) had begun to coalesce and form their own governments, the struggle between Guelf and Ghibelline became more dangerous. Henry IV may have been humiliated, but his successor, Frederick Barbarossa, would not give the pope the same satisfaction.

V. The complex factors that determined whether a state would be Guelf or Ghibelline related to social class, history, geography, and perhaps most significantly, opportunity.

    A. Political allegiance is often the exercise of opportunism— what is most beneficial at a particular time to a particular person. This was true of the Guelf-Ghibelline divide as with any ideological division.

        1. If an individual wanted power and those who stood in his way were Ghibellines, he would become a Guelf and vice versa.

        2. Similarly, it would be wise to be a Guelf if one was in the orbit of Rome or the Papal States or a Ghibelline if one was in the imperial orbit or a vassal of the emperor.

    B. These elements working together resulted in not just an ideological divide but a practical and political divide.

        1. The distinction between Guelfs and Ghibellines was not just an abstract question of the nature of sovereignty.

        2. This division influenced real politics in a world where there were no political parties and where power was based on the exercise of force.

    C. As we discuss the various states of Italy, we will see that this Guelf-Ghibelline divide is one of the dynamic factors that gives character to the various states. We will go beyond the idea of sovereignty into the actual practice that would become infused with tradition and, then, become an element of history itself.

    D. It's important to note that neither Guelf nor Ghibelline, neither pope nor emperor, was sufficiently powerful to knock the other out of the arena. For structural reasons, the powers were equally balanced.

1. Both the emperor and the pope were elected princes. They didn't rule by heredity but by the ability to summon electors that would give them authority.

2. Consequently, the idea of establishing a singular policy that could be pursued over a long period of time was, essentially, nonexistent. Decisions were made based on local and immediate conditions, and that meant that neither pope nor emperor had sufficient power over time to eliminate the other.

3. This inability of one to destroy the other meant that the two sources of sovereignty would always characterize the Italian Peninsula and that Italy could not be united. There was no king or prince sufficiently powerful to use the authority inherent in his role to bring together a vast territorial state.

E. Because of the division of Guelf and Ghibelline, Italy was destined to remain fragmented, as imperial and papal vicars struggled with one another or as the power of either the pope or the emperor grew and the other waned. These elements also allowed for the discussion of what we now call political theory on a very high level.

   1. It's no accident that the great poet Dante wrote a political treatise on the nature of sovereignty. His *De monarchia* was a discussion of why the Ghibelline cause should be victorious in Italy.

   2. Such discussions of political theory had to be taken into account by Italians because they affected everyday life.

F. The division between Guelf and Ghibelline also created a rich environment in which experimentation and competition could take place. The Italians of the Middle Ages were able to look at politics in creative ways, that is, to identify larger social and economic concerns while still dealing with local issues. This sense of diversity and energetic engagement with politics would characterize the Italian states.

G. There were some events, of course, that linked Guelf and Ghibelline, particularly the Crusades, which brought all of Latin Christendom together as one. The alliance of Christians took precedence over the division of Guelf and

Ghibelline, and this, too, must be factored into the definition of the Italian Peninsula during the Middle Ages.

Essential Reading:

G. Tabacco, *The Struggle for Power in Medieval Italy: Structures of Political Rule.*

Supplementary Reading:

O. Prescott, *The Lords of Italy.*

Questions to Consider:

1. Why was the question of whether the Holy Roman Emperor or the pope enjoyed universal sovereignty so crucial?

2. Why were local conditions rather than abstract discussions of sovereignty in fact more important in determining a state's allegiance to pope or emperor?

Lecture Two—Transcript
A Question of Sovereignty

The collapse of the Roman imperial system with the deposition of the last Roman emperor in 476 A.D. created a serious problem for Italy because the issue of sovereignty became central. Under whose authority would people actually exercise power, and what did it mean to exercise power? The various waves of barbarian invaders that came into the Italian Peninsula with the collapse of Rome were really of differing kinds. Some were heavily Romanized and Christian. They had respect for the Roman Church, for Roman traditions, and many of them actually followed an element of Roman law, so the memories of Rome were particularly deep amongst this group. But then there were other barbarian invaders, like the Huns, who were nomadic, who had no connection with either the religion or the traditions of Rome, and they had very little desire to sustain anything of the imperial system.

Consequently, there was in the Peninsula a great sense of collapse, a sense that the Roman imperial system was no longer operating in any form except through the memories of tribes like the Longobardi (the Lombards), who had some element of Christianity and Romanization, and then others threatening even them and other groups within the Italian Peninsula who had no desire to sustain anything of that memory. This unhappy situation was, moreover, made more complex by the attempt of Byzantine emperors to try to reconquer bits of the Peninsula. These attempts, these incursions of the Byzantines, destabilized some of the barbarian kingdoms, and indeed some of them that were the most Romanized, and some of them that were the most deeply established. Nevertheless, there were positive elements as well of this Byzantine incursion, inasmuch as cities like Venice were allowed to develop close to the exarchate at Ravenna, and thereby a new state could be formed—one that would become one of the most important of the Italian Peninsula, the Venetian Republic.

There was no central government, then, in order to maintain the things that central governments do—coinage, single law, elements of communication—and that resulted in power being assumed by those who could do it. There were those who assumed power simply because they needed the protection, or they had to protect what they had. Especially on the vast estates, the *latifundia* of the Peninsula, the landlords, used their peasants as private armies, as militias, in order to try to make sure that there was some element of both government and protection. However, Italy, unlike the rest of Europe, didn't suffer from the collapse of urban life. The cities in Italy continued, and in many instances continued to thrive. This was in part because the *episcopal see*, the seat of the bishop, was in a city; and consequently, the continuation of ecclesiastical power allowed for the city to be sustained. This maintenance of urban life becomes an extremely important factor in the development of the peculiarly Italian civilization that would emerge during the Middle Ages and Renaissance.

Also, cities had the advantage of being centers of trade and markets. So the continuation of cities also maintained that other function of Roman imperial rule—that is, allowing for trade to take place in a relatively protected environment by people whose essential occupation is trade. Consequently, cities then remained part of Italian life and remained part of the tapestry of the Peninsula. Local government, though, was something that became the most important element in this time of confusion. Local government was really all you could have. There was no central government. Local government, moreover, could deliver what you needed delivered: some element of protection, some element of security, some element of administration. So the world was defined locally; the world was defined in economic terms according to the locality that it served— and in political terms, by those who could actually assume authority and provide those elemental factors of life that any political organization required.

But there were universal ideas, and ideas are impossible to suppress, even in the most difficult and dangerous times of confusion and chaos. In particular, the principle of universal sovereignty was sustained by the Roman Church. The bishop of Rome was recognized throughout Christendom as the leader of the Latin Church in the West; the connections with not only St. Peter—who was by tradition the first pope—and the memory that Christ was going to build upon that rock his Church, but also the fact that he and St. Paul were martyred in Rome, gave Rome a particular authority. Also, there was this idea that Constantine had made the Roman Church the official religion of the Roman Empire, and so consequently the bishop of Rome was seen as an associate of the emperor. And as the memory of the empire was sustained, the memory of the Church was sustained with it.

The Edict of Milan of 313 that made Christianity the official religion of the empire then reinforced powerfully the position of the bishop of Rome. And pilgrims from all over Europe, looking for the place of martyrdom of the apostles Peter and Paul, consequently saw Rome not just as a political, or even an ecclesiastical unit, but a place of sanctity, and this also gave luster to the authority and power of the pope. The pope, though, was more than a spiritual leader; he also was a prince. He ruled a state that was associated increasingly with the exercise of political and secular, as well as ecclesiastical or spiritual, power. The states of the Church functioned as both an element to protect the pope—functioned as a cordon that provided some measure of independence for the Church from secular intervention—but also turned the pope into a secular prince himself, ruling over an extraordinarily important and growing amount of territory in central Italy.

This territory grew as a result of gifts and as a result of expansion. Pious rulers such as Mathilda of Tuscany made the papacy their heirs, adding large territories to the Patrimony of St. Peter. The popes, sufficiently ambitious as they were, would use this as a power base in order to expand. Moreover, they could then offer the ability to rule to others who would rule in the name of the pope, and who would take the sovereignty of the Church as their legitimization. These petty rulers, these despots of independent jurisdictions within the orbit of Rome, became papal vicars, and consequently the states of the Church began to send tentacles beyond Rome, into the territories in parts of central Italy where ecclesiastical power remained, and went beyond the ecclesiastical and spiritual authority that the pope provided to bishops and archbishops, and allowed the spiritual authority of the pope to actually enter into the secular world of papal vicars, princes acting in the name of the pope.

But the Papal States were not particularly stable. What we're talking about is not the exercise of centralized power, but the use of both coercion and indirect influence in order to create a state that varied dramatically in size and in central government according to the personality of the pope and according to the circumstances in which the pope was ruling. First of all, the papacy was an international, universal agency. Events outside of Italy, let alone within Italy itself, could have an effect on how the pope could rule and the amount of power the pope could exercise. Consequently, some popes may have been particularly ambitious, but they couldn't really act effectively because circumstances were beyond their control.

There were no secure sources of income. The pope was able to tax when possible and use the income from Church taxation in secular ways, but that, too, depended on what was going on elsewhere. This was not something that the pope could necessarily assume he would enjoy. So papal policy, then, tended to be somewhat erratic and depended very, very much on the personality of the pope, the circumstances in Italy, and the circumstances in Europe. Moreover, the pope wasn't really able, despite the power that came with being the successor of St. Peter and a prince of an important state in the center of the Peninsula, to really impose order on those who had the force to be able to withstand him. This is especially true of the great Roman barons. The Orsini, the Colonna, and other families ruled largely independently until the 16th century. It wasn't really until the pontificate of Julius II in the beginning of the 16th century that these barons were finally brought under papal control. So this area of Italy in the center was, by definition, unstable, and it introduced an element of instability to the whole Peninsula.

There was another source of sovereignty. There was another element that had to be factored into this political dynamic on the Peninsula, and that was the Holy Roman Empire and the memory of secular sovereignty. The Frankish King Charlemagne, following the policies of his father, wanted to protect the independence of the Church from the very forces that were trying to bring it into secular control. In order to do this, he used the great empire that he would put together north of the Alps as an instrument, and an empire that included Italian territories and recognizing the power of the pope in order to legitimize that rule, and also desiring to both protect the Church and add to his own authority. So, Charlemagne was recognized by the pope as, to some extent, the secular extension of the religious power of the Church. And it was for this reason on Christmas Day, 800, in the Basilica of St. Peter, that Pope Leo crowned him Holy Roman Emperor.

And in so doing, what Leo had done was not just recognize the real power that Charlemagne had, exercising an authority that hadn't been seen since the collapse of Rome, but also created another jurisdiction. He created another source of sovereignty and authority by reviving the idea of imperial rule. Charlemagne, in being the successor to Roman emperors and recognized by the Church as such, was really establishing the idea of imperial sovereignty. So it was these two—the sovereignty of the secular rule of the empire, and the sovereignty of the spiritual authority of the papacy—that provided the two elements that characterized the Italy of the Middle Ages. These two ideological elements that would provide much of the debate about what it was to be not only a member of the Church, but a member of the political community—to be, to some extent, a citizen of this mosaic of the Italian Peninsula.

This would be the fundamental divide, Guelf and Ghibelline: those who supported the pope, those who supported the empire. This jurisdiction divided the Peninsula and, to some extent, became part of the relief of Europe. It was something that was seen everywhere, that could be reflected in what Dante called the sun and the moon, the two swords, those very elements that were used metaphorically to indicate that there are two sources of power: one divine and one human. But in Italy, it became the fundamental factor that characterized Italian political life. Charlemagne's successors, as emperors, made regular incursions into Italy, usually just to attack, plunder, and to take whatever was not nailed down, because the Germanic emperors had very little of a power base in their own territories, and they saw the rich cities of Italy—especially ruled by those individuals who claimed to be ruling in the name of the emperor—as a place where they might get a quick fix of cash.

These emperors, moreover, did disrupt—to some extent—the social, political, and economic structures that were beginning to develop indigenously. So the emperor, for example, might give vast estates to his loyal followers. That would provide a basis of his rule or influence in a particular locality. He also would establish Italian rulers as imperial vicars to act in his name, thereby giving authority to one group or one faction, to the exclusion of another. So, in particular in north-central Italy, those areas where the emperor's authority was most visible—those areas that the emperor could most easily access from northern Europe—there tended to be the growth of imperial vicariates—imperial sources of power and authority that reflected very much the values of northern Europe, that reflected the feudal structure of the northern European kingdoms, and reflected some of that political element that saw sovereignty as residing in the power of the Holy Roman Emperor.

The contest between emperor and pope, then, was—to some extent—inevitable. It was inevitable because these two sources of sovereignty would have to come into conflict because you had two groups in society, each claiming to be ruling in the name of a sovereign power, but each often directed towards other goals. In general, the supporters of the Ghibellines were feudal magnates, were often rural-based, were usually of the knightly class, who were closely associated with the exercise of military authority. Those who were the supporters of the Guelfs often tended to be urban, tended to be closely associated with mercantile wealth, and saw the papacy as a much more irenic force, and were able to identify the papal values as hostile to—or at least in contravention of—the principles of fighting on horseback, of violence, of blood-feud, and the other things that characterized the practice of feudal life in the countryside.

The initial winner in this first round of struggle between empire and papacy was the pope. It was the great victory of Gregory VII, generally known as Hildebrand, who humiliated the Emperor Henry IV at Canossa in 1077, that sees the first rise of papal power in a dramatic way. Henry, having been humiliated by the authority that the pope had not just in military and political terms, but with the spiritual weapons of interdict—so that the priests were not supposed to marry or bury, were not supposed to say mass—of excommunication, of cutting the emperor and his supporters off from the Church, saying that they could not achieve salvation if they continued in their political ways. This resulted in Henry having to go as a penitent to the castle of Mathilda of Tuscany and stand barefoot in the snow for days until ultimately Hildebrand, Gregory VII, provided him with absolution—who went out and then readmitted him into the Church, but under the pope's conditions.

Later Holy Roman Emperors, of course, did not recognize that this was a battle that was lost forever. The struggle between the two sources of sovereignty didn't end with the humiliation of Henry IV at the hands of Gregory VII, but rather what happened had simply changed focus and—to some extent—changed dynasty. The various rulers acting in the name of the emperor or the pope provided—to some extent—proxy wars and proxy struggles of these two elements of sovereignty. It wasn't necessary to confront the emperor with the pope, or vice versa; you simply could exercise this struggle at a much more local level. Sovereign rights from the emperor or the pope, then, would be available from one or the other. Sovereign rights would always be accessible if you were willing to support one ideological faction or the other, and emperor and pope used this effectively to try to gain small advantages. Rather than pit two power blocks against one another, which had led to that terrible defeat of Henry IV, it was much easier, often, to simply allow your vassals to do it for you.

These allegiances, though, created two exclusive factions in the Italian Peninsula—the Guelfs and the Ghibellines—who saw themselves as representatives of true power, but one of them hating the other; one of them representing values that the other did not in any way respect, and also both of them seeing the danger inherent in not suppressing or completely destroying the other faction, because it could always be a threat, a platform for others to question your authority, to overthrow you, to establish another regime in the name of the other ideological position. The term *Guelf*, in fact, comes from one of the imperial families that sought the authority of the papacy in order to challenge the imperial rule. It comes from the House of Welf, and this was a Germanic family like the other families that had struggled for the imperial crown.

Similarly, *Ghibelline* is the Italianization of Waiblingen— Waiblingen being the battle cry and the name of the castle of the House of Hohenstaufen. This was the position of the emperor, the Hohenstaufen emperors that renewed this struggle, renewed this battle, represented in particular by that most remarkable of men, Frederick II Barbarossa of Hohenstaufen, who died in 1190. Frederick II, the Hohenstaufen who established a power base not in north-central Italy, but in the South in what would become the kingdom of Naples—this emperor was powerful indeed, moving up the coast, establishing authority in Umbria and other places that could actually challenge the role of the papacy.

The titanic struggle between Guelf and Ghibelline was enjoined once more, and this time it was much more dangerous because by this point, the Italian communes, those independent states, had begun to coalesce. They had begun to form their governments. They had begun to establish their own areas of influence and authority around the dominant cities. And these, then, were looking for sources of sovereignty and power, and now there was one that was reasonable as an alternative to the papacy. Henry IV may have been humiliated, but his successor, Frederick Barbarossa, was not about to allow the pope to do that.

The sorts of factors that determined whether a state would be Guelf or Ghibelline are complex, and they have to do with social class, history, geography—and, perhaps most significantly, opportunity. Political allegiance is often the exercise of opportunism, what is most beneficial at a particular time to a particular person. This was true of the Guelf-Ghibelline divide, as with any ideological division. If an individual wanted power, and he saw that the ones who stood in his way were Ghibellines, it would be reasonable for him to become a Guelf, and vice versa. Similarly, if you were in the orbit of Rome, close to the city, within the exercise of papal power in the Papal States, it was wise to be a Guelf because to be a Ghibelline would always be a threat. Similarly, if you were in the imperial orbit, if you were at a place where the emperor could provide assistance—or you were a direct vassal of an emperor like Frederick II Barbarossa—it would be a natural decision to remain Ghibelline. It was a sensible and reasonable thing to do because the alternative was much worse.

Consequently, we see, then, that these elements working together provided not just an ideological divide, but provided a practical and political divide. When we talk about Guelfs and Ghibellines, we're not just talking about abstract discussions of the nature of sovereignty. We're talking about real politics in a world where there were no political parties, where power was based upon the exercise of force: who could provide the most force, and who could provide alliance and assistance when needed; who could provide money if you needed a quick infusion of cash in order to fulfill a particular need, like a military campaign; and who ultimately could recognize your victory should you overthrow your enemies. These are the issues that became the dominant factors of Guelf and Ghibelline, of political allegiance, of recognition of sovereign authority.

As we discuss the various states of Italy, we're going to see, then, this Guelf-Ghibelline decision, this divide, as being one of the dynamic factors that would give character to the various states. We will go much beyond the idea of sovereignty into the actual practice that would become infused with tradition and then become the element of history itself. Guelf-Ghibelline, then, was like being a figure in a Gilbert and Sullivan operetta; "every child born alive is either a little liberal or a little conservative." Every Italian born during the Middle Ages was either a little Guelf or a little Ghibelline, as a result of forces not terribly different from those 19th-century English concerns. The important thing to note, though, is that neither Guelf nor Ghibelline, neither pope nor emperor, was sufficiently powerful to knock the other out of the arena.

The powers were equally balanced, and they were equally balanced for structural reasons. Both the emperor and the pope were elected princes. They didn't rule by heredity; they ruled by the ability to summon electors that would give them authority. Consequently, the idea of having a singular policy that could be pursued over a long period of time was essentially nonexistent. Everything depended on local and immediate conditions, and that meant that neither pope nor emperor had the ability to knock the other out because there was insufficient power over time to do it. This inability of one to destroy the other meant that the two sources of sovereignty would always characterize the Italian Peninsula. It would mean that Italy could not be united, could not end the division that resulted from the collapse of Rome, the way the other states could be united north of the Alps. There was no singular ruler. There wasn't a king or a prince sufficiently powerful to use the authority inherent in his role to bring together a vast territorial state.

Because of the division of Guelf and Ghibelline, Italy was destined to remain divided. It was also destined to remain fragmented as imperial and papal vicars struggled with one another, as the power of the pope grew and the emperor waned, or as the power of the emperor was real and immediate and the position of the papacy weaker during, for example, periods of an elderly pope, a disputed election, or perhaps even during the period of the Babylonian Captivity, when the papacy was in the south of France. These elements, then, created in Italy a particular set of circumstances not to be found anywhere else. It kept the fragmentation in place, but it also allowed for the discussion of what we now call political theory on a very, very high level.

It's not an accident that the great poet Dante, besides writing the *Commedia* and other elements of poetry and imaginative verse, also wrote a political treatise on the nature of sovereignty. His *De monarchia* was a discussion of why the Ghibelline cause should ultimately be victorious in Italy. It was a discussion of political theory, so it was something that every Italian had to take into account because it was something that really affected your life. It's not unlike the modern political world where we are engaged in political action and we have political allegiance because we see that the decisions made by one group or another when in government will affect us in our lives. That's the mentality, we have to remember, that pertained in Italy. This is the world also of the Italian Middle Ages—a world in which the decisions of popes and emperors would have an immediate and significant effect upon what actually happened in your own locality, in your own town or city, or in the countryside in which you lived.

This idea, then, reflected not just the complexity of Italian life, but also indicated very effectively, and in a very imaginative way, how Italy divided along these ideological grounds. You can see it even physically as you approach a town or a city. The crenellations of the city walls determined whether the city was Guelf or Ghibelline. If you were a noted Guelf, and you were approaching a town, and it was Ghibelline, it was a dangerous thing to do, or you had to at least make the adjustments necessary to enter that town. So if you saw the notched crenellation of the Ghibelline tower, or if you saw the flat crenellation of the Guelf tower, you knew perfectly well which party was dominant in that city or town, which prince recognized the sovereignty of the pope or the emperor.

This world, then, of Italy, divided between Guelf and Ghibelline, divided ideologically, divided practically, divided by personality, divided by circumstance, created a rich environment in which experimentation and competition could take place. The idea of competition, the concept that two competing factors that base themselves ultimately on issues of sovereignty could be played out in your locality, meant that the Italians of the Middle Ages were looking at politics in a creative and dynamic way. They were looking at the political world—they were looking at the economic and social world—in ways that could permit them to identify with larger issues while still identifying with the local issues that really were the ones in which they had to live.

This competition, this sense of diversity, this sense of energetic engagement with politics, would characterize the Italian states. It's not an accident that we see this cauldron of political and social experimentation. We see this world of economic experimentation, in which the great trading cities would use their authority in order to exercise power in different ways—and to use wealth and apply that wealth to achieve goals that seem to be greater than their immediate need or their immediate concern—because they were used to talking in larger terms. They were used to seeing the world as a larger arena in which ideas mattered.

There were some elements, of course, that linked Guelf and Ghibelline. There were the elements of the Crusades. The Crusades brought all of Latin Christendom together as one. The idea of being Christian and European became the element that mattered more than being supporters of the pope or supporters of the emperor. It's not an accident that the calling of the First Crusade in 1095 followed just a few years after the humiliation of the Emperor Henry IV by Hildebrand. It's this world, then, in which the Church and politics—in which the fighting men of the military Ghibelline alliance—the world in which Christians altogether, Italians and Europeans, could see themselves as under a single banner represented by the cross. So there were elements also that helped unite the Peninsula. There were ideas that were above even the division of Guelf and Ghibelline; what it was to be an Italian, a Christian, a member of the Latin Church, a European. All together, these are the things that factored into the definition of the Peninsula during the Middle Ages.

Lecture Three
The Crusades and Italian Wealth

Scope:

The preaching of the First Crusade at Clermont by Pope Urban II in 1095 began a series of European interventions into those areas of the Near East ruled by Islam. These events were driven as much by a desire to promote long-distance trade and to engage the knights of Europe in foreign rather than domestic warfare as by religious zeal to capture Jerusalem. Regardless of motive, the beginning of the First Crusade initiated an expansion of seaborne trade and traffic across the Mediterranean. The maritime republics of Italy reaped enormous profits through transporting the Christian knights and their equipment to the Levant. And because the returning ships needed ballast to sail, trade with the East was expanded with the importation of luxury goods. Access to these highly prized wares stimulated expansion of the carrying and retail trades in Europe. In all of these transactions, the Italians benefited the most. Moreover, the complexity of this trade stimulated the development of more sophisticated mechanisms of business organization and credit, again to the profit of Italy.

Outline

I. After a period of fragmentation following the collapse of the Roman Empire, a number of states arose on the Italian Peninsula that were different in character and personality.

   A. As we've seen, Christianity was the glue that bonded the Italians together. The concept of a singular Christianity also provided a vocabulary for exploring different political structures and different forms of ambition in terms of religion.

   B. In many instances, these issues come together in the Crusades. The Crusades provide a moment that helps us understand exactly how Italy developed and why, as well as the role Italy played in Europe—how it became the intermediary force between East and West, the concentration of much of the continent's wealth, and the place where experimentation could happen most easily.

II. The preaching of the First Crusade to the French nobility at Clermont by Pope Urban II in 1095 began a series of European interventions into those areas of the Near East ruled by Islam.

    A. The immediate motivation was to support the Byzantines against the Turks.

        1. The Byzantine emperor Alexius, having been catastrophically defeated at Manzikert, pleaded to the pope for help.

        2. Urban saw an opportunity to heal the recent schism between the Eastern (Orthodox) and Western (Catholic) churches.

    B. Underlying this motivation was generally increasing fear and hostility toward Muslim expansion at the expense of Christian dominance.

        1. Muslim armies had conquered the Middle East and the coast of North Africa and spread into Europe.

        2. Muslim enclaves in mainland Europe were seen as dangerous and against God's will.

        3. Muslim control of Jerusalem was a powerful source of religious resentment; for Christians, the only solution was to retake the city.

    C. By 1095, it was almost universally accepted that it was the duty of all Christians to recover the Holy Land and drive back the Muslims.

III. These events were driven as much by secular motivation as religious zeal.

    A. There was increasing pressure to engage the noble knights of Europe in foreign rather than domestic warfare.

        1. With threats from the Vikings and Magyars resolved, instability and warfare throughout Europe had been reduced. But with fewer external enemies, feudal knights began to fight one another.

        2. Moreover, stability in Europe had allowed for an expansion of trade and an increase in population, but with the rising population came a shortage of property to provide noble sons with fiefs. Europe looked to the East, to the lands controlled by Muslims, for expansion opportunities.

B. At the same time, maritime cities, such as Genoa, Pisa, and Venice, were expanding long-distance trade in the Mediterranean.

    1. With the increase in city life and population throughout the continent, these cities saw greater opportunities for selling goods, but there were also dangers: The Muslim states around the southern areas of the Mediterranean were hostile to Christian traders.

    2. Further, most of the lucrative long-distance trade with the East was managed by Muslim merchants who had no intention of permitting Christian Europeans to compete.

C. The pope saw a great Christian crusade as an opportunity to accomplish several goals at once.

    1. A crusade would further the expansion of Europe, Christianity, and trade; promote the conversion of infidels to Christianity; and export violence from Europe to an area where the violence could do some good.

    2. Military action would serve to protect and advance long-distance trade, bringing wealth back to Europe, much of which would ultimately find its way into ecclesiastical coffers.

IV. Regardless of motive, the beginning of the First Crusade initiated a significant expansion of seaborne trade and traffic across the Mediterranean.

A. The response to the First Crusade was enthusiastic.

    1. Knights, their retainers, and simple people without arms crossed the continent to embark for the Holy Land.

    2. The natural ports of departure were the Italian trading cities of Pisa, Venice, and Genoa.

    3. These cities had the ships, navigational skills, and experience to move tens of thousands of Europeans across the Mediterranean.

B. The Italian maritime republics reaped enormous profits from this venture.

    1. Secondary industry and services blossomed, including those engaged in warehousing, the provision of armor and harnessing, the sale of horses, and the provision of servants.

    2. The resultant increase in population and wealth changed the nature of the maritime states. Although these states had always been competitive, the competition was now greater because the stakes were higher. Distinctions and divisions among the states sharpened, turning them into enemies.

    3. The Italian cities also gained a great deal of knowledge from the experience of the Crusades. They learned elements of navigation and began to develop exchange rates and various laws that would help them expand their economic empire.

C. The constant contact with the Levant by Italian merchants greatly increased their wealth and opportunities.

    1. Knights and their retainers developed a taste for luxury goods they encountered in the Holy Land. The Italians had the advantage of knowing how these luxury goods could be supplied.

    2. After ferrying the knights and their equipment to the Holy Land, the ships needed cargo to serve as ballast for the return voyage.

    3. Some of this cargo consisted of religious "artifacts," such as soil from Jerusalem, but most of it was luxury goods from the East, including spices, silks, fruit, slaves, and ceramics.

D. Another unintended consequence of the Crusades was the development of more sophisticated mechanisms of business organization and credit.

    1. Northern European knights and their followers were often forced to borrow money to travel from their estates to Jerusalem. Because the northern European economy worked largely on a manorial barter system, liquid capital was not commonly available.

2. Those who did have available capital were Italian merchants; thus, the Italians added banking to the list of services they provided.

3. The Italians also developed business practices and instruments to ensure that they would be able to collect loans and to enable the transfer of money to cities elsewhere in Europe.

4. Among the innovations of Italian merchants and bankers were letters of credit, double-entry bookkeeping, and the *commenda*, a form of contract that allowed several investors to pool their capital.

E. Italy became a mercantile economy, based on the amassing of large amounts of wealth, which was, in many instances, simply funneled from the rest of Europe to help finance the Crusades.

1. This wealth was used to generate even greater wealth through the purchase of luxury goods that could be sold back to the Crusaders. In this way, the Italians became the economic middlemen of an entire continent.

2. Of course, the negative aspect of this activity was that it bred competition among the Italian cities that would ultimately end in warfare.

F. The Crusades also resulted in the enrichment of the church, particularly the Holy See in Rome.

1. Many knights who chose not to go on crusade felt guilty about the decision. To salve their consciences, they gave money to the church.

2. The church also saw in the Crusades an opportunity to tax the clergy in order to aid this great Christian endeavor.

V. The Crusades were not just adventures in the history of Christianity and Islam. They were, in fact, the beginning of the Italian Peninsula as we know it and the ultimate sources of wealth, competition, and diversity in Italy.

Essential Reading:

T. Asbridge, *The First Crusade. A New History: The Roots of Conflict between Christianity and Islam.*

Supplementary Reading:

J. Riley-Smith, *The Oxford Illustrated History of the Crusades.*

Questions to Consider:

1. Do you think the Crusades were motivated more by religious or economic interests?

2. Can the Crusades be seen to have defined how the West and Islam relate to each other up to the present day?

Lecture Three—Transcript
The Crusades and Italian Wealth

We discussed how, after the fragmentation of the Italian Peninsula following the collapse of the Roman Empire, there arose a number of states that were different in character and different in personality. It's necessary to investigate how these differences arose and to see, at least initially, how economic changes drove different sorts of political and social organization. The most reasonable place to start would be the great maritime republics. Also, we've seen that after that period of fragmentation, it really was Christianity, the idea of a singular Western Latin church, that was the glue that bonded all of the Italians together into the idea of a shared concept of what it was to be Western, to be European, and to be Italian. This concept of a singular Christianity, of a united Christendom, also provided a metaphor, a vocabulary for the discussion of what it really was to be Western, and it also provided an opportunity to discuss issues of change, and to look at different forms of political structures and different forms of ambition in terms of religion. If change was to happen, it had to be change that was ordained by, or at least approved by, God.

In many instances, we can see that these issues come together; in fact, they form a kind of tightly bound knot over the issue of the Crusades. The Crusades provide a moment that will help us understand exactly how Italy developed and why, and the role that Italy played in Europe; how Italy became, then, the instrument, the intermediary force, between East and West; the concentration of much of the continent's wealth, and also a place where experimentation could happen most easily, based upon not only diversity and competition, but also based upon the availability of new ideas that could be applied in multifarious ways, and in a number of different contexts, each driven by their own particular circumstance.

The preaching of the First Crusade to the French nobility at Clermont by Pope Urban II in 1095 was a dramatic moment. It was, in fact, the first postclassical moment of the expansion of Europe outside its own continent, and the beginning of a period of colonization of territories on the other side of the Mediterranean. The immediate motivation was well known; it was to support the Byzantines in their terrible struggle against the Turks. The Emperor Alexius had been defeated catastrophically at Manzikert, and he appealed to the pope for assistance, fearing that Islam would overwhelm what was left of the Byzantine Empire. That empire, with its capital of Constantinople—founded by Constantine, the first Christian emperor—was a place not only seen as the extension of Roman rule, but also as the maintenance of the Christian vanguard in the East.

Urban saw this as an opportunity for other things as well. Urban realized that the recent schism between the Eastern, or Orthodox, and Western and Latin churches could perhaps be healed by providing assistance to Alexius. That schism of 1054 had divided the Church, and one of the issues was the authority of the pope. Here was the emperor asking the pope for help. Urban, being a very sophisticated statesman, realized that these were opportunities not to be missed. But there were other issues. Underlying the general sense of the need of Christian mission, there was indeed a serious fear, and a real fear, that the Turks would indeed overwhelm the Christians in the eastern Mediterranean and elsewhere.

The expansion of Islam from the foundation of the religion in the 7th century had been dramatic and extraordinarily quick. Muslim armies had conquered the Middle East and the coast of North Africa. They had spread into Europe through the conquest of much of Spain and the establishment of the kingdom of Granada. They had moved into the south of France until they were stopped at the Battle of Tours by Charles Martel. Muslim enclaves in Europe made Europeans very nervous. They saw it as not only inappropriate for the Christian dispensation, but also as a dangerous element because the Muslims were, to them, a single people. They weren't divided between Moor and Turk; they simply were infidels to the Christians of the Middle Ages. There were reasonable fears, then, that these infidels might come together, band in allegiance, and then threaten Christian hegemony.

It was the Muslim control of Jerusalem that really focused the Christian mind. Here was the Holy City, the place that was closely associated with the life of Christ, under the control of a religion that the Christians found to be not of their making—an infidel religion, something with which they believed that God must necessarily be extremely angry. The Christians saw the only solution as military intervention; they had to take the city. They had to relieve it from the

Muslims and reestablish some form of Christian rule—something that it had not seen for centuries, since the Byzantines were driven out. By 1095, then, there was a sense of urgency and a sense of mission. It was generally believed that it was a Christian responsibility to take back Jerusalem and the Holy Land and return it to Christian rule.

This, of course, was the outward sign. This was the general belief, and this was the vocabulary, but it also was, to an extent, a metaphor for other forces that were not as easily understood. There were pressures in Europe that also drove these decisions to be made—pressures in Europe that ensured that Christians would have to look for other outlets for not only a rising population, but for economic ambition, increased territory and broader estates. Domestic warfare had increased in Europe, and it increased not because the continent had become any more violent—Europe was always the violent continent, as we well know—but also because of the threats. The dangers from outside forces had been greatly reduced.

The Northmen, for example, those Vikings that had come from Scandinavia and looted and plundered much of northern Europe, and had gone as far as Russia, had been domesticated to some extent in the province of Normandy, where the Northmen then settled down and established a duchy of their own; and in Sicily, where the Northmen conquered that island and turned it into a Norman kingdom. Similarly, the Magyar tribes from the East had settled in the broad Hungarian plain and established settled agriculture and domestic organization. There were no longer threats; there were no longer nomadic plunderers. They were, in fact, an increasingly civilized, Christianized people.

But with the threats gone, it meant that the large numbers of heavily armed, mounted warriors, or knights, had to find someone to fight. They were trained to do nothing else; it was their culture. It was their belief that it was their role in society to protect, to govern, and to fight. If there were no enemies to fight from the outside, they would fight one another. The Church saw the idea of the "peace of Christ" as a critical element in the Christian dispensation. It was, in fact, to be an irenic religion; Christianity was supposed to bring brotherhood and peace. But Christians were fighting and killing one another, and the Church realized there had to be some instrument that would allow this to at least be curtailed, if not altogether stopped.

Moreover, the growing stability had allowed for increased trade—first local and then more long-distant. This not only increased the wealth of Europe, but it also increased the sizes of towns and cities throughout the continent. In particular, it allowed for the easy movement of food, which increased the population more with an increased fertility rate. The population of Europe in the 11th century began to seriously grow. As with the knights, it was necessary to find broad acres for those surplus sons who would not be content being sent off with just a suit of armor and a horse. This led to the opportunity of the expansion of Europe into the East. It was perfectly normal and reasonable that the expansion would be directed towards those areas that the Christians defined as infidel, the area controlled by the Muslims, because it provided the ideological justification for what was really a war of expansion.

While this was happening, the cities of Italy—especially the great maritime cities of Genoa, Pisa, and Venice—were expanding long-distance trade. With the increase in city life throughout the continent, and the increase in population, there was greater opportunity for the selling of goods of all kinds, but there were also dangers. The dangers were that the Muslim states around the southern areas of the Mediterranean were hostile to Christian traders. They weren't very keen on the competition of Christians in their area. Consequently, that Muslim control meant that there was a barrier to the expansion of Christian economic activity—and most significantly, the really, really lucrative trade. The long-distance luxury trade with the East, with India and China, was controlled largely by Muslim traders. They were willing to trade with Christians, but at an extremely high price. The Christians wanted a better deal. They wanted more of this economic action, and they realized it would require war in order to achieve it.

Those luxury goods were things that the Europeans were craving more and more: spices in order to maintain food in a world without refrigeration, luxury clothing (especially the silks that came from the East), ceramics that became extremely sought after; and of course, slaves, with Venice developing quickly into the premier slave market of western Europe. Slavery was not a widespread practice in Europe, and indeed there was nothing like a slave economy. But the Church permitted, and almost encouraged, the conversion of non-Christian peoples through the act of slavery. Slaves had to be captured as non-

Christians, and it was the responsibility of the people who purchased these slaves to convert them. Then the Church strongly encouraged the owners to manumit them, or to free them, once they had converted to Christianity, and turn them from slaves into servants. Indeed, this happened very often. Because the children of slaves—regardless of who the parents were—were, in fact, free there was no way that there could be a slave economy in Europe. Nevertheless, there still was a desire for slaves as domestic servants and, particularly if they were young and attractive, as concubines.

The pope saw the great Christian Crusade as an opportunity. It was an opportunity to fulfill several goals at once. It was an opportunity that the pope really was not going to allow to slip. It was the expansion of Europe, of Christianity, and of trade; the conversion of infidels to Christianity for the well-being of their soul, or so he believed, and the export of violence from Europe to an area where the violence would actually do some good—that is, in the conversion of souls and in the increase of wealth. Military action would protect the long-distance trade and ensure that those cities that were engaged in it (like Genoa, Venice, and Pisa) could bring even more wealth back to Europe—wealth that the Church could use because much of that wealth would ultimately find itself in ecclesiastical coffers. Merchants from cities and towns saw this as an opportunity to grow as well, and they strongly encouraged their noble neighbors, the knights of Europe, to engage in this activity, realizing there was profit to be made.

Regardless of the motives, the First Crusade initiated the huge expansion of seaborne trade, seaborne traffic across the Mediterranean—and indeed the expansion of Europe itself—with the ultimate creation, after the First Crusade, of the Latin kingdom of Jerusalem and the creation of Christian kingdoms in areas that had previously been ruled by Muslims. The Crusade was met with enormous enthusiasm. In fact, Urban II was surprised by the degree of enthusiasm that he met at Clermont. At that place of the meeting of the French nobles and ecclesiastics, to every one of his sentences, there was the cry of "*Deus vult*;" "it is God's will;" "God wants us to do this." Knights in the thousands, their retainers, and simple people without arms, marched towards the Italian cities to take ship in order to free Jerusalem, and in order to ensure the supremacy of Christian European commerce.

What were the natural points of departure? The natural ports were those that were in the Italian Peninsula because of Italy's geographic position—so Genoa, Pisa, and Venice benefited immediately. These maritime cities, after all, had large numbers of ships, and they were experienced in the navigation of the Mediterranean, having expanded beyond local trade into long-distance trade. Moreover, they had the experience to deal with people outside of Europe, unlike almost any other place on the continent. It was, then, not only the natural point of embarkation, but also the natural point of intermediation between Europe and the East, that gave rise to the power and the wealth of these Italian cities.

The maritime republics did extraordinarily well. They grew enormously rich, and they reaped huge profits; not only from the seaborne trade—because it's obvious that they would charge what the traffic would bear, and the traffic was willing to pay a great deal in the salvation of their souls—but also the secondary industries that would grow up around any large military long-distance adventure, such as a Crusade. Warehousing, the provision of armor and harnessing, the sale of horses, the provision of servants; all of these things were necessary. Warehousing was necessary to put together the necessities to equip a large army fighting over a long distance. Venice and Genoa became not only the points of embarkation, but also the warehouses of Europe, ensuring that much of the wealth of an entire continent would be funneled into them in order to be used for this purpose, which was defined, at least in the rhetoric of religion, as good and God's will.

The resultant increase in interest, population, and wealth changed the nature of these states. Whereas previously they were not completely content with just local trade and determining their own areas of interest and economic influence, now they were forced into an area of competition. Which of the cities would be chosen to take an army across? How would the spoils be shared? In other words, what was supposed to be a cooperative Christian operation in order to take the Holy Land from the infidels focused on the city-states of Italy, especially the maritime republics, an element of competition. They were competing with one another for markets, for routes, with points of connection, and with the ability to continue to service those armies fighting abroad.

They had always been competitive with one another. It's the nature of the economic activity, competition. However, now the competition was sharper because the stakes were so high. The amount of money involved was huge, and the possibility for growth, wealth, and empire was now perfectly visible. The competition sharpened the distinctions and the divisions. In fact, we've already discussed how the diversity of the Italian Peninsula brought forward a whole experimentation in social, political, and cultural opportunities. Now we're going to see that competition for trade and wealth distinguish them as well and turn them into, in fact, enemies—ultimately enemies that would fight unto the death. By the end, by the 14th century, it was really only Venice that remained.

The Italian cities also benefited in a way that's not so immediate. With their connections with the East now cemented, regular, and constant, they began to be able to navigate and determine everything, including the values of coinage and the exchange rates. They began to understand the various laws they would have to interpret. They began to understand the elements of navigation that would take them from one port to another. In other words, they gained the experience that would allow them in the future to expand their economic empire, and to expand their physical empire, allowing them to reap even more wealth. This was a time of learning. It was a time of shared and growing experience, and it was this experience that would be focused very, very much on those cities that would make not only Italy, but all of Europe, much richer.

The other unintended consequence of the Crusades was the enormous increase in the carrying trade for luxury goods in general. It's obvious that the connections with the East would provide opportunities, but no one quite imagined how great and how huge these opportunities would be. The northern knights—who were being sent to Jerusalem, who were fighting in the Holy Land, who passed through the cities of Venice and Genoa, who perhaps had visited Rome as pilgrims as well—saw a world so distinct and so alien to their own that they had to bring some of it back with them when they returned.

How do you "keep them down on the farm once they've seen Paree?" How do you send them back to the fastness of the motte-and-bailey castles on an assart in the middle of central Europe when they've spent time in Constantinople or Jerusalem; when they've tasted fruits, worn silks, tasted spices; when they've seen a level of sophistication in living that they could not in any way sustain by living on their estates, rude as they often were, determined only by local production made by local craftsmen? We see, then, a desire for luxury goods spreading beyond those merchants into the market itself. Knights and their retainers who had seen this wanted it when they returned home. The Italians saw this as an opportunity for expanding and extending trade in a dramatic way.

The Italians also had the advantage of knowing that these luxury goods could be supplied. It's one thing to know that a market was available; it's something else to know that, in fact, you can supply it. The Italians realized it can happen because they had already begun to look towards the secondary market. The Genoese in particular, but also the Pisans, had begun spreading into the western Mediterranean using the ports in the south of France, in Barcelona, and perhaps even outside the Straits of Gibraltar, up the Atlantic coast, in order to service areas that they knew would be very susceptible to goods that they could supply. Moreover, when this opportunity began, they knew that they were going to have lots of ships available in order to carry this trade. We have to remember that the ships that were sailing in order to pursue the Crusades were very, very large. They were galleys that rode across the Mediterranean. They were wide-beam/shallow-draft, which meant that they required a great deal of ballast.

The ballast was provided, on the route out, very much by the knights, their horses, and their armor. This, of course, is the purpose of the sail to begin with. But what were they going to return with? What were they going to use as ballast in order to fill those vast holds in the ship on the way back, returning to Venice, Genoa, or Pisa? Initially, curious things were carried. The Pisans, for example, filled their ships with the land from Jerusalem. They literally dug the soil of the Holy City and put it in the bottoms of their ships. They carried the soil back to Pisa and put it in that vast complex of ecclesiastical buildings they were beginning to construct around the "*Campo Santo*," the holy field.

It was holy because the dirt was the very land that they had taken, the earth from Jerusalem. They did it because they believed that when the last trumpet sounded, and the dead shall be raised, that the first to rise into heaven would be those who had been buried close to

Christ in Jerusalem. The Pisans—always ambitious and always in competition with their fellow states of Genoa, Venice, and Amalfi—decided they wanted to be first. Therefore, their burial ground—because the Campo Santo was initially a cemetery—was going to be covered with the earth of Jerusalem so that the Pisans would be first off the mark and first in line waiting to enter heaven at the time of the Second Coming.

This curious experiment in ecclesiastical marketing didn't really produce many followers, but it did provide the kind of model that the other states used, because the empty ships had to be filled with something, and earth, holy as it may be, is not particularly valuable, except when that last trumpet blows. But if you fill it full of slaves, silks, spices, luxury goods, or fruit, then these things could be sold quickly and easily, and the profit is then much increased—the profit from carrying across and the profit from carrying back. Consequently, the Italian cities grew doubly rich, and quickly, because so much of this happened over a very short period of time, with the success of the First Crusade really being determined by the very end of the 11th century.

There was another element, too, that we have to factor in, a second unintended consequence. In order for these northern knights and their followers to travel from the fastness of their estates in northern Europe through the Italian cities and across to Jerusalem, they had to have money. The feudal economy was largely a manorial barter economy. It was a subsistence economy in many ways, in which money was really a secondary function. In fact, the feudal system and the manorial economy had developed largely to deal with the world without cash, without liquid capital. How were the knights about to do this?

They often needed to borrow, and the people from whom they could borrow were those that had surplus capital. They couldn't find these in the North because of the nature of the less sophisticated northern European economy. But they could find the capital in Italy because those merchants, who were making large fortunes, had surplus capital, and the knights could borrow from them in order to engage in this great adventure of the return of the Holy Land to Christendom. The Italians, then, moved from being merchants to also being bankers. In fact, they provided the sinews of wealth that kept the continent together, all of which were bound in Italy.

Besides money and the access to capital, there were also the instruments needed to make sure that capital could be managed. It's one thing to have a good deal of money and to be able to lend it; it's something else to be able to collect on the loan, to draw contracts that would ensure that they could be enforced, and also to make sure that money could be moved from where it was available to where it was needed. Here, the Italians became very skilled as well, developing in many ways the first modern business practices and business instruments. This was largely the result of the Crusades. For example, not only banking, but the idea of letters of credit for moving money from one place to another began to develop. These developed because the Italian merchants had offices in several places. They were used to this from their mercantile activities, from the primary trade to the secondary trade—the need of transferring capital from far-off places back to their home base. It was easy, then, to transfer money from Genoa or Venice to Paris, the cities of Germany, or to England. It could be done because the Italians had already been doing it.

They also developed other instruments. It was the time of the invention of double-entry bookkeeping. We don't know exactly when and where this happened, but the most likely place is Genoa, and the most likely time is to account for the vast amounts of money flowing through that city as a consequence of the Crusades. It is probable that that moment that all students of commerce celebrate every year, the invention of double-entry bookkeeping, is the result of this very economic activity and the expansion of Europe through the Crusades. Instruments of cooperation and contracts also began to develop. The Italians invented the *commenda*, that contract that allowed several investors to pool their capital and allowed other investors with less capital to get a greater return than their investment ensured by actually taking on the voyage, by being the captain on the ship or being the merchant in charge of the hold's cargo.

We have, then, a sophisticated world of international finance being developed—a sophisticated world of surplus capital that was being amassed almost for the first time in significant amounts since the collapse of the Roman Empire. Northern Europe remained largely a feudal, manorial, subsistence economy. Italy was increasingly becoming a money economy based on cash because if you're going to trade with the East you can't do it by barter. There's no point in bringing pigs and chickens in a galley across the Mediterranean in order to exchange for silks and spices. What you need is an accepted medium of exchange, and the Italians were geniuses at being able to determine what those exchange mediums would be, and how they should be applied. Of course, like all good merchants, they ensured that it would be on their terms, and they're the ones who would define precisely the means of transfer and the rates of exchange.

We see developing in Italy a different kind of world. We see Italy becoming a mercantile economy, based on the amassing of large amounts of wealth, which was, in many instances, simply funneled from the rest of Europe in order to help finance the Crusades. We saw this wealth being used and applied in order to make greater wealth through the access of capital to purchase luxury goods that could be sold back to those very crusaders who had pawned their property and had mortgaged their estates in order to set sail for Jerusalem in the first place. The Italians became the economic middlemen of an entire continent. Of course, the negative side of this was that it also bred competition amongst the Italian cities for this lucrative trade that would ultimately end in warfare. The competition that we've seen as driving so much of the peninsula could also be seen as sowing the seeds for some of the instability, danger, and violence that we will see developing throughout the peninsula as this course unfolds.

Also, we have to know that the Church benefited as well. The Church didn't exactly skim from the top of this great wealth, but in many ways that's what happened. First of all, those knights who wanted to go on Crusade, but felt unable to do so, gave money in order to solve their conscience. Secondly, the Church realized its Crusade provided this emotional opportunity to tax the clergy in order to help this great Christian endeavor. The instruments of clerical taxation began to develop in Rome, which was the headquarters. It was where all of the money ended up as far as the Church was concerned, and it became another focus of capital—allowing for the popes and the great ecclesiastics of the city to begin to rival the ancient imperial city; to be able to build greatly and to ensure that the pope would be seen—at least in terms of building, and patronage, and magnificence—as the true heir of the Roman emperors.

The Crusades were not just adventures in the history of the religion of Christianity and Islam. They were, in fact, the beginning of the Italian Peninsula as we know it; the creation of wealth, the creation of competition, the creation of diversity, and a wonderful moment that really helps define why Italy is so different from the rest of the continent in the Middle Ages.

Lecture Four
Venice—A Maritime Republic

Scope:

With the advent of the Crusades in 1095, Venice became increasingly rich and influential. By the early 13th century, it was a powerful maritime empire with fortified posts throughout the Mediterranean, Aegean, and Greek mainland. The enormous profits flowing into Venice made the wealthier citizens far richer and more influential than those not as fortunate. In 1297, the Venetian Great Council was closed to all families except those then in place. These were registered in an official genealogy called the Golden Book. Lesser citizens—not as wealthy or powerful but still important— were deemed "original citizens" and recorded in a Silver Book. They had their own privileges, but only patricians from Golden Book families could hold political office. The Venetian constitution was an elaborate structure, and elections were complex events to ensure that no group or family could subvert the republic. Because there was no land to purchase, no feudal nobility to deal with, and no mass of oppressed workers, members of the Venetian ruling elite were committed to similar goals. Trade expanded, and Venice became a stable republic, enormously rich, powerful, and densely populated.

Outline

I. With the advent of the Crusades in 1095, Venice became increasingly rich and influential. By the early 13th century, it was a powerful maritime empire with fortified posts throughout the Mediterranean, Aegean, and Greek mainland.

    A. Venice was an unusual Italian city, founded in the late 5th and 6th centuries.

        1. The original citizens of Venice chose the republic as their natural form of government. Their leader, the *doge* ("first duke"), was viewed as a *primus inter pares* ("first among equals"), someone who would provide some measure of government and leadership but could not transform the state into a monarchy.

2. Those who founded Venice were trying to distance themselves from the chaos on the peninsula following the incursions of barbarian tribes at the end of the Roman imperial period. They realized that their protection would not come from the Italians in the west but from the Byzantines in the east.

3. Initially, the city was protected by the Byzantine exarchate at Ravenna and by the Byzantine fleet stationed at nearby Classe.

4. Hence, Venice identified with Constantinople and took its sovereignty from the Eastern Empire.

5. The economy of Venice was originally based on fishing and local seaborne trading, but this trade soon expanded into the Adriatic and, eventually, deep into the Mediterranean.

B. Although several Italian cities benefited greatly from the Crusades, Venice established a key advantage during the Fourth Crusade of 1204.

1. Venice had been angered by the Byzantines' seizure of the property of Venetian merchants in the city 30 years earlier.

2. In retaliation, the Venetian doge convinced the leader of the Fourth Crusade to conquer the capital of the Byzantine Empire.

3. The Venetians offered the Crusaders free ships and passage to the Holy Land in exchange for first capturing the Christian city of Zara in Dalmatia, then attacking Constantinople itself.

4. The scheme worked, with the European Crusaders establishing the Latin Empire at Constantinople.

C. The benefits to Venice of this initiative were enormous.

1. Venice gained control of fortified trading posts and outposts in the Aegean and eastern Mediterranean. Venetians were also given special privileges within Constantinople.

2. Further, Venetians received a good part of the spoils of the Crusade and plundered rich treasures from the imperial city.

3. Venice emerged from the Fourth Crusade as a maritime power that had the opportunity, foundation, and platform to become the dominant force in the Mediterranean.

II. The wealthy mercantile families of Venice that had been successful around the time of the Fourth Crusade realized that they could amass more wealth and focus more of their activity on increasing that wealth, as well as the power of the republic, by using the state itself as an instrument of their economic and personal ambitions.

   A. In 1297, the wealthiest citizens closed the Venetian Great Council to all families except those then in place.
      1. This event, known as the *Serrata*, established a closed caste of merchant patricians (called "nobles"), whose members saw the state as an extension of their own mercantile and familial ambitions, as well as a clearinghouse for their own businesses.
      2. These powerful patrician families were registered in an official genealogy called the Golden Book and were accorded certain privileges and responsibilities.
      3. Lesser citizens—not as wealthy or powerful but still important—were deemed *cittadini originari* ("original citizens") and recorded in a Silver Book. Members of this class filled the offices of the chancellery and, indeed, became chancellors, but they had no access to political office.

   B. This separation of classes created one of the curiosities of the Venetian Republic.
      1. Both the Venetian patricians and the "original citizens" seemed to be content with their respective responsibilities.
      2. Nobles of the Great Council were not paid for their service and could not refuse to serve; thus, members of the *cittadini originari* were often relieved to be able to undertake paid employment.
      3. Below the level of the *cittadini originari* and the patricians, other inhabitants of the republic, such as the *arsenalotti* ("arsenal workers"), had some measure of responsibility to the state and to their jobs. Indeed, glassmakers who tried to take their craft outside of

Venice were hunted down and killed by paid assassins of the republic.

III. Venice was extraordinarily stable, with an elaborate system of elections to ensure that the republic could never be subverted.

    A. Up to 2,000 adult males had the privilege of sitting on the Great Council, but only those who were in the city, solvent, and not insane or felons attended.

        1. The council met in a room designed to hold 1,500 men, and the majority of its work was the election of officers, from the most minor up to the doge.

        2. The more powerful the office, the more elaborate the election and the shorter the period of appointment.

        3. The doge, whose office was largely ceremonial and without any real power, was elected for life, usually as a very old man.

    B. As noted, Venice looked to the East for sovereignty.

        1. The question we investigated earlier of the difference between the Guelfs and the Ghibellines, those who sought sovereignty from the pope or the emperor, didn't pertain in Venice, which saw its sovereignty as coming from the emperor in Constantinople.

        2. The Venetians took full advantage of their relationship with Constantinople after the Fourth Crusade, nearly monopolizing the trade between East and West and becoming one of the most powerful states in the Mediterranean.

        3. The structure of the republic helped to fulfill this ambition. Indeed, to ensure that the republic always gained from East-West trade, the trading ships were not owned by Venetian merchants. They were all made in the Venetian Arsenal in such a way that they could be transformed from cargo galleys to war galleys in just one day.

        4. The Venetians created a world that we might call omnicompetent, one in which all members of society were forced, by both custom and law, to participate. And the law, although harsh, applied equally to everyone.

IV. The myth of Venice as an ideal state with a perfect constitution was born out of the republic's success. The reality, of course, as in all myths, was different, and there were, in fact, two attempts to overthrow the state.

A. The first attempt was made in 1310 by a group of young patricians, perhaps discontented with the period of apprenticeship required of them before they could enter service to the state.

1. Although this rebellion quickly broke up, it terrified the Venetian patricians, who responded by establishing the much-feared Council of Ten.

2. This council was an extra-constitutional body of the most influential politicians in Venice. The council could remove any person from office, including the doge; could torture and try those it accused in secret; and could elicit information through the use of spies, all of which it did with some regularity.

3. The council established the infamous *bocche dei leoni*, "the lion's mouth." These were letterboxes spread throughout the city bearing the image of the lion of St. Mark. It was the obligation of every good Venetian who heard or saw something suspicious to write a declaration of the activity and place it in the *bocche dei leoni*.

B. The second attempt to overthrow the Venetian state was instigated by a wealthy, elderly doge, Marin Falier, who tried to establish himself as king in 1355. He may have believed that he could pursue the Venetian war against the Genoese much more vigorously if he did not have to negotiate his actions with the state. Falier was discovered and beheaded on the very spot where he had been crowned.

V. The Republic of Venice became an instrument of economic activity, with the success of its merchants as its primary goal. Venice owed its stability to the fact that all its inhabitants were directed toward the same purpose: the pursuit of wealth.

A. This goal allowed Venice to take on its competitors—the Genoese, the Pisans, and others—for the single purpose of ensuring that Venetian wealth would not be compromised. It was inevitable, then, that this stable, ambitious, warlike maritime state would run into conflict with its fellow maritime states in the peninsula.

B. Fundamental differences in the nature of these states would also become apparent.

    1. Venice was the stable mercantile republic in which the merchants formed the government, used the state in their own interest, and saw themselves as a singular class with a singular ideology.

    2. Genoa was a fractious state where the nobles fought amongst themselves to gain greater advantage and, ultimately, defeat others.

    3. The differences in the social and political structure of Venice and its fellow maritime republics ultimately worked in favor of Venice, which became a model of the successful republican state. Its economic victory and, ultimately, its military victory can perhaps be traced precisely to its constitutional structure.

C. The Republic of Venice was not an accidental superpower in the Mediterranean; rather, it resulted from a series of decisions and structures that allowed it to fulfill its own ambitions and the ambitions of its most prominent citizens. But these policies put Venice on the frontline of the struggle with Islam.

    1. As we will see in a future lecture, Venice would become the vanguard in the clash of Christian and Muslim civilizations.

    2. Venetian interests in the Mediterranean were determined by economic power, long-distance trade, and maritime control. When these interests were challenged, by the Turks in particular, the Venetians had no choice but to resist.

    3. Venice also became the power that protected much of southern Europe from the Turks for centuries. The Venetians sacrificed blood and treasure to protect not just Europe but their own civilization, which was predicated on control of the Mediterranean.

    4. Ironically, Venice was also a tolerant city, in which Islam and variations of Christianity could be practiced as long as the adherents abided by certain rules. When the

Venetians felt that they were losing this control and that the wealth of the republic and the power of its citizens were in jeopardy, they stood firm. Venice then became the frontline of Christian Europe against a powerful and resurgent Islam.

Essential Reading:

D. S. Chambers, *The Imperial Age of Venice: 1380–1580.*

Supplementary Reading:

D. Queller, *The Fourth Crusade: The Conquest of Constantinople.*

Questions to Consider:

1. The Venetian Republic lasted for 1,100 years (697–1797). Why is such political longevity so rare in the West?

2. Venice harbored a Turkish warehouse and Orthodox churches and communities. Account for this anomaly in the age of the Crusades.

Lecture Four—Transcript
Venice—A Maritime Republic

The Crusades made all of the Italian maritime cities rich, but it was Venice that benefited the most. It's necessary now to pause and look to see what this remarkable state was like, how it developed, and why it ultimately emerged as the most powerful of all the maritime republics, lasting until the end of the 18th century with a single constitution; one of the most remarkably stable and successful of all of the experiments in government in Western history. It was not just the advent of the Crusades that made Venice rich; it was enriched partly because of its circumstance. It was enriched because of its location at the headwaters of the River Po, where the river meets the Adriatic. There, at the end of the Roman Empire, in the 5th and 6th centuries, groups of Roman citizens rushed from the barbarians in order to found a city that would be protected by nature. In the almost impenetrable sandbars of the lagoons, they built a city upon millions of open staves driven through the sand into the clay subsoil. On those staves arose the city of Venice that we know to this day.

It was a city that began as a group of independent individuals. There was no prince; there was no leader; there was no bishop. It was not an ancient city. These independent individuals saw a republic as the natural form of government, in which their leader, once elected in the choice of the "first duke" or *doge* in 697, as a *primus inter pares*, a "first among equals"; someone who could provide some measure of government and leadership, but could not under any circumstances subvert the state and turn it into a monarchy. Moreover, the connections of the city were really not those of the Italian Peninsula initially. These Italians, running from the barbarians, were trying to distance themselves from the chaos that they saw on the peninsula following the incursions of the barbarian tribes at the end of the empire. They realized that their protection was not from the Italians on the West, but rather from the Byzantines in the East.

The Byzantines had taken over the great Roman military seaport of Classe; *classis* in Latin means fleet. Augustus has built the seaport of Classe in order to maintain the Adriatic fleet of imperial Rome. The Byzantines took it over and used it as their base of operations, creating their capital at nearby Ravenna for the Exarchate of Ravenna, that Exarchate of Byzantium, which was an attempt to recover the Italian Peninsula for the eastern empire. Protected by the Byzantines and looking to the East for sovereignty, Venice then developed with a very, very clear and distinct eastward-looking philosophy and set of attitudes.

Moreover, these individuals began as fishermen. That's how they could make their living initially. But then, skilled at negotiating the difficult waters of the Po headlands, they began to expand farther and farther down the Adriatic until they developed into local traders; then soon, as their ships grew larger and more sophisticated, long-distance traders. The result was that, by the time we reach the time of the First Crusade, the Venetians had become very sophisticated navigators. They had become brilliant shipbuilders, and they had a sense of government in which all members of the Republic contributed towards the extension of trade. This was focused on that moment of the Crusades that actually provided Venice with the great opportunity to become the powerful maritime state that it did in very, very few centuries.

The Fourth Crusade was called, and the Crusaders amassed once more to try to recover those territories that, although captured in the First Crusade, had been subsequently lost. It was the desire of all Christendom then to recover Jerusalem again. But also, it was a desire of all of Europe to maintain the economic and trading links that had been established as well as a result of the First Crusade at the end of the 11th century. As the Crusaders began to amass in Venice, the Venetians decided that they had an opportunity to avenge what they saw as a fundamental wrong. The Byzantines, a generation before, had confiscated the property of Venetian merchants working within the city, and the Venetians were known to hold grudges. Indeed, Venetian memories are, to this day, long.

The Venetian doge, Enrico Dandolo, who was almost 90 and completely blind, convinced the leader of the Fourth Crusade, Baldwin of Flanders, that it would be to everyone's advantage if he, first of all, took the Christian city of Zara on the Dalmatian coast because the Venetians wanted it; and secondly, to take the crusading army not against the infidel, but against the schismatic Orthodox Greeks of Constantinople. In return, the Venetians would provide free transport, galleys, and support. In other words, the Venetians would provide the transportation; the Crusaders would provide the muscle. The benefit would, of course, be to them both. The result would be the conquest of Constantinople by Baldwin of Flanders in the Fourth Crusade in 1204; one of the most disreputable and dishonorable events in Western history, thereby weakening the Byzantine Empire to such an extent that it never altogether recovered; and in some ways, ensured the ultimate victory of the Turks in the East. In the short term, however, the Venetians benefited enormously. Baldwin of Flanders and his son established, at least for two generations, the short-lived Latin Empire of Constantinople.

The Venetians, being extraordinarily crafty— and also realizing their limitations in the nature of their polity—saw that they would take, as opposed to large amounts of territory or even great wealth, fortified trading posts and outposts in the Aegean and the eastern Mediterranean that they could then use in order to support their trading links with the East. They were given special privileges within Constantinople, and they were also allowed to carry away for the return voyage almost anything that wasn't nailed down, and some things that were, in Constantinople. To this day, we see the great Quadriga, the four horses that the emperor Constantine had established in the Hippodrome in Constantinople on the Basilica of St. Mark. We also see the four tetrarchs, those porphyry figures of the two Caesars and two Augustus's, probably from the time of Diocletian, attached to the walls of the Basilica; and inside, the Pala d'Oro, one of the most beautiful and exquisite examples of Byzantine goldsmithing and enamel work.

These things were taken because they were available, and the Venetians thought that they had earned them by arranging the Fourth Crusade—that moment when the Venetians seemed to be conquering the known world. Venice emerged from the Fourth Crusade as not just another one of the competing maritime powers, but one that had the opportunity, the foundation, and the platform to become the dominant force in the entire Mediterranean. Indeed, it soon fulfilled that promise. The great wealth, though, as in most examples in almost any history of any place at any time, was not distributed evenly.

Indeed, the wealthy mercantile families that had been successful around the time of the Fourth Crusade realized that they could amass more wealth and focus more of their energy and activity in increasing that wealth, as well as the power of the Republic, by using the state itself as an instrument of their economic and personal ambitions. By the end of the 13th century, in 1297, the Venetian patricians—who were confusingly called nobles—sitting in the Great Council closed that council to all but those families that were sitting there at that moment. This is the famed *Serrata*, the closing of the Great Council of Venice, and establishing not a fluid class of wealthy merchants, which it was possible through social mobility to enter, but rather now a closed caste of nobles who saw the state as an extension of their own mercantile and familial ambitions, and who saw the state as, in some ways, a clearinghouse for their own businesses.

The closing of the Great Council created the Venetian patriciate as it was going to be sustained until the end of the 18th century, when Napoleon, in 1797, finally ended the Republic. It created several classes of citizens. The nobles were determined by genealogy in an official genealogy called the Golden Book, kept by the state. You had to be born into a family recognized as patrician in order to be inscribed. Once you were inscribed, you had certain responsibilities and duties, and certain privileges. Anyone not in that genealogy was not noble, and therefore lacked those privileges—although the Venetians, always being crafty, provided them with others.

The class immediately below the patricians, also mercantile, often professional men—doctors and lawyers in particular—and those with a level of education and sophistication but insufficient wealth or insufficient opportunity to enter the Great Council before the Serrata of 1297, were still recognized and formed a secondary class known as *cittadini originari*, or "original citizens." They had their own genealogy, a Silver Book, and they had privileges as well. It was they who became the secretaries of embassies. They were the ones who filled the offices of the chancellery, and indeed they became the chancellors themselves. They were people who were educated, wealthy, and sophisticated, but they had no access to political office.

This creates one of the curiosities of the Venetian Republic. Some say it determined the nature of its stable government because what we see are two groups in society: those who have access to political privilege, who alone can fulfill political office, who can be elected to doge or to the Senate; and those who have to fulfill secondary offices. Both seemed to be content because the Venetian patricians, who could be doge or powerful members of the government, had to do so at their own expense. They had to serve if elected—they could not refuse—and they had to serve the state because the state, in many ways, determined the contours of their lives; whereas the *cittadini originari* were paid, and they fulfilled important roles, and they didn't have the obligation to serve in the same way. It seemed as though this division of society provided a stability in Venice where everyone knew his place, and where everyone knew the responsibilities and privileges attended upon that place.

It's also interesting that even below the level of the *cittadini originari* and the patricians, those within the Republic were seen as privileged and had some measure of responsibility to the state and to their jobs. For example, there were two great industries in Venice. One was the *Arsenal*—a word of Arabic origin that has given us our word "arsenal"—where the galleys of the Republic were built, the cannons were cast, and the sails and the rope were made. The Arsenal workers, the *arsenalotti*, were given special privileges. They even had distinctive costumes with little red round hats that they would wear when out in order to identify them as members of this privileged group. They were well paid, honored, and respected, but the understanding was that they would work for the Republic, that they would be very well trained, and that they had responsibilities, but they would be rewarded proportionately.

The same was true of the glassmakers of the glass factories. Glassmaking was something that the Venetians learned from the Syrians. They picked up the techniques of the making of decorative glass as a consequence of the Crusades, and they became the great glassmakers in Europe. Those who worked in the glass factories were well paid and honored. But as in all things Venetian, there was always a threat. Those who decided that they were going to take their craft elsewhere, outside of Venice, would be hunted down by the paid assassins of the Republic, killed, their families punished, and their property confiscated. It's not an accident, then, that the skills of the Venetian glassmakers never did escape from the Republic until well into the 16th century.

Venice was an extraordinarily stable place. Elections were stable. The Great Council consisted of about 2,000 adult males. In order to sit in the Great Council, you had to be adult and be in the city. Your name, of course, had to appear in the Golden Book, and you also had to be not crazy. You had to be solvent and not in arrears of taxation, and you could not be a felon; always good restrictions on elected office. Those individuals who were elected had access to every office in the state, it was though a very, very carefully controlled set of offices. Indeed, the largest purpose, the most time-consuming element of the Great Council—which sat in a room that was designed for 1,500 people to be present simultaneously—was to elect others. We see in Venice the creation of this complex state in which elections were remarkably elaborate. Elections were designed to ensure that no one, under any circumstances, could subvert the state. The higher the office, the less time an individual held it. The lower and most insignificant offices were held for long periods.

The greatest office, the doge, was for life. This curious situation resulted from the fact that the doge was really a symbol. He was not a powerful person. In fact, the doge had almost no power or authority whatsoever. He was, as he is often described in Venetian literature, "a bird in a gilded cage." He was often elected as an old man, often just to recognize the honor that he had done the state in previous years; someone who was the head of a long-serving and important family. Once elected, he had to move into the Ducal Palace with his family. He was never allowed to meet with really anyone, but especially foreigners, alone. He always had to speak so he could be overheard. He was not allowed to put his image or his coat of arms up during his own lifetime. When he was given the honor of being represented, including in the wonderful pictures of the Palazzo Ducale and the Ducal Palace, or on his own tomb, he had to be kneeling, either before a symbol of Venice, like the Lion of St. Mark or the Virgin Mary, who was the protector of Venice itself; or to the symbolic image of Venice, a large woman with blond hair and a ducal robe, who symbolized the Republic.

He was not to be seen as a prince; he was to be seen as the embodiment of Venetian sovereignty. Sovereignty, of course, was an unusual thing in Venice because it looked to the East. The question that we have investigated of the difference between the Guelfs and the Ghibellines, those who sought sovereignty from the pope or the emperor, didn't obtain in Venice. Venice looked to the East; Venice saw, initially, its sovereignty coming from the emperor in Constantinople. Even the Church, because there was no bishop, initially took its authority from the patriarch of Constantinople, ultimately transferred to the patriarch of Aquilea. Venice was always a place that had connections with the East. After 1204, after the Fourth Crusade, those connections were made deep and rich, and the Venetians were, in fact, almost the holders of a monopoly of that incredibly rich trade between Constantinople and the West.

The Venetians took full advantage of this. Again, with usual Venetian craftiness, they were able to turn an opportunity into something that would last for centuries. Just the structure of the Republic, as we've seen, helped to fulfill this, helped to sustain this ambition of making Venice the most powerful state in the Mediterranean. How this worked is something that again exemplifies not only the imaginative nature of Venetian government, but that single-minded fixation on profit, on wealth, on the belief that if your argosy should leave from Venice and go to Constantinople and come back, you should be able to allow for a 1,000-percent return. To make sure that the Republic would always gain from this, none of the ships of the Venetian merchants were owned by Venetian merchants. They were all made in the Arsenal. They were all made in such a manner that they could be transformed from being a cargo galley to being a war galley in just one day. In other words, all of the ships of the Venetian fleet were both mercantile vessels and war vessels simultaneously.

There was no distinction, just as there was no distinction between the patricians of Venice, the nobles—being merchants, responsible for their own family businesses— and officers of the Republic, responsible for the collective authority of the Venetian state. The Venetians created a world that was not totalitarian in our sense, but one that was omnicompetent—one in which all members of society were forced, really by both custom and law, to participate, and the law was harsh. The law, though, harsh as it may have been, pertained equally to everyone. Regardless of your rank or wealth, you were tried in the same way because the law represented Venice, and Venice was greater than the sum of its citizens—greater than any of its citizens, including the doge.

Consequently, Venice as the myth of Europe begins to develop: the perfect constitution, the ideal state, the most stable republic imaginable. This is a myth that begins as early as the 15th century with Florentines comparing their own fractious republic with the stability and calm of Venice. It becomes the model for the English Republicans of the 17th century. It becomes almost an image of perfect government. The reality, of course, as in all myths, is different. There were, in fact, two attempts to overthrow the state, both of which had powerful consequences, especially the first.

Despite the fact that Venice was a stable and highly integrated state in which everybody knew their place and had roles to play—and those roles were enforced—there was an attempt in 1310 by a group of young patricians to overthrow the Republic. Their leader, Bajamonte Tiepolo, was a kind of young swell, and he was surrounded by other young swells. They really didn't have a plan or know what they were going to do, but they gathered together one day in 1310, and they got horses—which was unusual in Venice because Venice is a city full of water, and horses were not to be seen—and they put banners on the ends of spears and rode towards the Piazza San Marco.

There, they made a great deal of noise until, according to tradition, an elderly lady, wishing to sleep in the afternoon, tired of the noise and took a roof tile from above her head, threw it at them, and hit the standard-bearer of Tiepolo, who fell off his horse. All of the others realized this was a bad plan and went home. It was a kind of comic-opera moment. It was something that really can't be seen as a serious attempt to subvert the state, but the patricians were terrified. One of their own number, a member of a great family, the Tiepolo, had gotten as far as organizing a revolt against the state, and they knew nothing about it. They thought they controlled everything, but they clearly did not.

What Bajamonte wanted is impossible to say. It was likely that he represented one of the real fissures in Venetian society between the young and the old. Venice was a gerontocracy in which accumulated experience, great wealth, time spent abroad governing the vast empire, the *stato da mar*, that the Venetians established, serving on galleys, spending time in Constantinople and Alexandria; these were recognized, but it meant that most high officers in the state, the members of the Senate and the doge, were in their 70s or 80s, or even older. Young patricians found their lives very restricted by a *cursus honorum* that required them to go through this apprenticeship, and many didn't like it. Many wanted to stay home; boys just want to have fun. Bajamonte Tiepolo represented the young patricians who thought that perhaps they might be able to have a bit more influence in government and not spend as much time seasick on a galley.

The Venetian patricians who responded did so in a completely Venetian way. Five years later, they established, after much consultation, the feared Council of Ten, the *Concilio dei Dieci*. The Council of Ten has entered the collective unconscious of Europe the way the Gestapo has, or other instruments of terror, the KGB. The Council of Ten was an extra-constitutional body of the most influential politicians who were in fact guided by the *Capi*, the three most influential amongst those. They could do anything, literally. They could remove any person from office, including the doge, which they actually did on one occasion. They could try in secret, torture, or elicit information through the use of spies; all of which they did with some regularity.

They established the infamous *bocche dei leoni*, "the lions' mouths." These lions' mouths were images of the Lion of St. Mark with an open mouth, to which was attached a letterbox, spread throughout the city. It was the obligation of every good Venetian who heard or saw something suspicious to write a declaration that something had been seen, to denounce those—if he knew the names—persons who were actually engaged in this activity, and place it in the *bocche dei leoni*. The most feared of all of these *bocche dei leoni* was in the room of the Great Council itself, and it opened into the adjoining room, which was the room of the Council of Ten. This secret police, this secret organization, became the real instrument of Venetian government. The creation of the Council of Ten, the secret denunciation, and the secret trials, resulted in Venice being stable—but again, we have to ask at what cost.

The second attempt is even more curious. Again, we really don't know why. In 1355, a very elderly—well into his 80s—extraordinarily rich doge named Marin Falier tried to overthrow the Republic and establish himself as king. There is much speculation about why he did this. It certainly wasn't for the benefit of his family because he had no immediate family. He had every honor that the state could give him. It is likely he did so out of an odd sense of patriotism. He believed, perhaps, that the Venetian war against the Genoese was not being pursued with enough vigor, and he really thought that if he could just do it alone and not have to negotiate everything, which was what the Venetian state required, then the Genoese would be defeated much more quickly.

He was discovered, and the result was that his head was severed from his body on the very spot—the Venetians love symbolism—where the doge's crown had been placed upon it. To this day, as you go into the room of the Great Council in the Palazzo Ducale in Venice, and you look, with your back to the great image of paradise behind you, into the far corner of the left-hand cornice, you will see a black spot where there should be, amongst all of his fellows, the image of Marin Falier. Instead, there is only blackness, written upon that says, "Here would be the image of Marin Falier, but that his crimes have stricken him from the book of memory."

Venice then was a remarkable place. It also was a place in which all the government members, regardless of rank—whether they were the dog-catchers or the doge—were directed towards a singular policy of the enrichment of the state, which was done through the enrichment of the mercantile families. The state became an instrument of economic activity, and consequently the success of its merchants became the primary policy of Venice. This was pursued not really for the acquisition of territory. The Venetians didn't want an empire that they could then rule for the sake of ruling an empire; they weren't Romans. They were looking for opportunities to make wealth. The families that constituted the members of the Great Council, those that determined Venetian policy, did so in their own interest, which happened to correspond exactly with the interests of the Republic.

Consequently, Venice developed in a way very different from the other maritime republics, as we shall see. Venice was indeed extremely stable because everybody was directed towards the same purpose. There was a singular ideology, which was the pursuit of wealth. The wealth might not have been evenly distributed, but in comparison with most other states in Europe at the time, it was remarkably prosperous. It was a policy that allowed for Venice to take on its competitors—the Genoese, the Pisans and others—for the single purpose of ensuring that Venetian wealth would not be in any way compromised. It was inevitable, then, that this stable, ambitious, warlike maritime state would run into conflict with its fellow maritime states in the peninsula. The warfare, especially between two of the greatest, Venice and Genoa, would characterize a good deal of the 13th and 14th centuries; ultimately, it would end in Venetian victory.

What will also become apparent is that there is a fundamental difference between the nature of the states. Venice was the stable mercantile republic in which the merchants formed the government, used the state in their own interest, and saw themselves as a singular class with a singular ideology. Genoa was a fractious state where the nobles fought amongst themselves trying to get greater advantage, so that one could then ultimately defeat the other. There was no singular policy; there was personal ambition and factional dispute. It can be seen that the difference in the social and political structure of Venice and its fellow maritime republics ultimately worked in favor of Venice. Venice becomes a model of the successful republican state. Its economic victory, and ultimately its military victory, can perhaps be traced precisely to its constitutional structure.

The great Republic of Venice was not an accidental superpower in the Mediterranean. It was one that resulted from a series of decisions and structures that allowed the Venetian Republic to fulfill its own ambitions and the ambitions of its most prominent citizens. Also, it put Venice on the frontline of the struggle with Islam. When we look at this fundamental struggle—this element that began with the Crusades and was not really determined until, in some ways, the 19th century—we will discuss that Venice would be the vanguard, the frontline of the clash of civilizations, between east and west, between Christian and Islam. This was because the Venetian interests in the Mediterranean were determined by economic power, long-distance trade, and maritime control. When these things were challenged, by the Turks in particular, the Venetians had no choice but to resist them. It was necessary to stand against the Turks for what Venice was. Its source of wealth, its political dynamism, would all be lost.

Venice became not just the frontline, but the power that protected much of southern Europe from the Turks for centuries. The Venetians sacrificed blood and treasure in order to protect not just Europe, but their own civilization, which was predicated upon control of the Mediterranean. Venice becomes part of our own world, and this struggle with the East becomes a characteristic of the city itself. It's ironic that it was also a city that was the most tolerant, in which Islam could be practiced, provided it was done in a place that was permitted by the Republic. Other elements of Christianity, like Orthodoxy, could be practiced; and ultimately, after the Reformation, Protestantism could be practiced. The point was that this was under Venetian control. When the Venetians felt that they were losing control of the Mediterranean, and the wealth of the Republic and the power of its citizens would be jeopardized, they stood firm. Venice then became the frontline of Christian Europe against a powerful and resurgent Islam.

Lecture Five
The *Terraferma* Empire

Scope:

The great success of the Venetian Republic eventually changed its nature and policy: The city was so large that it could no longer feed itself, while it increasingly felt vulnerable on its landward frontier. After defeating Genoa in 1380, Venice pursued a policy of expansion, building a large state on the Italian Peninsula, the *terraferma*, by conquering such ancient cities as Verona, Vicenza, and Padua. Political crisis came in 1509 when the Venetians were crushed at Agnadello by an international alliance combined against them, and the conquered cities on the mainland reaffirmed their independence. A good deal of energy and resources were required for Venice to recapture these territories. Recognizing that the high return on their maritime investments was forever over and determined to avoid any future disintegration of the *terraferma*, the merchant nobles in the Venetian Great Council for the first time began to invest heavily in landed estates on the mainland, transforming themselves into rentier aristocrats. Venice remained the center of political life, but there came a marked shift in values and social mores, influenced by the pervasive Renaissance styles and Humanist principles of the mainland culture.

Outline

I. The great success of the Venetian Republic eventually changed its nature and policies, inducing the city to become Italian for the first time.

    A. Venice had become so densely populated that it was unable to feed itself.

    B. Although it could not be attacked easily by sea, Venice was vulnerable to land attack.

    C. Further, Venice was threatened by powerful states, such as Milan, that were expanding on the Lombard Plain toward the Adriatic, as well as the Holy Roman Empire, which claimed some of the territories that the Venetians had either taken or desired at the top of the Istrian Peninsula.

D. What ultimately persuaded the Venetians to become Italians was their victory over Genoa in the War of Chioggia. This victory determined which state would control most of the Mediterranean trade.

II. After defeating Genoa in 1381, Venice pursued a policy of expansion onto the mainland (*terraferma*).

    A. The creation of a *terraferma* empire would protect the landward flank of the city, the passes through the Alps, and the trading routes that the Venetians desired to maintain. A land empire would also ensure a cheap and easily accessible food supply for the city.

    B. The Venetians recognized the growing importance of overland trade routes across the Alps and up the Rhine into northern Europe. If those trading routes should be cut or if a great power should impose taxes or fees for the movement of goods across their territories, then Venetian profits would be greatly curtailed.

    C. Thus, the Venetians realized that it was in their best interest to abandon the policy of staying aloof from Italian affairs and looking only to the sea as their source of wealth and protection.

    D. The first imperative was to build a large state on the Italian Peninsula by conquering the ancient cities of the Veneto. This was territory in northeastern Italy that stretched to the Lombard Plain in the west; its cities included Verona, Vicenza, and Padua.

        1. These cities had enjoyed rich cultures and powerful spheres of influence, especially Verona, where members of the Ghibelline Della Scala family were vassals of the Holy Roman Emperor.

        2. With the fall of Padua in 1405, Venice acquired not just another great city but also the University of Padua. This acquisition launched Venice into the Humanistic world of 15th-century Italy.

    E. Venetian control of these cities was characteristically high-handed.

        1. The Venetian attitude toward the republic's outposts on the Greek Peninsula and the islands of the Aegean and

Mediterranean had been that of a conquering power. Venetian governors and soldiers were used to suppress the local populations and authorities.

2. In applying this model to the subject territories of the *terraferma*, the Venetians made a mistake. The territories in the Veneto, which had their own rich traditions and civic pride, saw the Venetians as oppressors and tyrants.

3. Moreover, the local nobles, who had been the courtiers and officers of powerful families, now found themselves cut off from political office. In turn, the nobles stirred up the peasants, who had seen their quality of life decline.

F. Other powers that were uncomfortable with Venetian expansion included Milan, the Holy Roman Empire, and the papacy.

1. Milan saw its own future in creating a territorial state across the Lombard Plain but realized that the expansion of Venice could stand in its way.

2. The Holy Roman Empire saw the creation of the *terraferma* empire as a threat to its own expansion and control of the passes through the Alps that led to the Rhine and central Germany. Further, the empire had already witnessed the Venetians taking the March of Treviso and the Istrian Peninsula.

3. The papacy controlled a block of land from one side of the Italian Peninsula almost to the other. As the Venetians began to expand down the Adriatic coast from Venice, they took cities that the Holy See had claimed as well, such as Cervia.

III. The crisis arrived in 1509, when the Venetians were crushed by a significant international alliance combined against them.

A. Angry at Venetian imperial ambition and annoyed with Venetian arrogance, the League of Cambrai (an alliance led by the papacy and the Holy Roman Empire but including many European and Italian powers) declared war on the republic. The Venetian armies were shattered at the Battle of Agnadello in 1509.

B. The city of Venice itself was saved only by the change in policy of Pope Julius II.

1. Julius realized that the complete destruction of Venice would remove the most powerful buffer state in northern Italy against northern invasion.
2. He switched sides to become a defender of Venice, forming the Holy League against his former allies.
3. Venice was saved as a result, but the trauma of the defeat and humiliation hung over the political classes of the republic.

C. Agnadello was not the only lethal blow experienced by Venice.
   1. The economic preeminence of Venice was already threatened to the point that many merchants realized the period of easy wealth had forever passed.
   2. The fall of Constantinople to the Turks in 1453 and the Turkish assault on Venetian trading posts and outposts throughout the Mediterranean and Aegean had been sapping Venetian profits and confidence for half a century.
   3. The Venetians had lost the privileges they had gained in 1204 and now faced competition from other Italian and Islamic merchants, as well as harassment from Muslim pirates and the Turkish fleet.

D. In some ways, the Portuguese were a greater threat to the Venetian economy than the Turks.
   1. The Portuguese realized that the Venetian monopoly of the Mediterranean would make it difficult for them to sustain long-distance trade.
   2. Led by Prince Henry the Navigator, Portugal was a crusading nation. Prince Henry formed a school to train seamen and began the movement of Christians further south down the African coast after colonizing parts of North Africa and establishing fortified trading posts.
   3. The Portuguese were motivated by a desire to link up with Prester John, a Christian emperor thought to be somewhere in Africa, to enable an attack against the Muslims on two fronts. Of course, the Portuguese also wanted to see if Africa could be circumnavigated, a goal that was accomplished by Vasco da Gama in 1497.

E. Da Gama's accomplishment was the final blow to the economic hegemony of Venice.

   1. Now, the powers on the Atlantic seaboard could sail from Lisbon or the ports of Spain directly to India or China, set up their own trading posts, and avoid the Mediterranean altogether.

   2. Ironically, the Venetian monopoly wasn't destroyed only by the Turks but by their fellow Christians, who were also looking for a Crusaders' victory.

IV. These threats fundamentally altered the Venetian character.

   A. The eastern Mediterranean was now a dangerous place because of the Turks, whose fleets were seemingly invincible and who, when they captured Venetian admirals, would skin them alive.

   B. In addition, Arabic and Saracen pirates were licensed by the Turks to prey on Christian shipping. These pirates, including the feared Barbarossa, had their ports in what is now Albania and North Africa and attacked the Venetian mercantile fleets with seeming impunity.

   C. Venetian patricians began to question the wisdom of sending their sons to sea. The *cursus honorum* of the Venetian nobility, the practice of giving patrician sons command of galleys as a sort of apprenticeship to authority, began to pass away.

   D. The enormous profits to be made in shipping that had been virtually guaranteed to Venetians simply evaporated. Profits could be made, but now Venetian merchants had to question whether the potential for earnings was worth the risk.

   E. The *terraferma* empire provided the opportunity for Venetian patricians to cease being merchants and to become *rentier* aristocrats, landowners who could buy vast estates and rely on the safe but low-yielding ground rents that came from them.

   F. This flight of capital from trade into the Venetian *terraferma* empire was powerfully supported by the Venetian state.

   1. Through intermarriage and social connections, the Venetian landlords and local nobility eventually fused.

2. Seats in the Great Council were sold for vast sums, many going to great families from the *terraferma*.

3. In this way, Venice became more than just a mercantile empire and truly an Italian state.

V. With this encouragement from the state, the *terraferma* empire began to grow and prosper and, in turn, influence the capital, the *città dominante*.

A. The rich connections with Italy of such cities as Padua, Verona, and Vicenza, as well as their involvement with Humanism and Italian Renaissance art, were now transmitted directly to Venice, a city that previously had looked to the East and much older traditions.

B. The Italian Renaissance came to Venice, which began to look more like an Italian city and less like an extension of Byzantine rule. The great buildings that we associate with the 16th century and Venice, the work of Jacopo Tatti (known as Sansovino) and Andrea Palladio, began to rise.

C. The Venetian personality changed as the city's architecture and style changed. The Palladian villas reflected the new rentier mentality and offered a world of pleasure. The palaces on the Grand Canal continued to be built and decorated, and there was an element of trade in most of the families, but the future of Venice was now with Italy.

D. This movement toward the Italian mainland and the emergence of a rentier economy also changed the values of the Venetian nobility.

1. The sons of the nobility were no longer sent to sea but, instead, went to the University of Padua.

2. The achievement of Vasco da Gama and the experience of Agnadello taught the Venetians that their wealth and power would not last forever. Venice became a city of pleasure, its citizens bent on enjoying what they had while it lasted.

E. To be sure, the Venetians still saw their primary role as the vanguard of Christianity. Indeed, until 1797, when Napoleon ended the republic, Venice maintained its heroic stance, its wealth, and its beauty, but it wasn't the Venice that had taken Constantinople in 1204 and it wasn't the Venice that had defeated Genoa in the War of Chioggia.

Essential Reading:

P. F. Brown, *Art and Life in Renaissance Venice.*

Supplementary Reading:

J. J. Norwich, *A History of Venice.*

Questions to Consider:

1. Did Venice make the right decision in seeking a territorial empire on the Italian mainland?

2. Are there any mechanisms that could confidently be said to reconcile a conquered people with a victorious imperial power?

Lecture Five—Transcript
The *Terraferma* Empire

We've left the impression of Venice as a maritime republic only, as a great sea power of the Mediterranean, but it was this very success that required the Venetians to become Italians, to begin expanding not just in the Mediterranean at sea, but also onto the Italian Peninsula. The success of Venice over its rivals resulted in the city becoming huge, rich, and indeed so densely populated that it became clear that it was unable to feed itself. It consequently felt extraordinarily vulnerable. It knew that, although it could not be attacked easily by sea because of the strength of its galleys, it could perhaps be attacked by land, if only the army could bridge those impenetrable lagoons. The decision was made to become Italian, and it was a conscious decision indeed. The city could no longer feed itself. The island of the Judecca had become inhabited rather than being the market garden of the city.

Also, it was threatened by powerful states that were expanding at the Lombard Plain towards the Adriatic—states like Milan. It was obvious that the imperial power on the other side of the Alps—that claimed as well some of the territories that the Venetians had either taken or desired at the top of the Istrian Peninsula—could perhaps be a great danger to the state in the future. What ultimately decided the Venetians to become Italians was the victory over Genoa, finally determining the state that would control all of Mediterranean trade, or at least the greater part of it. The war with Genoa was extremely difficult. The Genoese fought extraordinarily hard, and indeed almost won. But the Venetians ultimately, in the War of Chioggia, which ended in 1380, realized that not only had they conquered a great rival, but that they had before them the monopoly on long-distance trade and the monopoly on much of the carrying trade of the eastern Mediterranean.

So, what to do? With the Genoese conquered, and there was no threat to Venice at sea, it was now necessary to move beyond seeing the galleys as the wall of defense for Venice, and begin looking to solid land to create another Venice—not just the *stato da mar*, the maritime empire that had been in existence since even before 1204 and the Fourth Crusade—a *terraferma*, a solid land empire that would protect the landward flank of the city, the passes through the Alps and the trading routes that the Venetians were increasingly desirous of maintaining, and also to ensure that Venice would have a supply of cheap and easily accessible food in case of either famine or siege.

It was obvious that the Venetians would want to control the passes through the Alps and the trade routes through northern Italy because, like most merchants, they realized that the wholesale trade of long-distance mercantile activity could also result in a good deal of profit from the retail trade, from being able to sell those goods to ready markets. The Venetians then began to look at that secondary trade, and at moving the goods into northern Europe, so that they could control those as well and see their profit rising ever more. The Venetians were afraid that if those trading routes should be cut, or that if a great power should impose taxes or fees for the movement of goods and property across their territories, then these profits would be greatly curtailed. The Venetians realized that it was in their best interest to abandon the policy that had protected the Republic for almost 800 years, a policy of staying aloof from Italian affairs—not getting involved in the battles, wars, and the almost continuous petty squabbles of the Peninsula, and looking only to the sea as their source of wealth and protection.

The war with the Genoese, as I suggested, was long and difficult. But ultimately, after the War of Chioggia, Venice emerged triumphant, and they were then able to start moving in a serious way against the surrounding states on the mainland. The area that's now known as the *Veneto*, that territory in northeastern Italy that's dominated by the city of Venice and sees on its farthest western frontier the Lombard Plain, was the area of Venetian interest. One by one, the ancient and powerful cities of the Veneto began to fall: Verona, Vicenza, and Padua. These cities, like Verona, were not only very, very sophisticated, and at one time great powers in the region, but they were also Ghibelline signorial fiefs. The Della Scala family of Verona were fiefs of the emperor. Consequently, the Venetians had conquered territory that technically, according to feudal law and practice, belonged to the Holy Roman Emperor. These Ghibelline cities were proud, but now they were the subject of Venice, a city that owed no allegiance to either emperor or pope, and that still had its view to the East, but now had become involved with the West.

With the fall of Padua in 1405, Venice acquired not just another great city—the city that had been ruled by the Carrara family for centuries in a very sophisticated and urbane court—but it also acquired one of the greatest universities of Europe, the University of Padua, founded in 1222. With the conquest of Padua, Venice instantly entered the humanistic world of 15th-century Italy. It became part of, and indeed a major player in, the culture of antiquity, in the teaching of law and medicine, and in the subject and study of art. Venice was becoming an Italian almost by adoption. Italy was becoming part of the DNA of the Venetians for the first time. There was now an addition to the gene pool of that maritime republic that it had not known since the time of the collapse of the Roman Empire.

The Venetians, though, had a tradition of ruling their subject territories based upon their activities in the eastern Mediterranean and the Aegean. Their attitude towards their outposts and trading posts on the Greek Peninsula, and the islands of the Aegean and Mediterranean, had been essentially those of a conquering power. These were protected outposts, often surrounded by enemies. Consequently, there was a governor supported by powerful military force. The Venetians took this model and initially applied it to the subject territories of the *terraferma*. In many ways, it was a mistake. The Venetian territories in the Mediterranean, and also the territories that it had enjoyed for some time along the coast of what is now Croatia—that is, the Dalmatian coast on the other side of the Adriatic—had not suffered terribly under Venetian rule. They were used to both the protection and, to some extent, the highhanded activity of Venetian governors.

However, the territories in the Veneto—cities like Verona, Padua, and Vicenza—had rich traditions. They had an element of pride, of civic consciousness and integration, that saw the Venetians as oppressors and as tyrants. Therefore, there was a good deal of tension rising between this new *terraferma* empire and the Venetian state. Moreover, the local nobility saw that they no longer had a role to play. The local nobles, who had been the courtiers and the officers of the Carrara and the Della Scala, now found themselves cut off from political office. They still had their property and their estates, but because they were not Venetian patricians, they could not participate in Venetian government. They then saw themselves again as being ruled by oppressors and tyrants, men over which they had no control, and they were resentful and angry.

The same was true of the peasants in the countryside, who worked the estates of these nobles. The peasants saw their quality of life decline. It wasn't altogether because of the Venetian conquest, but it was an easy sell. The nobles could then stir up activity and say, "You are declining in comfort and your level of nutrition because of the Venetians. They are our shared and collective enemy." Moreover, the powerful states on the edge of this new Venetian *terraferma* empire became both nervous and angry. Milan in particular, who saw its own future as creating a large territorial state across the Lombard Plain—perhaps one day reaching to the Adriatic—realized that the expansion of Venice, with its almost unlimited resources for the hiring of mercenary soldiers, stood in its way.

The Milanese began increasingly to see the Venetians as enemies. They previously had not been part of the equation because they hadn't participated in the wars of the Peninsula, but now they became the object of both jealousy and aggression. The Empire was in a very similar situation. The Empire saw the creation of the *terraferma* empire as a threat to its own expansion and control of those passes through the Alps that led to the Rhine and to central Germany. The Empire became extremely annoyed, and having already been bested by the Venetians when the Venetians took the March of Treviso—and by the taking of the Istrian Peninsula—they, too, saw that there was an opportunity for revenge.

Finally, and to some extent most dangerously, there were the states of the Church. The papacy controlled that block of land from one side of the Italian Peninsula almost to the other. The Adriatic coast was extremely important to the papacy. Indeed, many of the cities of that coast were claimed by the papacy as part of papal territory, the patrimony of St. Peter, and forever in the property of the Holy See. But as the Venetians began to expand down the Adriatic coast from Venice, they began taking cities that the Holy See had claimed as well—cities like Cervia. Now there was a competition between Venice and the Church, and this competition would again lead not only to jealousy, but ultimately to a war that virtually destroyed the Republic.

The crisis came on the Italian Peninsula in 1509. A great league was formed of all of those states that had a grudge against Venice and Venetian expansionism, and to some extent against the Venetian pride, the belief that Italy belonged to them as much as the territories of the Mediterranean belonged to them. It was a very, very large league, called the League of Cambrai because it was formed in northern Europe. Indeed, many northern European princes were involved, the Holy Roman Emperor, the papacy, and other states like Milan—who realized they now had an opportunity to finally pay the Venetians back for the way they were acting. War was declared on Venice, and Venice, with its great resources, hired the leading *condottiere* of the time, but it was not enough. They were not aggressive enough, and the alliance against Venice was so overwhelming that the Venetian forces were shattered at Agnadello.

Agnadello, 1509: these two concepts are burned upon the Venetian consciousness and determined Venetian policy right to the end of the Republic. The Venetians, already having been seriously wounded—and having had their confidence sapped by the events that we will discuss in a moment when we look at what was happening in the Mediterranean—finally saw this as the blow that might end the Republic forever. The forces of the united League of Cambrai began marching towards the city. It looked as though Venice itself was going to be conquered, looted, and plundered, just as Venice had looted and plundered Constantinople some three centuries before.

Venice was saved, though. It was saved by the statesmanlike foresight of Pope Julius II, who had initially caused much of the trouble by jealously demanding that the Venetians retreat from the Adriatic territory that it had conquered. Julius was wise enough, warrior-pope that he was, to know that if Venice should be destroyed, the main power that served as a buffer between northern Europe and northeastern Italy would, in fact, be taken away. There would be no power strong enough to ensure that if the emperor decided to cross the Alps and move south, there would be no one to stop him, and so Julius II changed sides. He created a league of his own, the Holy League. Under the somewhat absurd battle cry, given his previous activities, of "Out with the Barbarians," he saved Venice by turning against his earlier allies and driving them from Venetian territory. Nevertheless, Venice was still shattered. There was not much that Venice could do in the short term, given that its armies had been destroyed and its confidence had been sapped.

This loss of confidence is, of course, the great crisis that any state must eventually face. A state that is used to victory and success, used to expansion and ever more wealth and glory, now faced, perhaps, the prospect of its own demise. The confidence wasn't destroyed at Agnadello. Agnadello was the end of a process that actually began at sea, where the Venetians believed that they were in complete and absolute control. It began, first of all, in 1453. The Turks took Constantinople, ending the Byzantine Empire—that empire that, with unbroken succession, stretched back to Constantine. The loss of Constantinople to the Turks meant the loss of the special Venetian privileges within the city, and loss of the protection that the Venetians had—such as it was by the 15th century—from the Byzantines.

Venice now was just another infidel power, as far as the Turks were concerned, that had to pay the same bribes, fees, and taxes. Venice began to see their control of the long-distance overland trade route decline. The Turks now wanted more of this. The Turks wanted the wealth, and they owed nothing to the Venetians, whom they saw not only as infidels, but as dangers to both their true religion and their economic success. The fall of Constantinople was the first blow, and it was a blow that was so powerful that all Europeans felt it—not unlike the way Saint Augustine saw the fall of Rome in 410 to the barbarians. It seemed as though civilization itself was being tested.

That wasn't, of course, the only blow. The Mediterranean was no longer a Venetian lake; it was becoming increasingly a Turkish lake. However, in some ways, the Portuguese were a greater threat to the Venetian economy than the Turks. The Portuguese had realized that the control, the virtual monopoly, of the Mediterranean meant that it would be difficult for them to sustain long-distance trade and compete. The Venetians had been there too long. Their galleys were too successful, their connections too deep. As part of the crusading urge, that crusading movement that really began in 1095, the brother of the King of Portugal, Prince Henry the Navigator, formed not just a school to train seamen, but also began the movement of Christians further south down the African coast after colonizing parts of North Africa and establishing fortified trading posts.

There was a double impetus—the same kind of impetus we've seen with the Crusades. The Portuguese, under Prince Henry, were a crusading nation. They shared the Iberian Peninsula not just with the various Spanish kingdoms, but with the Muslim kingdom of Granada. They saw the need for a Crusade to try to win some victories for Christianity when the Turks seemed to be carrying all before them. Prince Henry saw a Crusade as necessary because he was also the head of a great crusading order. He began ordering his captains farther and farther south along the African coast, charging their way each year, going a little bit farther. The intent was, first of all, to try to link up with Prester John, that Christian emperor somewhere in Africa, so that the Muslims could be attacked both from behind and in front. The other reason, of course, was to see if Africa had an end.

The Romans, despite their colonization of North Africa, had never extended beyond the Sahara. Sub-Saharan Africa was truly *terra incognito*, an unknown land, with no classical model and no biblical story to even connect it to some kind of reality of geography. The Portuguese began pushing farther and farther, until ultimately they realized that Africa did have an end, that Africa could be circumnavigated. You could leave from Lisbon, sail around the continent, and reach India and China. When this was done in 1497 by Vasco da Gama, it was the final blow to the economic hegemony of Venice.

It was the final blow because now the powers on the eastern seaboard, the powers that were on the Atlantic seaboard, could sail from Lisbon or the ports of Spain directly to India or China, set up their own trading posts, make their own connections, and avoid the Mediterranean altogether. The Venetian monopoly, then, wasn't destroyed only by the Turks; it was destroyed by their fellow Christians, who also were looking for a Crusaders' victory, looking also to extend Christianity. It is one of the ironies of history that the Crusades made Venice rich, and the crusading impetus ultimately sapped that very wealth.

Venice, by the time we reach the period of the end of the 15th century and the beginning of the 16th century, was already in economic decline—something that many Venetian patricians and merchants were aware of. This decline and the shock of Agnadello—that blow to the Venetian confidence—altered the Venetian character fundamentally. It did both for good reasons and bad—for reasons that were psychologically understandable, but nevertheless short sighted, and for reasons that were in some ways very wise, a long-term investment in a different kind of future. The Mediterranean was now a very dangerous place because of the Turks, who controlled the eastern Mediterranean, and whose fleets were seemingly

©2007 The Teaching Company.

invincible—who, when they captured Venetian admirals, would skin them alive and use their skins as battle pennants in order to frighten others; and it does have a certain effect.

In addition to the Turkish fleets, there were also privateers, Arabic and Saracen pirates, who were licensed by the Turks as Turkish admirals to go out and prey upon Christian shipping. These pirates, these dangerous men who had their ports in what is now Albania on the north coast and the south coast of the Mediterranean and North Africa, like the feared Barbarossa, could sail and, again with seeming impunity, attack the mercantile fleets of the Venetians. The Venetians seemed to be unable to stop them. More and more Venetian patricians began to question the wisdom of sending their sons to sea, and the sons themselves began to question whether this was a career that they really wanted. The old *cursus honorum* of the Venetian nobility, taking boys quite young and sending them to learn the rudiments of navigation—giving them command of soldiers on galleys so that they could ultimately command fleets and be the governors of provinces, cities, and islands in the Mediterranean— began to pass. More and more Venetian patricians began to look for ways to obviate this, to ensure that their sons would not be skinned alive by the Turks.

Also, the enormous profits that were virtually guaranteed simply evaporated. Now it was still possible to make money, but not the way that it was possible before. Then there was a kind of risk assessment. Yes, you could make a profit if you lived. You could make a profit if the ships returned. Was it worth the risk? Was the profit large enough? Many Venetians decided it was not. There was then a flight of capital away from trade for the first time in Venetian history. Previously, there was no other way to invest; you'd simply put your huge profits back into your family company. Venice got richer, you got richer, and your family was assured of power forever. Not anymore; the money was taken out of commerce and put into ground rents because, for the first time, there was ground to buy.

The Venetian *terraferma* empire provided the opportunity for the Venetian patricians to cease being merchants and to become *rentier* aristocrats, landowners who could buy vast estates and rely on the safe but low-yielding ground rents that came from them. No longer did they look for a 1,000-percent profit; now they were content with the 10 percent return that land usually gave. At least it was safe, and at least you knew that you would live to enjoy it. This flight of capital from trade into the Venetian *terraferma* empire, into estates around Vicenza and Verona, and into the building of villas and the establishment of communications routes that would allow Venetians easily to move to and from the subject cities to the capital, was also powerfully supported by the Venetian state.

The Venetians were clever and crafty. They had learned their lesson. They realized that their way of controlling the *terraferma* had resulted in Agnadello. Now they saw another way, and that was simply to colonize the people that they had repressed. Venetian patricians were then encouraged to engage in the development of land, to build villas, and to spend part of every year in their beautiful villas in the *terraferma* around Vicenza. They were encouraged because it was a way of integrating the local nobility with the Venetian patriciate. There was intermarriage, and when funds were short in particular—but also as a kind of principle—some of these great families were now permitted, at enormous cost, to purchase seats in the Venetian Great Council, opening up the Great Council to the *terraferma* nobles for the first time. In this way, Venice became more than just a mercantile empire, more than just the *stato da mar* with a subject territory on the Italian mainland or the Dalmatian coast. It really became an Italian state, integrated with what had gone before, integrated by personality and by family, as well as by mutual mercantile and commercial interests.

The *terraferma* empire then began to grow and prosper. The estates were fertile, and they were well managed by the Venetians. It was also a time when Venice was expanding intellectually and culturally. This became powerfully reflected in the *terraferma*, and the *terraferma* had an enormous effect on the traditions of the capital, the *città dominante*. First of all, the conquest of the *terraferma* had resulted in very sophisticated cities being part of the Venetian dominion. Cities like Padua, Verona, and Vicenza had rich connections with Italy, and they had seen the development of humanism and Italian Renaissance art. These things were now transmitted directly to Venice, a city that previously had looked to the East and had maintained much older traditions, those of Venetian Gothic or eastern Byzantine style.

Now the Italian Renaissance in all of its forms entered Venice, and the city began to look very different. The great buildings that we associate with the 16th century and Venice, the work of Sansovino, for example—although born a Florentine, working in Venice—began to rise. Venice began to look more like an Italian city and less like one that was simply an extension of Byzantine rule. Certainly the onion domes and the pointed arch of the Gothic survived, and the use of Turkish crenellations was still there. But now there are the perfect Renaissance classical palaces built by Sansovino, and that developed in the next century into the palaces and churches of Baldassarre Longhena. But of course, it is the architecture of Andrea Palladio that symbolizes this most effectively.

Palladio was a Vicentino; he was born in Vicenza. As a citizen of Vicenza, he was part of that rich tradition that surrounded the nobility of Vicenza, around Giangiorgio Trissino and those writers and thinkers who ultimately created the Academy, whose theater would be built by Palladio as his last completed work. Indeed, Palladio was the architect of choice of these new Venetian patricians. They wanted villas, places where they could live in elegance and harmony. They wanted things that reflected this new style of being Italian, of being part of a collective unconscious that went back to antiquity, that used the vocabulary of ancient buildings, that made reference to Vitruvius. They wanted this because they saw their future now in Italy rather than on the Mediterranean and in the East.

The Venetian personality changed as its architecture and style changed. The style of Venice became very different, and the activities of its patriciate became different as well. The Palladian villas reflected this new rentier mentality, a world of pleasure. Decorated by Veronese and full of the treasure and wealth collected over a millennium, these buildings were the new Venice. The palaces on the Grand Canal continued to be built and decorated, and there was an element of trade in most of the families, but nevertheless the future was now on the mainland; the future was with Italy.

The loss of will, this movement towards the Italian mainland, and the building of a rentier economy and the building of Palladian villas also changed the fundamental values of the Venetian nobility. Not only did they stop their sons from going to sea when young, and sent them instead to the University of Padua, where they could be trained in classical letters, they also themselves began to see that, well, we've acquired this great wealth. We're the heirs of a thousand years of enormous profit. Our ancestors have worked hard, and it's up to us to enjoy it. Nothing lasts forever, and the Venetians were shown that by Vasco da Gama and by Agnadello. So why not enjoy what you have?

Venice, then, by the second half of the 16th century, becomes a city of pleasure, a city of beauty. It becomes a place where the carnival ultimately would last for six months, in which prostitution became one of the great industries, and it was carefully regulated by the state to ensure that profits and quality would be maintained. It was a world where pleasure was to be found in the *ridotti*, or the "gambling casinos," of the Republic. It was a place where every visitor had to stop—not just to see the courtesans and to gamble, but also to see this great collection of materials that the Venetians had taken from around the world and put to decorate their city. The personality of Venice changed, and it became increasingly the Venice not of the blind Enrico Dandolo, but the Venice of Casanova in the 18th century.

To be sure, the Venetians still saw their role as the vanguard of Christianity to be primary, and they took it very seriously. Until the 17th century, they were in fact the most powerful force to stop the Turks. They contributed to the Battle of Lepanto in 1571. They ensured that the Greek mainland would at least be protected for a while, and then reconquered for a short period, before even the great and genius doge, Morosini, had realized that it was impossible to really stop the Turks. It was, then, a long story—one that was to continue until 1797 when Napoleon ended the Republic. Venice still maintained its heroic stance, its wealth and its beauty, but it wasn't the Venice that had taken Constantinople in 1204, and it wasn't the Venice that had defeated Genoa in the War of Chioggia.

Lecture Six
Genoa, *La Superba*

Scope:

Genoa, the birthplace of Columbus, was an important port from ancient times because of its excellent harbor. It endured a long history of war against the Muslims, ultimately combining forces with Pisa to drive the enemy from Sardinia in 1016. Genoa was then free to establish trade routes throughout the Mediterranean, but it was the Crusades that ensured for Genoa spectacular wealth. Again allied with Pisa, Genoa assisted the papacy in its political and religious ambitions, and the pope gave the two cities joint control over Corsica and Sardinia. However, the division of Sardinia caused increasing tension that broke into open warfare when Genoa, in 1240, supported the pope over the emperor. Pisa, a Ghibelline state, used this as a pretext to attack the Genoese fleet, defeating it in 1241. Now mortal enemies, Genoa and Pisa continued their conflict until 1284, when Genoa conclusively defeated its former ally. That left just Genoa and Venice to struggle for complete control of Mediterranean maritime commerce. Both powers won major victories, but in 1298, Genoa decisively defeated Venice, although the long years of war had left Genoa weak and internally divided.

Outline

I. During the Middle Ages, Genoa established control over the Mediterranean, often in competition with Venice and other maritime powers.

    A. Genoa, the birthplace of Columbus, was the most significant seaport in Cisalpine Gaul among the Romans.

        1. The city had survived the collapse of Rome, the ensuing barbarian invasions, and sacking by the Carthaginians during the Punic War.

        2. After the collapse of Rome, Genoa, like Venice, recognized Orthodox Byzantium as one of it protectors.

        3. Charlemagne brought Genoa under the rule of Milan as part of the Frankish Empire in the 8th century. With the fall of this empire, however, and a second period of instability, Genoa had little protection and was sacked by Saracens in the 10th century.

   4. The Genoese were ultimately successful in driving the Muslims from the island of Sardinia. The two islands of Sardinia and Corsica, just off the coast of Italy and France in the western Mediterranean, were important as staging posts and as buffers to ensure that the continent of Europe was safe from Saracen power, which continually threatened to break out of the Iberian Peninsula.

B. By 1052, Genoa emerged as an independent commune, a self-governing state separate from the authorities of emperor and pope but dependent in one way or another on both of them.

   1. Internal friction within the republic resulted in civic authority being divided between a *podestà*, that is, a military leader usually connected to the nobility, and a captain of the people who represented the general population, the *popolani*.

   2. Thus, the divisions between the nobles and the popular faction, as well as between Guelfs and Ghibellines, were formalized, sapping the energy and stability of the state for centuries to come.

   3. As in most states, the Ghibellines had closer connections with the nobility, while the Guelfs were seen as the faction of "new men."

II. It was the Crusades and the conflict with Venice that ultimately determined the future of Genoa, much more so at this point than its own divided, unstable government.

A. Genoa and Pisa were initially allied, taking common cause against the Saracens of the western Mediterranean. As the two great maritime powers on the west coast of Italy, they saw it as their responsibility to be at the forefront of Christian protection against the Saracens in Europe and in the western Mediterranean.

   1. Both powers recognized the strategic importance of the islands of Corsica and Sardinia. Genoa and Pisa had established trading posts and connections with the south

of France around the port of Marseilles, with Barcelona in Spain, and elsewhere that required protection.

2. The success of Genoa and Pisa in driving the Muslims from Sardinia prompted the papacy to give the two powers joint control over both Sardinia and Corsica. They were to rule these together as Christian states and fortified outposts, not only against the Saracens, but in their own interests as trading republics.

B. The First Crusade (1095–1099) saw the Genoese as leaders in the carrying trade between Europe and the Holy Land.

1. In compensation for their participation, the Genoese secured ports in Syria and Palestine to service their long-distance luxury trade with the East, in direct competition with Venice.

2. Genoa also received important commercial privileges from the Crusader kingdom of Jerusalem.

3. Together with Venice and Pisa, Genoa became a great maritime and mercantile power, combining a lucrative carrying trade with naval supremacy and close economic ties with the Levant.

C. Genoa, still in alliance with Pisa, assisted the papacy in the suppression of heresy and in its political ambitions, and the pope reaffirmed the joint control of Genoa and Pisa over Corsica and Sardinia.

1. The Genoese were fortunate inasmuch as they also received recognition from the emperor.

2. In the complex world of Guelf and Ghibelline, Genoa seemed to have struck a balance between the pope and the emperor, winning recognition of its ambitions from both factions by the beginning of the 13th century.

3. Genoa was beginning to emerge as not just a competitor to Venice but a state that perhaps could even best the Venetians should warfare break out.

III. The division of Sardinia caused increasing tension with Pisa, and the competition between the two states erupted into open warfare in 1240.

A. Ghibelline Pisa, an ally of the imperial party, used the struggle between the pope and the Holy Roman Emperor as a pretext to attack the Genoese fleet. The war initially went badly for Genoa, with Pisa decisively defeating her rival in 1241 and destroying the Genoese fleet. Thereafter, Genoa and Pisa were mortal enemies.

B. The conflict with Pisa was not settled by the Pisan victory over the Genoese. The humiliation of Genoa fortified it in its resolve to defeat the Pisans and to restore its preeminence in the western Mediterranean. In 1284, the Genoese did just that.

    1. The tables had turned dramatically because of the rise of Florence and Tuscany.

    2. As long as Florence was divided between Guelf and Ghibelline, the Pisans could act freely. By 1284, however, Florence had grown in influence and needed a seaport for its international trade.

    3. The defeat of Pisa in 1284 came at a time when the Pisans could not recover because they were fighting, in effect, on two fronts: defending themselves against Florence and Tuscany and against Genoa.

C. By this time, Amalfi had declined, leaving just Genoa and Venice to struggle for complete control of Mediterranean maritime commerce.

IV. Venice recognized that Genoa was not only a growing power but also that it was the only possible threat to Venetian control of long-distance trade.

A. Genoa had been so consumed with war against Pisa that it was unable to recover sufficiently to build a fleet that could challenge the Venetians. The Venetians took advantage of this situation, attacking and defeating the Genoese twice, in 1257 and 1258.

B. Genoa's response was aggressive diplomacy.

    1. The Fourth Crusade in 1204 had given rule of Byzantium to the family of Baldwin of Flanders, although the original Greek dynasty still made a claim to the throne.

    2. The Genoese realized that the family of Baldwin of Flanders and the Latin Empire of Constantinople were wildly unpopular within the city and the remains of the Byzantine Empire. The most effective way of defeating

Venice was to ensure that Genoa had some measure of control in the return of the Greek dynasty and the exile of the Latins.

3. The Genoese supported the Greek claimant, who was returned to the throne, and were greatly rewarded. The Eastern Empire granted to Genoa the same trading concessions and opportunities previously enjoyed by Venice alone.

4. Genoa was now competing directly with Venetian interests, making war inevitable.

V. The two great maritime states were approximately evenly matched.

A. Both powers won victories, but they were minor. Then, in 1298, under Admiral Doria, one of Genoa's great heroes of the sea, the Genoese decisively defeated the Venetians at Curzola.

B. The cost of the struggle with Venice—the expense of rebuilding the fleet and protecting and maintaining Genoese trade routes and lines of communication with the East— proved to be particularly high. Once more, divisions emerged in Genoa along lines of class and occupation.

1. Obviously, those who would benefit most from victory over Venice and the monopoly on trade would be the aristocratic, wealthy merchants. The popular party, the *popolani*, though, were the ones who would be sacrificed should Venice again grow strong.

2. The city was divided between two factions, those who wanted to make any sacrifice necessary to pursue the war against Venice and those who did not.

3. This class division and the resulting instability, to some extent, is the curse of Genoese history. The great strength of Venice, in contrast, was its ability to establish a policy that would work for all Venetian citizens simultaneously and a government that would speak for all members of the republic.

4. The Venetians entered the war united and with confidence; the Genoese entered the war divided.

C. Direct naval and economic competition in the Aegean and the Greek mainland, but mostly at sea, from one end of the

Mediterranean to the other, meant that compromise between the Venetians and the Genoese was impossible. The two great navies came together in the War of Chioggia of 1380–1381.

1. The Genoese had sailed up the Adriatic coast as far as the fishing village of Chioggia, just down the coast from Venice.
2. Initially, the Genoese were clearly winning the Battle of Chioggia, and it looked as though the Venetian fleet would be destroyed.
3. At the very last moment, a fleet arrived to support the Venetians with reinforcements, turning the tide and allowing the Venetians to take the initiative and destroy the Genoese once and for all.

D. Although Genoa would remain an important mercantile center and maintain a fleet to service its now-reduced trade, the struggle for supremacy was lost. Venice had emerged as the dominant sea power in the Mediterranean.

E. The defeat by Venice didn't end Genoa's internal instability.

1. Attempts to create a government modeled on that of Venice actually worked in Genoa in the 1330s, but the administration soon frayed as a result of class divisions in the city and internal divisions among the factions themselves.
2. Families in the aristocratic faction fought one another for control of the government and control over the fleet and the carrying trade.
3. Unlike the Venetians, who used the Great Council and the instrument of the republic to create a singular vision, the Genoese took defeat and ambition as a personal or a kin issue. The resulting feuds left the city chaotic and impossible to rule.
4. Ultimately, the French, the Milanese, and other dynasties attempted to impose order in Genoa. The republic itself became relatively impotent, seriously divided, and greatly weakened.
5. There would be no resurgence of Genoa before the 16th century. Genoa could not regain its position and

challenge the Venetians simply because it was unable to focus its energy in one place.

F. The great opportunity of Genoa had been wasted in struggling against its fellow Christians and Italians.

    1. The possibility for Europe, Italy, and Christianity to sink deep roots into the Mediterranean to control the Turks was left to the Venetians alone, and the history of the Mediterranean becomes, then, the history of Venice.

    2. The history of Genoa becomes the history, not of a great mercantile power, but of a bank.

Essential Reading:

S. A. Epstein, *Genoa and the Genoese, 958–1528.*

Supplementary Reading:

K. Fleet, *Europe and Islamic Trade in the Early Ottoman State: The Merchants of Genoa and Turkey.*

Questions to Consider:

1. Why was the lucrative trade with the East seen as a life-and-death competition between the maritime powers of the peninsula?

2. What weakened Genoa was its internal division, something the Venetian Republic did not experience. Are there lessons to be learned from this for modern states?

Lecture Six—Transcript
Genoa, *La Superba*

Venice's great competitor, and the state that almost defeated it in battle at sea, was Genoa. Genoa is one of the least known of the great Italian city-states. It's remembered mostly as the city of Christopher Columbus, whose house still stands near the city walls. But it had a rich and vibrant, if unstable and chaotic, history that is important to know if the history of the Italian Peninsula, and of the development of the Italian state, is to really be understood. During the Middle Ages, Genoa controlled much of the Mediterranean trade, often in direct competition with the other maritime states of Pisa, Amalfi, and Venice. It was an extraordinarily important city inasmuch as it had been the most significant seaport in Cisalpine Gaul among the Romans; Cisalpine Gaul being that part of the Italian Peninsula on this side of the province of Gaul, this side of the Alps.

The city survived not just the collapse of Rome, but the barbarian invasions and sacking by the Carthaginians during the Punic War, in order to be sustained as a sea power with some measure of influence in the western Mediterranean. After the collapse of Rome, like Venice, Genoa paid good attention to the role of Byzantium and indeed recognized Orthodox Byzantium as one of it protectors. Nevertheless, Charlemagne, when he arrived in the 8th century, did bring Genoa under the rule of Milan as part of the Frankish Empire; again putting Genoa back into the center of European politics and economy, and of the Italian Peninsula. But with the fall of the Frankish Empire and the second period of instability after the fall of Rome, there was in fact very little to protect the city, and it was sacked by Muslims. It was sacked by Saracens in the 10th century, and this resulted in almost continuous warfare between the Genoese and the Muslims that had moved around the southern coast of the Mediterranean and into the Iberian Peninsula. Indeed, Genoa saw itself as the vanguard of the western Mediterranean, just as Venice saw itself as the vanguard of the eastern Mediterranean.

Nevertheless, the Genoese were successful in driving the Muslims from the island of Sardinia. The two islands in the western Mediterranean, Sardinia and Corsica, just off the coast of Italy and France, were extraordinarily important as not only staging posts, but as areas of protection to ensure that the continent of Europe would be safe from the depredations of Saracen pirates, and the maintenance of the Saracen power in the Iberian Peninsula that threatened always to break out and follow the route that was stopped by Charles Martel at Tours. By 1052, Genoa emerged as an independent commune, a self-governing state separate from the great authorities of emperor and pope, but nevertheless dependent in one way or another on them both, as were so many of the city-states of the Italian Peninsula during this period of the formation of communal governments.

The seeds of the dangers in the Republic were already being sown. The creation of the commune created two offices. One was the *podestà,* who was the military commander with close links to the nobility, responsible for defense and closely linked to those powerful feudal families that often owed allegiance to the emperor, and whose servant of the emperor they had been. Then there were the "popular parties," the *popolani.* These were the common people. They too had their representative; this captain of the people was the one who spoke for them. The tension between the aristocrats, represented by the *podestà,* and the popular party, representing the general population, was to become institutionalized and create for Genoa an extraordinarily dangerous situation. Whereas Venice was stable and integrated, Genoa was, almost from the beginning of its self-governing history, divided.

The Guelfs and the Ghibellines also played their role, and they played their role in somewhat of a more dramatic way. The Ghibellines were associated with the party of the *podestà,* and the Guelfs were supporters of new men—those socially mobile who found natural homes among the popular party tended to owe more allegiance to the papacy. It was the situation of the Crusades and the conflict with Venice that ultimately determined the future of Genoa, much more so then at this point, its own divided unstable government. Genoa was initially allied with Pisa. The Genoese and the Pisans took common cause against the Saracens of the western Mediterranean, and as the two great maritime powers on the west coast of Italy, they saw it as their particular responsibility and their Christian duty to be at the forefront of Christian protection, and ideally Christian victory, against the Saracens in Europe and in the western Mediterranean.

The strategic importance of the islands of Corsica and Sardinia was recognized by both powers. Both the Pisans and the Genoese had established trading posts and close trading connections with the south of France around the port of Marseilles, with Barcelona in Spain, and with other areas that really required some measure of safety and security for those trade routes. They worked together against the Saracens, and they succeeded in driving the Muslims from the island of Sardinia. This success allowed for the papacy to give the Pisans and the Genoese joint control over the islands of Corsica and Sardinia. They were then to rule these together as Christian states and as fortified outposts—not only against the Saracens, but in their own interest as trading republics.

The First Crusade, as in so many examples that we have seen so far, added much to the wealth and influence of Genoa. The Genoese were, like the Venetians, leaders in the carrying trade. They too had sophisticated navigational experience. They had a large fleet and were used to sailing long distances. They were used to protecting fleets, and they used means of communication with North Africa and with Europe. They were then purely capable, as were the Venetians, of carrying the Crusaders from Europe to the Holy Land and bringing back, in exchange, goods that could be sold at great profit.

In compensation for the great contributions that the Genoese made in the First Crusade—in particular their close connection with Syria, Palestine, and the crusading kingdoms that developed thereafter—the Genoese were given rich trading concessions. In particular, their close connection with the Latin kingdom of Jerusalem allowed them to set deep roots in the areas that are now Palestine, Israel, and Syria. But, of course, in so doing, they found themselves in direct competition with the Venetians. As long as the Genoese stayed in the western Mediterranean, the competition was essentially a competition at a distance. Now that the Genoese, as a result of the Crusades, had moved into the eastern Mediterranean, they found themselves confronting the Venetians, and neither would be content until the other was ultimately knocked out of the competition.

Genoa, with its promise of great riches and protection by the Latin kingdom, saw itself in a particularly privileged position. It was not willing to compromise with the Venetians, and it still at this point was closely connected with the other republic of Pisa. Together, they thought they would be able to challenge any competitor in any way. Moreover, the rich carrying trade from the Levant provided, as it had for the Venetians, great profit. Genoa became an enormously rich and powerful city. Despite the connections that it had once enjoyed with Charlemagne, it realized that its immediate future was more closely associated with the ambitions of the papacy and the Guelf party—particularly at a time when the *popolani*, the popular party, had a measure of influence within the city.

During the period of the Crusades, Genoa reconnected closely with papal ambitions, and also realized that it was possible to not only further their economic interests, but also the ambitions of the papacy to try to suppress heresy, drive the Muslims from the Mediterranean, and establish a powerful papal position throughout the southern elements of Europe. Consequently, the pope, in recognition of Genoese contribution, granted joint control over the islands of Corsica and Sardinia to the Pisans and the Genoese again, recognizing the role of Genoese sovereignty and ensuring that Genoa would always be part of this Guelf allegiance.

However, the Genoese were very fortunate inasmuch as they also received recognition from the emperor. The Ghibellines, who were represented within the city by the party of the nobility headed by the *podestà*, saw that this was an opportunity for them as well. It seemed then, by the beginning of the 13th century, that the Genoese had walked a very, very careful line, being supported and their sovereignty recognized and supported by both the emperor and the pope. This was something that, in theory, seemed to be impossible, but the Genoese had managed to do it. Genoa was beginning to emerge as not just a competitor to Venice, but a state that perhaps could even best them should it come to open warfare.

The Venetians, however, were not to worry, at least not at this point, because the connection with the Pisans that had begun so amicably, and had created the joint alliance that had driven the Muslims from Sardinia and Corsica, turned into one of the great hatreds of the Italian Peninsula. It was this problem, caused by the papacy giving joint control of Sardinia and Corsica to the Pisans and the Genoese, that began to fray the close working relationship between the two maritime states. The friction began to build throughout the 13th century until, by 1240, it broke into open warfare. Ultimately, the interests of the Pisans and the Genoese were in competition. They both traded in the same parts of the western Mediterranean, and they realized that there really would only be room for one of them.

The war was particularly savage because the Pisans were a Ghibelline state, and they were closely allied to the emperor and to the imperial party. The Genoese increasingly began to shift their allegiance toward the papacy. This created the *casus beli*, the "cause of war." The Pisans took an opportunity of tension between the empire and the papacy to accuse the Genoese of being hostile to the imperial interests, and to attack the Genoese fleet. Pisa, having the advantage of having attacked, decisively defeated the Genoese in 1241, destroying the Genoese fleet. After 1241, the Genoese and the Pisans became mortal enemies, carrying a hatred for one another that lasts to this very day. We have a close friend in Genoa who still uses the popular Genoese phrase, "Better a death in the house than a Pisan at the door." It's only in the past few years that the chains that used to block the harbor at Pisa were returned to Pisa by the Genoese in order to try to reconcile, after more than seven centuries, this hatred that had begun in the 13th century.

The conflict with Pisa was not settled by the Pisan victory over the Genoese. The humiliation of Genoa just fortified it in its resolve to defeat the Pisans and to restore its preeminence in the western Mediterranean. In 1284, the Genoese did exactly that, defeating the Pisans decisively. Now, though, the table had turned dramatically because of the rise of Florence and Tuscany. As long as Florence was divided between Guelf and Ghibelline, and as long as there were tensions within the city, the Pisans could act largely freely, without worry of their neighbors down the Arno. However, by 1284, Florence had grown in influence and saw the need of a seaport and access to the sea for its international trade in luxury cloth. Pisa then had to worry about Florence more than it had to worry even about Genoa. The defeat of Pisa in 1284 happened at a time when the Pisans could not recover because they had to fight, in effect, on two fronts: defending themselves against the Florentines and Tuscany, and defending themselves against the Genoese at sea.

By this time, Amalfi, as one of the powerful states of the Mediterranean, had slipped into decline. Amalfi, after all, is on the Amalfan coast south of Salerno. There is not much there by way of trade. It did not have a rich hinterland in order to service; it's restricted geographically. Ultimately, it was the victory of the Hohenstaufen supported by the Pisan fleet that destroyed Amalfi as one of the competitors—the smallest, but nevertheless a real competitor that now was no longer part of the Mediterranean equation. It left, then, with Pisa worried about the Florentines; Genoa and Venice to work between themselves which one would ultimately have the hegemony, which one would control the trade of the Mediterranean, and to what extent Genoa could recover and challenge the Venetians as they might have done before their defeat by the Pisans.

Venice realized this immediately. Venice recognized that Genoa is not only a growing power, but also that Genoa was the only possible threat to its control of long-distance luxury trade, that monopolistic situation that it had always wanted. The East had provided the wealth of Europe, and the Venetians wanted to make it their own. The Genoese, because of their still close connections with the Levant, stood in their way. From the beginning, the Venetians had the advantage. Genoa had been so consumed with its war with Pisa that it was unable to recover sufficiently to build a fleet that could challenge the Venetians. But with the victory over Pisa, that would change. Still, the Venetians wanted to make sure that there was not too great a threat at this time when there were great fortunes to be made. The Venetians attacked and defeated the Genoese twice, in 1257 and 1258.

Genoa, though, like Venice, was a crafty state. Genoa is known as *La Superba*, "the proud"; the proud Genoa, a city that recognized its preeminence the way Venice, the most serene, the *Serenissima*, recognized its preeminence. The Genoese were not about to allow the Venetians to have this monopoly without a struggle. Although their fleets had been damaged and, in the instance of 1257 and 1258 virtually destroyed, they were not about to yield. The only option they had at this point was clever, crafty diplomacy. Genoa's response to Venice was to try to undo that very close relationship that the Venetians enjoyed with the empire at Constantinople.

The Fourth Crusade in 1204 had given rule of the empire in the East to the Flemish family of Baldwin of Flanders, that leader of the Fourth Crusade who found himself and his son as the emperors of Byzantium in this rather absurd situation. The claimant, the pretender, to the throne, though, was the original Greek dynasty. It was, in fact, with the Greek pretenders that the Genoese made common cause. The Genoese realized that the family of Baldwin of Flanders and the Latin Empire of Constantinople were wildly unpopular within the city and within what was left of the Byzantine Empire. Therefore, the most effective way of defeating Venice was to ensure that Genoa would have some measure of control in the return of the Greek dynasty, the exile of the Latins, and the overthrow of the offense and the effects of the Fourth Crusade.

The Greek dynasty was indeed established. The son of Baldwin of Flanders was exiled, and the Greeks returned to the throne of the Eastern Empire. Genoa—as Venice had been before under the Latins—was greatly, greatly rewarded. In fact, the Empire decided that it was an appropriate thing to give the Genoese the same kinds of privileges that the Venetians had previously enjoyed: trading concessions and opportunities. The Genoese felt that this was not only their due, but also the best way to come into conflict and competition with the Venetians, having been defeated at sea. However, the situation was particularly dangerous. It was dangerous because the two states were about evenly matched at this point. Although the Venetians had defeated the Genoese in 1257 and 1258, the Genoese were sufficiently rich and had sufficient opportunity as a result of the restoration of Greek rule in Constantinople to recover quickly, to rebuild their fleets and to begin to look to that opportunity when they were going to face the Venetians for that final showdown in the eastern Mediterranean as to who would ultimately be the victorious power and who would have the virtual monopoly on the incredibly lucrative trade with the East.

Indeed, both powers won victories against one another, but they were minor until, in 1298, under the Admiral Doria, the Genoese decisively defeated the Venetians at Curzola. Doria, a name that we will come across constantly in the discussion of the city of Genoa, was one of the great heroes of the sea. Admiral Doria was able to take the Genoese fleet, rebuilt and reconstituted after its terrible defeats a half century before, and turn them against the Venetians, who had now become their singular enemy. The cost of the struggle with Venice, though, the cost of rebuilding the fleet and protecting and maintaining long Genoese trade routes and means of communication with the East had proved to be particularly dangerous. The onerous cost divided the city once more, according to class and to occupation.

It was obvious that those who would benefit the most from the victory over Venice and the monopoly on trade would be the aristocratic wealthy merchants—those patricians who saw the *podestà* as their protectors. They were the ones who were prosecuting this war, who saw it as their destiny. The popular party, the *popolani*, though, were the ones who would suffer. They were the ones who would fight on the ships and drown at sea if defeated. They were the ones who would be sacrificed if the Venetians should again be successful. The city was divided between two factions: those that wanted to make any sacrifice necessary to pursue the war against Venice, and those who did not. This, to some extent, is the curse of Genoese history: this class division, this instability and inability to run a government for the benefit of all of its citizens. The great strength of Venice was always its stability, its ability to put together a policy that would work for all Venetian citizens simultaneously, and a government that would speak for all members of the Republic. The Venetians entered the war united and with confidence; the Genoese entered the war divided.

Direct naval and economic competition in the Aegean and the Greek mainland, but mostly at sea from one end of the Mediterranean to the other, meant that compromise between the Venetians and the Genoese was impossible. By the 14th century, the situation was such that there was no way that there could be any splitting of the rich spoils because both the Venetians and the Genoese had now defined their policy in terms of destroying the other. The Venetians saw this as the necessary conclusion to a policy that had begun almost centuries before, and that reached its highlight in the conquest of Constantinople in 1204. The Genoese saw it as their fair share of a long-distance trade that they had helped protect, driving the Muslims from Corsica and Sardinia and protecting the authority of the papacy.

With compromise impossible, and both sides full of hatred for one another, and both looking upon the monopoly on long-distance trade as the ultimate prize, the two great navies came together in the War of Chioggia of 1380–1381. Initially, the Genoese had the advantage. The Genoese had sailed up the Adriatic coast as far as the fishing village of Chioggia, which is on the tip of the Lido, just down the Adriatic coast from the city of Venice itself. Initially, in the great Battle of Chioggia, the Genoese were victorious. They were clearly winning the battle, and it looked as though the Venetian fleet was going to be destroyed, which would have left Genoa rather than Venice as the dominant sea power in the Mediterranean. But then, at the very last moment, a fleet arrived coming to support the Venetians with reinforcements, turning the tide and allowing the Venetians to take the initiative and destroy the Genoese once and for all.

The destruction of the Genoese fleet in the War of Chioggia in 1381 resulted in Venice emerging as not only the dominant sea power in the Mediterranean, but in some ways the only sea power that could challenge the Turks, and the only sea power that could ensure a monopolistic trade with the East. Genoa will remain important despite this defeat, not only because of the position of its harbor and the strength of its position and control of certain elements of trade—especially around the Black Sea. The Genoese had very cleverly tried to stay away from the Venetian areas of interest, and took mostly seaports around the Black Sea. It was there that they would engage in their element of long-distance luxury trade. Nevertheless, the Venetians knew that they now had the upper hand, and the Genoese, to a large degree, retreated.

Moreover, the internal competition within Genoa was sustained. The defeat of Genoa by Venice didn't end the internal internecine instability. In fact, in many ways it made it worse. Genoa was still an important state and an important sea power. The Venetians realized this, and they recognized that they would have to try to contain it one way or another. What happened in Genoa, though, was what happens in so many instances when a great power has been shattered because of internal division and external defeat. There were attempts, first of all, to try to solve the problem. There were attempts internally to create a government modeled on that of Venice, to create a doge so that there would be a singular policy. For a while, this attempt in the 1330s had actually worked, but very soon it frayed because not only was the city divided by class—between the popular and the aristocratic party, between those who had continued sympathy with the Guelf allegiance and the papacy because of the hopes of social ambition and the hopes of papal largess but also it began to be divided internally amongst the factions themselves.

The aristocratic faction in particular saw itself as fragmenting ever more as the families in that faction fought with one another for control of the government and for the advantages, and even control over the fleet and the carrying trade. Unlike the Venetians, who used the Great Council and the instrument of the Republic to create a singular vision and almost a myth of the city that would allow all members of the Republic to function with one voice, the Genoese took defeat and ambition as a personal or a kin issue. The families were divided amongst themselves, exiling one another, murdering one another, trying to take over the fleet and turn them into private navies to use against their enemies. It was impossible to rule a city that was so chaotic and so divided, and there was no easy solution possible.

The only solutions that were attempted were the usual desperate moments of searching for a man on horseback, or allowing for the intervention of another power that saw the instability of Genoa to be a danger not just to the Italian Peninsula, but to Christendom itself. Consequently, it will be shown that the Republic began to be overtaken by other forces: the intervention of the French, the Milanese, and other dynasties just to try to impose order long enough for the Genoese to create some kind of singular vision. None of these attempts worked until the 16th century. Genoa became relatively impotent, seriously divided and greatly weakened by its inability to determine any form of stability. It became the plaything of other dynasties and the object of ambitious states' interest.

It was for this reason that there was no resurgence of Genoa before the 16th century. Genoa could not regain its position and challenge the Venetians simply because it didn't have the internal fortitude and the wherewithal to focus its energy in one place. It was too busy fighting amongst itself, too busy struggling from one aristocratic clan to another—exiling one doge and raising another, who perhaps would hold office for a single day. Genoa, with its great possibility, its long history of struggle in the Mediterranean against not only its Christian enemies, but against the Turks; Genoa, the city of Columbus, and Genoa, the city that would rise from this conflict and destruction to become one of the great banking and mercantile cities of Europe in spite of itself was, by the end of the 14th century and the first years of the 15th century, something of a depressed and depressing place.

Its great opportunity had been wasted. Its great strength had been wasted by struggling against its fellow Christians and against the Venetians and Pisans, and the Turks were challenging everyone, including the victorious Venetians. What will emerge, then, in Genoa is not the Genoa of the 17th century, but the Genoese attempt to create some kind of viable state. It's for this reason that the history of

Genoa is so often neglected. It is chaotic and complex, and ultimately—until the rise of Andrea Doria in the 1520s—it's sad because this is an opportunity wasted, and it was another moment when Europe, Italy, and Christianity could have put deep roots into the Mediterranean in order to try to control, if not stop, the Turks. It was left to the Venetians alone because only the Venetians had the power to do it—the Genoese having been destroyed by the Venetians themselves. The history of the Mediterranean is then the history of Venice, and the history of Genoa becomes the history not of a great mercantile power, but of a bank.

Lecture Seven
Bankers and Dukes

Scope:

To restore unity, the constitution of Genoa was restructured as a republic, and in 1339, the first doge, Simon Boccanegra, was elected for life. Boccanegra revitalized Genoa, expanding the city and defeating the Turks, but factional strife returned, with some doges serving less than a single day before relinquishing power. This situation led to the constant intervention of foreign powers, particularly after 1380, when Venice decisively defeated the Genoese. The economic power of Genoa was sustained, however, through the creation of the Bank of St. George in 1408. The bank was almost a state within the state, funding the public debt, floating loans to foreign princes, issuing coins, raising armies, and even accrediting ambassadors. French influence in Genoa led to much conflict with the Habsburgs; as a consequence, the city was captured and sacked by the Spaniards in 1522. The Genoese hero Andrea Doria drove out the Habsburgs in 1527 and, by the next year, became, in effect, the uncrowned duke of Genoa. But the *Genoese century*, which followed Andrea Doria's restoration of sovereignty, owed as much to the bank as to the admiral's brilliant leadership.

Outline

I. To understand why Genoa could lose its place as the dominant maritime power in Europe to Venice, an enemy that the Genoese had crushed in 1298, it is necessary to examine the internal workings of Genoese politics.

    A. From the beginning, Genoa's greatest weakness was its lack of internal stability and cohesion.

        1. Constitutional changes were introduced in the 14th century to try to address the situation, partly as a consequence of the wars with Venice. The state was restructured as a republic on the obviously successful Venetian model, and the office of doge was created.

        2. In 1339, the first doge, Simon Boccanegra (d. 1363), was elected for life. Boccanegra revitalized Genoa,

expanding the city, reestablishing trade connections, defeating the Turks, and putting Genoa back into the Mediterranean as a powerful player.

    3. With Boccanegra's death, however, factional strife returned, with some doges serving less than a single day before being forced to relinquish power.

  B. The political problems of Genoa seemed insurmountable.

    1. Two competing factions, led by two great noble families, were evenly matched but represented different interests.

    2. The aristocratic faction, led by the Adorno family, was loosely associated with the Italian Ghibellines.

    3. The popular party, led by the Fregoso family, was allied to the Guelfs.

    4. These two families and their supporters alternated in power, always ensuring that the policies of one would be overturned with the election of the other.

    5. The resulting political chaos made any kind of reasonable accommodation difficult if not impossible.

II. This instability, along with the importance of Genoa, led to the constant intervention of foreign powers.

  A. Genoa was the major seaport on the Ligurian coast of Italy and the point of entry for foreigners, who could then use it to expand at the expense of other Italian states close by. The geographical importance of Genoa, as well as the continuing division between Guelf and Ghibelline, ensured that Genoa would not be able to maintain its independence for long.

  B. As early as 1311, the Holy Roman Emperor Henry VII demanded and was granted the right to rule Genoa for 20 years. After Henry's death in 1313, the Guelf party in Genoa called in the support of the French House of Anjou to counter the Ghibelline claims of the ruler of Milan.

  C. The result was almost a complete factional breakdown over the question of who would rule Genoa—the Guelfs or the Ghibellines, the aristocrats or the popular party, the imperial party from Germany or the French party?

  D. Venice renewed its war with Genoa, and the defeat of the Genoese by the Venetians occasioned a Ghibelline victory. The House of Anjou had, to some extent, promised protection, but that protection was now seen as worthless. Victory in the city was handed back to the Ghibellines, the House of Visconti, and the rule of Milan.

E. When Venice decisively defeated Genoa at Chioggia in 1380, the Genoese responded by surrendering to foreign rulers.

    1. The French controlled the city in the years 1396–1409, 141-1458, 1464–1478, 1487–1499, and 1515–1522.

    2. The marquis of Monferrato, a small state between Lombardy and Liguria, was in command from 1409–1413.

    3. The duke of Milan held power from 1458–1461 and 1499–1512.

    4. Clearly, the ability of the Genoese to rule themselves had collapsed.

III. The economic power of Genoa was sustained, however, through the creation of the *Banco di San Giorgio* (Bank of St. George) in 1408 by a consortium of rich merchants.

A. The bank was a mechanism that existed to obviate the instability and chaos of the republican government and to protect private wealth.

    1. The Bank of St. George became, essentially, a state within a state and the center of Genoese life.

    2. The bank minted its own coins, accredited its own ambassadors to foreign countries, and even raised armies in its own name. It provided an element of stability to Genoa with its singular policy directed toward making money for its investors and founders.

B. Even the bank, however, could not control all the forces surrounding it, especially in a world of two opposing empires: the Christian empire of the West and the growing Turkish Empire of the East.

    1. The Turkish conquest of Constantinople in 1453 had as devastating an effect on Genoa as it had on Venice. Whatever protection the rich and important Genoese mercantile empire had enjoyed around the Black Sea now simply evaporated.

    2. Turkish expansionism eliminated the Genoese trading posts around the Black Sea and other mercantile privileges that had been protected by the Byzantines since 1261.

    3. The most painful blow was the fall of Caffa, Genoa's most important trading post, to the Turks in 1475. This event marked the end of the maritime empire of Genoa.

  C. With Genoa's decline, the Bank of St. George became extraordinarily important. The bank was also seen as a rich prize for other powers, which would be more interested in taking advantage of Genoa's wealth and strategic location than in trying to solve Genoese problems.

IV. French influence in Genoa was particularly powerful. By the 16th century, this influence had taken on dangerous geopolitical implications.

  A. The king of France, Francis I, was anxious to impose Valois hegemony on the continent. He was, of course, confronted by Charles V, Holy Roman Emperor, head of the House of Habsburg, and king of Spain.

  B. The duel between Habsburg and Valois was one of the recurring dramas of Italian history because the battle was fought in Italy.

    1. Both the French and the Habsburgs had competing claims, usually on such cities as Milan and Naples, but the conflict ran much deeper than that.

    2. The battle was, in some ways, the old ideological argument of Guelf versus Ghibelline, but it now took place in a world that had become much more dangerous because of the intervention of forces from beyond the Alps.

  C. Through the Spanish kingdom and the Holy Roman Empire, Charles V had designs on Italy that could be backed by great powers. He also knew that the question of Genoa would have to be confronted because of its strategic location.

    1. France had controlled Genoa from 1515, and as long as the French were in Genoa, they had an outpost from which they could supply their armies and provide additional troops, as well as a place to retreat in case of danger.

2. Charles realized that to control north-central Italy, he would have to take Genoa. In 1522, the city fell to the House of Habsburg and was sacked. For the next five years, Genoa was garrisoned and became an extension of Habsburg rule.

D. In 1527, Andrea Doria, with help from the French, succeeded in driving the Habsburgs out of Genoa.

1. Doria was a former pirate, an admiral, and an aristocrat from one of the great families of Genoa.

2. Full Genoese sovereignty was restored under Doria, but he realized that the factional disputes within the city would always offer an opportunity for the intervention of one of the great powers.

3. Doria's plan was to restructure the government of the republic so that it reflected much more realistically the power within the state. In accomplishing this goal, he became, essentially, a dictator.

4. Doria refused the doge's crown and, in fact, abolished the office, realizing that it had been a source of factional maneuvering.

5. The admiral created a new ducal office that held power for only two years. This doge was to be elected only by the mercantile nobility of Genoa, who would sit in a Great Council styled after that of Venice.

6. The popular election of the doge thus ceased, with the common people no longer having a strong voice in the government. As we will see, this movement away from popular governments toward governments by oligarchy will become a recurring theme in Italy.

E. Despite his obligations to France, Doria saw that the future of Europe was with the Habsburg and their Spanish dominions. He broke his ties to France, made peace with the Habsburgs, and joined with them. In return, he was given the office of Supreme Admiral of the Habsburg fleets.

F. The Bank of St. George had succeeded under foreign intervention and was now recognized as the essence of a new Genoese empire that would be based on its enormous reserves, financial acumen, contacts, and political influence. Because of the Habsburg connection, the Bank of St. George became the essential banking instrument of the Habsburg Empire.

1. Keep in mind that the Habsburg Empire was also the empire of the New World, and the vast amounts of gold and silver flowing into Europe often passed through the Bank of St. George.

2. The bank also assumed the public debts of nations and transferred money across the Habsburg Empire.

G. The result of Doria's statesmanship was the so-called *Genoese century*. This period encompassed the world of the Baroque, the world of the patrician palaces along the Via Garibaldi, the world in which Van Dyck and other artists painted luxurious portraits of members of the great families. These portraits reflect the Genoese century and the power and wealth of the families that commissioned them.

V. As mentioned earlier, Genoa is one of the most understudied of the Italian cities, partly because of its complexity, but Genoa must be recognized for its great contributions to Italian and European history and culture, as well as its links to North America.

A. Of course, Genoa was the city of Christopher Columbus, but it was also the city where Marco Polo was held as a prisoner and from which Giuseppe Garibaldi set sail to liberate Italy and begin the War of the Risorgimento. Garibaldi's close collaborator and friend, the republican Giuseppe Mazzini, was a native of Genoa.

B. Genoa was the port from which millions of Italian immigrants sailed to Australia, the United States, Canada, and Argentina, contributing much to the creation of lands in the New World.

C. Genoa had begun as a great maritime empire, but because of its own internal confusion, had fallen into anarchy; it was saved by the financial institution of a bank and the creation of a new kind of state by Andrea Doria.

1. In some ways, Genoa becomes a cautionary tale: To what extent should freedom be limited for financial advantage and stability?
2. The wealth of a small group of citizens in Genoa was often made at the expense of large numbers of their fellows who had been frozen out of government and excluded from political and economic activity.

Essential Reading:

T. A. Kirk, *Genoa and the Sea: Policy and Power in an Early Modern Maritime Republic, 1559–1684.*

Questions to Consider:

1. Genoa lost its maritime empire and naval power but maintained its economic power through the Bank of St. George. Can you think of other examples where military power was lost but economic power remained?

2. Even in the face of complete catastrophe, the classes in Genoa could not cooperate. Why do political or social factions everywhere risk everything rather than compromise with their opponents?

Lecture Seven—Transcript
Bankers and Dukes

In 1298, the Genoese, under Admiral Doria, had completely defeated the Venetians. What happened to change the history of this remarkable maritime empire so that it would decline into relative insignificance as a maritime power, whereas its enemy Venice grew to be the most powerful maritime state in Europe? To understand this, it's necessary to look at the internal history and the political situation in Genoa to see the effect of factional division. From the beginning, Genoa's greatest weakness was its factional instability, its lack of cohesion, the division between classes in which the popular party and the aristocrats alternated in power and found themselves very, very often in virtual combat.

Constitutional changes were introduced in the 14th century to try to address the situation. Indeed, partly it was a consequence of the desperate wars with Venice—to try to ensure that there was some kind of continuous policy that would allow the Genoese to confront their formidable adversary—that resulted in the experiment of the creation of the office of doge, modeled on the Venetian duke who had proved to be just a symbol of the Republic, but also a symbol that the Genoese needed to emulate. In 1339, the first doge, Simon Boccanegra, was elected. This is not really the character of the 1857 Verdi opera, who owed more to 19th-century romantic novels than to the real personality, although they both were partially corsairs; but most Genoese admirals engaged at some point in piracy, given that piracy and trade are essentially the same occupation undertaken by different means.

Boccanegra was a remarkable man, and he did what everyone hoped that he would do: He revitalized Genoa. He gave it a new sense of purpose, and he gave it a sense of authority. He tried to overcome the divisions within the city, and at least during the period of his five-year rule, he seemed to have succeeded. He expanded the city, defeated the Turks, and managed to put Genoa back into the Mediterranean as a powerful player, able to confront its enemy Venice and the growing Turkish threat. However, he died in 1344. With his death, what was clearly just a shallow veneer crumbled once more. Genoa declined again into its factional divisions, into that period of instability where classes and family disputes drove politics.

The political problems seemed, in fact, insurmountable. The election of doges continued, but because of the authority and power that these families had, and the factions behind them, sometimes they reigned for just a day before being thrown out of office. Occasionally elections were overturned, or two elections, driven by two factional interests, were held simultaneously with different results. The competing factions were almost evenly matched, and they were led by two of the great noble families of Genoa. The aristocratic faction was led by the Adorno family, who was closely associated with the Italian Ghibellines, as most of the aristocratic parties were. The popular party, led by the Fregoso family, another great aristocratic clan, was closely allied with the Italian Guelfs.

These two families essentially alternated in office—neither was powerful enough to defeat the other—always ensuring, however, that the policies of the one would be overturned with the election of the other. The consequence was obviously a kind of political chaos—not the stasis of two equally matched parties that would not allow either to do anything, but rather the chaos that comes about when alternating parties will simply do anything to undo the intentions of the other. It reached the stage where these were not only ideological or family disputes; they became the objects of mutual hatred. With that, any kind of compromise or accommodation became more than difficult; it became impossible.

This instability, and the importance of Genoa, resulted in the intervention of foreign powers. Genoa was just too strategic a place to simply allow to decline into chaos. It was the major seaport on the Ligurian coast of Italy. It dominated the western Mediterranean, and it also was the point of entry for foreigners who could then use it to expand at the expense of other Italian states close by. The geographical importance of Genoa, and the continuing division between Guelf and Ghibelline—that ideological dispute in the Italian Peninsula—ensured that Genoa would not be able to maintain its independence for very long. Indeed, almost immediately in the 14th century, there were hints of what was to come. In 1311, the Holy Roman Emperor, Henry VII, with his incursion in Italy—in which he planned to bring about a new level of internal quiet, his intent to bring about some form of factional union under the Ghibelline flag—ended with his death in 1313. Nevertheless, he had tried to use

Genoa as his port of entry, and he demanded that he have the rule of the city for 20 years after 1311.

The Genoese, really being in no position to say no, agreed. However, his death in 1313 changed all of this. His death meant that the Ghibelline threat had been made perfectly clear, that Genoa would have lost its independence to the imperial party for a period of 20 years. The result was that the Guelfs, the opposition party, called in their hero, the leader of their great international ideological faction, the cadet House of France and the House of Anjou. The House of Anjou was the leader of the European Guelfs, and it was the House of Anjou that then decided it would intervene to ensure that the heir of the Ghibelline faction in Italy, who was the ruler of Milan, of the House of Visconti, would not take up that inheritance in Genoa.

The result was that the Guelf/Ghibelline struggle in Genoa was one of factional dispute in the city itself. Who was going to rule, the Guelfs or the Ghibellines? Who was going to rule, the aristocrats or the popular party? Who would rule, the imperial party from Germany or the French party? It was this circumstance that ultimately gave rise to a new and, to some extent, more desperate moment of complete factional breakdown and the continuous intervention of foreign powers. This was brought about by that crisis of war. Venice once more renewed its war with Genoa, and the defeat of the Genoese at the hands of the Venetians occasioned a Ghibelline victory. The House of Anjou had, to some extent, promised protection. The defeat of Genoa at the hands of the Venetians indicated that that protection was worthless, and it handed victory back to the Ghibellines, the House of Visconti, and the rule of Milan.

This was made much worse with the almost complete and total defeat of Genoa in the War of Chioggia of 1380–1381. The Genoese responded in the way so many states that are at a point of crisis responded, looking for someone who would come and solve their problems, offer protection, and give them some hope for the future. Initially, it was the French. The French were brought back, and they controlled the city from 1396 to 1409, after which the rule of the city was given to a relatively minor prince, the Marquis of Monferrato, a small state between Lombardy and Liguria, and he ruled Genoa for a period of a few years. Then again, the French would return, followed again by the Duke of Milan and the imperial party. In fact, the Milanese controlled the city from 1458 to 1461, and from 1499 to

1512. But then again, the French returned in 1515 and ruled until 1522. It's clear just from this rehearsal of the intervention of foreign states that the ability of the Genoese to rule themselves had essentially collapsed. The Genoese realized that they were unable to overcome their factional divisions, and they looked to foreign powers to try to sort out the problems that they themselves should have confronted.

However, this political chaos, this complete breakdown of political independence, this division in the city between factions that were irreconcilable, created a situation that was one of the most curious and inventive in Italian history. The city itself, and the government of the state, became secondary. What became important and developed as the center of Genoese life, particularly Genoese economic life, was a bank. In 1408, the chaos of the political situation drove a number of very rich merchants to try to overcome the factional dispute by working together as a consortium to pool their resources and found a bank, the *Banco di San Giorgio*, the Bank of St. George; St. George and the cross of St. George are symbols of Genoa. Indeed, the English adopted the cross of St. George and that red-cross flag from the Genoese in order to offer protection to English ships. They would pretend to be Genoese, and they would be a little bit safer than the small maritime power of England in the Middle Ages.

The bank was a mechanism that existed essentially for no other purpose than to protect private wealth and to obviate the instability and the chaos of the Republican government; and so it did. In fact, it worked so well that it became a state within a state. In fact, in some ways, it became more important than the state. It's not that what's good for General Motors is good for America; it's much more as if General Motors was, in fact, the most important thing in America, and the federal government was just something that swirled around it, essentially of no consequence. The Bank of St. George became the center, in many ways, of Genoese life, surrounded by the chaotic political situation, which seemed to matter less and less.

To say that it functioned as a parallel government is really, in some ways, almost an understatement. First of all, it minted its own coins. The minting of coinage was one of the elements of sovereignty. A bank did it; the Genoese had coins, but the bank's coins were much more readily accepted because they were backed by the Bank of St.

George. They accredited their own ambassadors to foreign countries. There may have been a Genoese ambassador, but he was secondary to the ambassador of the Bank of St. George, especially given that the real function of Genoa was as a maritime economic power. If you wanted to deal with Genoa economically, you dealt with the bank rather than with the Genoese government. It raised armies in its own name. How often does a bank actually hire mercenaries to fight on its behalf? The government couldn't be trusted because the Republic was so divided that one faction could easily undo the other. The bank, however, had an element of stability and had at least a singular policy to make its investors and the consortium that had created it very rich and powerful.

The result was that the Bank of St. George, to some extent, became Genoa. But even banks sometimes cannot control forces around them, especially in this geopolitical world of two opposing empires: the Christian Empire of the West and the growing Turkish Empire of the East. The fall of Constantinople in 1453 had an effect on Genoa similar to the effect that it had on Venice. The collapse of the Byzantine Empire meant that whatever protection the rich and important Genoese Empire around the Black Sea had enjoyed, now simply evaporated. The Turks treated the Genoese as they treated all Christians, as infidels; to pay higher taxes, dues, fines and fees, and to pay bribes. The Genoese also realized that their control of these trading posts would be limited.

Moreover, since 1261 when the Genoese had engineered the return of the Greek dynasty to the imperial throne of Constantinople, they had enjoyed privileges within the empire and within the city. The imperial family owed a good deal to the Genoese, and that repayment was something the Genoese had counted on. But with the imperial family gone, slaughtered on the walls of Constantinople on that day in May of 1453, it meant that the Turks were there, who cared nothing about the Genoese. The Genoese found themselves, then, without that economic platform that they always had been able to count upon. The most painful blow to Genoa was the loss of its most important trading post, an element of Genoese pride as much as an element of the Genoese economic empire. That was the city of Caffa on the Black Sea. In 1475, it fell to the Turks, and with its fall, we really see the end of the maritime empire of Genoa.

Genoa, though, at least had something to fall back on, which was the bank. The bank was still there. The bank became extraordinarily important, and the Genoese realized that it was going to be the bank that would save them economically. Of course, owning a bank and owning one of the most important financial institutions in all of Europe meant that Genoa would be a rich prize for other powers—powers more interested in taking Genoese wealth and using its strategic location for their own good, than trying to solve the Genoese problems. The French influence was particularly powerful, as we've seen. The Italian Guelfs had always looked to the House of Anjou as their savior. St. Louis of Toulouse was the almost mythical saint that led the Italian Guelf ideological cause. Genoa, like so many other cities, looked to the Guelfs as the popular party. The French influence was powerful, and the French, as we've seen, intervened on a number of occasions.

By the time we reach the 16th century, though, this has another geopolitical implication—something significantly dangerous. The King of France, Francis I, was anxious to impose the Valois hegemony on the continent. He believed that the House of France should be the preeminent power in Europe. He was, of course, confronted by the Emperor Charles V, the Holy Roman Emperor and the King of Spain. Charles believed it was the House of Habsburg and the vast empire that he ruled—Spain, what is now Germany, Bohemia, parts of Italy, and of course the vast wealth of the New World—that should provide him with the hegemony of the continent.

The duel between Habsburg and Valois was to be one of the recurring dramas of Italian history because the battle was to be fought in Italy. Italy would be the place where the hegemony of Europe was going to be determined because both the French and the Habsburgs had competing claims, usually on the same places like Milan and Naples, but it was really much deeper than that. It was, in some ways, the old ideological argument of Guelf and Ghibelline once more writ large, but now in a world that had become much more dangerous and powerful because of the intervention of forces from beyond the Alps. The barbarians had come back once more, and they came back in the 16th century with a vengeance.

Through the Spanish kingdom, and through the empire, Charles V had designs on Italy that could be backed by great powers. Also, he had economic interests that were extremely powerful indeed, and he knew that the question of Genoa was one that would have to be confronted because of its strategic location. France had controlled Genoa from 1515, and Charles V looked at this and saw the dangers involved. As long as the French were in Genoa, which of course is on the Ligurian coast of Italy—the western Mediterranean, facing France—he knew that the French could supply their armies, provide additional troops, and always have a place to which they could retreat on the Peninsula in case of danger, and in case the warfare should continue. As long as Genoa was there, the Spanish position would always be in danger, and Charles V recognized this.

In order to control north central Italy, Charles would have to take Genoa. He directed his armies to do exactly that, and in 1522 the city fell to the House of Habsburg, to the Spanish troops and the imperial veterans of the Habsburgs. The city was sacked quite terribly, and then it was garrisoned and turned into what really amounted to a Habsburg outpost. It was a fortified city, both to protect the flank of the Habsburg Empire, and also to ensure that the French would have no means of entry should they decide to rekindle the wars in the continent. For the next five years, Genoa became an extension of Habsburg rule. But then along came—to some extent—a hero, someone who is celebrated in Genoese history to this day, Andrea Doria. In Italy, he is seen as one of the great heroes of Italian life.

Andrea Doria, with help from the French, succeeded in driving the Habsburgs out in 1527. Doria was a great captain. He also had been a pirate for part of his life, but then again, almost all Genoese captains had. He was a great admiral and a great aristocrat from one of the great families in the city. He, with the help of the French, drove out the Habsburgs and allowed for some measure of independence to return to Genoa. Full Genoese sovereignty was restored under Doria, but he realized, having grown up in this environment—having, in fact, been exiled himself previously—that the factional disputes within the city would always be a dangerous moment, always be an opportunity for the intervention of one of the great powers, and he had to face this.

He also had the advantage of being, to some extent, an independent factor. He had been helped by the French, but he really didn't feel he owed them very much. He had to confront the factionalism internally; he had to confront the instability. He realized the only way to do this was to restructure the government of the Republic so that it reflected much more realistically the power within the state. In order to do this, he actually became, and was recognized popularly as becoming, the dictator of Genoa. He was offered the doge's crown, which he wisely refused. He said he didn't want to be doge. He really rather liked having the extra constitutional power that gave him the authority of restructuring the government, and he did. Having refused the doge's crown, he then abolished the office. He realized that having a doge elected for life had been part of the problem because all of the factions had tried to get hold of this office and the patronage and power that it implied. Without that office, there would not be the same kind of focus of factional interest.

He abolished the office of doge for life and created a new office, also called doge or duke. This was to be held for only two years. This new office of doge was a two-year appointment, and the election of the doge was to come about not by popular support. Simon Boccanegra, the first doge of Genoa, had been elected by everybody in the city; it was, in fact, a popular election. But using the model of Venice, the aristocratic party that seemed to be his strongest supporter, and the wealth of the Bank of St. George and its investors—who had become, to some extent, the Genoese state—he now turned Genoa into an aristocratic republic. The power and the right of election of a popular party was abolished. There was no opportunity now for the poor—those people who did not have significant wealth, influence, or family ties—to have a role in government. Genoa, like Venice, became a closed aristocratic republic in which only those nobles who sat in a Great Council could serve as, and elect, the doge for two years.

The common people were shut out, and this adds to a recurring theme that will develop and will be elaborated in this entire course; in the 16th century, the "aristocratization"—to create a rather infelicitous term—of Italy; a movement away from popular governments towards governments by oligarchy—governments by the rich and the powerful, who began to transfer more and more of the power and the wealth of their communities to themselves at the expense of those who were being increasingly cut off from access to power, opportunity, and social mobility. Of course, this situation was unhappy, but it was also driven by crisis. The Genoese, led by Andrea Doria, felt that they had no choice. They would either become the plaything and pawn of the great powers of Habsburg and

Valois, or they would take circumstances into their own hands. It meant sacrifices, but as in so many instances in Western history, the sacrifices would be made by the poor.

Despite his deep obligations to France—because it was, after all, a French army that had returned Doria and had, in fact, returned the sovereignty of Genoa back to its people—Andrea Doria realized that the future of Europe was with the Habsburgs. In particular, the future of Italy would be with the House of Habsburg, which would become the dominant power on the Peninsula. This would last until the *Risorgimento* of the 19th century. Andrea Doria was a brilliant statesman. He knew which way the wind was blowing, and he knew that if he was going to protect Genoa, he had to be taken along with it. He consequently broke his ties to France, made peace with the Habsburgs, and joined with them. In return, he was given the office of Supreme Admiral of the Habsburg fleets. Andrea Doria became the admiral of the Mediterranean, the admiral in charge of all of the Habsburg fleets, essentially directed towards the Turks, but as everyone knew, also to protect the coastline of Italy from the French and any others that might interfere with Habsburg interests.

The Bank of St. George was reinforced, and the Bank of St. George had always gone along; money is always above politics. The bank had been successful under the most complicated and difficult circumstances. The bank had succeeded, had worked very well, under foreign intervention. The bank was recognized for what it really was, the essence of a new Genoese Empire. The Genoese Empire of the trading posts of the Black Sea, of the long-distance trade, of mercantile wealth, and of galleys sailing the entire Mediterranean, had given way to a financial empire, a mercantile empire based upon the enormous reserves, financial acumen, contacts, and political influence of the Bank of St. George. The bank became, because of the Habsburg connection, the essential banking instrument of the Habsburg Empire. We have to reiterate that the Habsburg Empire was also the empire of the New World. The vast amounts of gold and silver flowing into Europe often passed through the Bank of St. George. The Bank of St. George assumed the public debts of nations and transferred money all across the Habsburg Empire, making sure that it got where it was needed and that they always took a reasonable skim, something at which banks are particularly good.

The result of this was the so-called *Genoese century*, and a wonderful century it was. This celebrated Genoese century was, in fact, a world of the baroque, a world of the great patrician palaces that exist to this day along the Via Garibaldi—those brilliant palaces with their remarkably intricate and highly developed interiors. It was the world in which Ruebens painted. It was the world in which Genoese painters became celebrated for their luxurious portraits of the rich patricians of the great families—those portraits by Ruebens, who spent so long in Genoa; the portraits of the Adorno, the Doria, and the Balbi. These great portraits reflect the Genoese century and the power and wealth of the families that commissioned them. When we think of great maritime empires, we often think of the portraits of the powerful leaders and families of these empires. In mercantile empires, like the Dutch in the 17th century or the Genoese, we see the character and personality; the Dutch with the clear and rather austere black costumes, seriousness, and Calvinist demeanor, as opposed to the Genoese portraits with the incredible richness of costume and background, just being surrounded by servants.

Genoa was a remarkable place. It was a place of beauty and refinement, but it was a place that was built upon a bank. One of the parallels that's often drawn is how the British Empire moved from being a great maritime empire that encircled the world, to becoming essentially the financial clearinghouse of a continent. To a degree, the same thing happened with Genoa. Genoa lost its maritime empire, but it became the financial clearinghouse of another kind of empire, the House of Habsburg, and it became the money center of Italy. The palaces of Genoa, the portraits, the elegant furniture, carved woodwork, and painted ceilings—these things reflect the Genoese century because they reflect the great wealth of those noble families that controlled the Republic and the Bank of St. George.

Then there's the other Genoa. I remarked at the beginning how Genoa is one of the most understudied of the Italian cities, partly because of its complexity. It's very, very difficult to actually get through any one year in Genoese history without falling into hopeless confusion. But we have to remember that there are those other elements that link the city very much to us in North America. It was, after all, the city of Christopher Columbus, as we noted, and his house is very carefully preserved. But it also was a place where Marco Polo was held as a prisoner, and it was a place from which

Giuseppe Garibaldi set sail with his thousand in order to liberate Italy and really begin the War of the Risorgimento. His close collaborator and friend, the Republican, Giuseppe Mazzini, was a native of Genoa.

Besides the *Risorgimento* and the creation of an Italian nation, we also have to remember the role that Genoa played in the creation of other nations—not just the role of Christopher Columbus, and not just the name of Andrea Doria, given to great ships that sail the Atlantic. Also, it was the port from which the millions of Italian immigrants sailed to Australia, the United States, Canada, and Argentina. It was the port of embarkation for those millions of Italians who gave so much to the creation of lands in the New World, of lands that had been, to some extent, determined by the voyages of Christopher Columbus, the Genoese.

Genoa, then, is a model of a very unusual state—a state that had begun as a great maritime empire, a state that, because of its own internal confusion, had fallen into anarchy, and one that ultimately was saved by the financial institution of a bank until a real man on horseback (actually a man in a fleet of galleys) came along, Andrea Doria, and created a new kind of state. But the sacrifice was always there, and it becomes a cautionary tale. To what extent are you going to limit freedom for financial advantage, and to what extent are you going to limit freedom for stability? Genoa survived, but it survived, to some extent, as the bagman for the Habsburgs. The wealth of a few citizens was often made at the expense of large numbers of their fellow citizens who had been frozen out of government and kept out of political and economic activity.

Lecture Eight
Pisa

Scope:

Pisa functioned as an important papal ally during the Crusades; however, when it was officially organized as a free, self-governing commune in 1162, it switched from Guelf to Ghibelline allegiance. After falling out with Genoa over shared control of the Mediterranean islands, Pisa was disastrously defeated at Meloria in 1284. Recovery was difficult because of the growing ambitions of Florence, the Guelf power located upstream. Florence ultimately captured Pisa in 1406, thereby acquiring its first secure seaport. Although circumstances allowed Pisa independence for a brief time after 1494, the Florentines starved the city into submission in 1509. Thereafter, the history of Pisa is that of the Grand Duchy of Tuscany. Still, the Medici rulers made significant contributions to the city by strengthening the university and reestablishing Pisa's role as a sea power. At the Battle of Lepanto in 1571, the Pisans participated heroically in the Christian victory against the Turks. Notwithstanding these triumphs, the silting of the harbor and the Medici's construction of the alternative port of Livorno turned this once great *città marinara* into a quiet, provincial university town.

Outline

I. Pisa was once one of the great maritime states of Italy, but by the end of the Middle Ages, Genoa and Venice had become triumphant, and Pisa had been left far behind.

   A. Pisa was a Roman foundation that enjoyed an excellent harbor at the mouth of the Arno River. Both Pisa and Genoa had ports on the Ligurian Sea, which faced the islands of Sardinia and Corsica and gave access to the southern coast of France and the coast of Spain.

   B. The Saracens had colonized the islands of the western Mediterranean and used them as the basis to attack Christian shipping. The Pisans and Genoese cooperated initially to drive out the Saracens at the request of the pope and to further their own economic interests.

C. Allied with Genoa, the Pisans struggled throughout the Mediterranean against the Saracens. In 1016, the Saracens were driven off Sardinia, and the pope rewarded the two powers with joint control of the island.

    1. Rather than having the Pisans and Genoese fight each other, the pope saw the advantage for the papacy and for Christianity if the two states cooperated against the Islamic powers in the inland sea.

    2. In 1077, the Pisans and Genoese were given joint control over Corsica. Together, they were to control the seaward route into the southern coast of France and the coast of Spain.

D. Although it switched from Guelf to Ghibelline allegiance when it was officially organized as a free, self-governing commune in 1162, Pisa continued as an important papal ally during the Crusades.

    1. The Pisans did extraordinarily well from the Crusades, bringing in wealth that allowed for the construction of the remarkable complex of ecclesiastical buildings around the Campo Santo.

    2. At this time, the Cathedral of Pisa, the Baptistery, and the *campanile*, or bell tower—the Leaning Tower of Pisa—were built.

    3. From the Levant, the Pisans brought back an architectural decoration—an alternating design of light and dark marble—that was applied to the cathedral complex around the Campo Santo and to other complexes elsewhere in Italy.

II. Events over the next century saw the extinction of Pisa's attempt to become a great Mediterranean power on the model of its rivals, Genoa and Venice.

A. Unlike Genoa and Venice, Pisa never established a network of trading posts in the eastern Mediterranean; instead, Pisa concentrated on the western Mediterranean, the coast of North Africa, and the southern part of Italy. Thus, the Pisans never had the opportunity to reap enormous profits by making connections with the East.

B. This policy linked the Pisans too closely to the Holy Roman Empire.

    1. The emperors who came into Italy often needed maritime support, which the Pisans provided to gain some measure of advantage should the Ghibellines ultimately win in the battle with the Guelfs.

    2. In 1137, this policy seemed to work. The Pisans gave their fleet to the Holy Roman Emperor Lothair II, who wanted to establish imperial power in the south of Italy. The Pisan fleet destroyed Amalfi, removing it from the competition of the maritime empires.

    3. However, the removal of Amalfi was not to Pisa's advantage alone; the Genoese and the Venetians had also lost a competitor.

    4. This action cemented Pisa once and for all in the Ghibelline orbit at a time when the Guelfs were beginning to rise.

C. It was the terrible series of wars between Pisa and Genoa, though, that ultimately sapped the authority, wealth, and confidence of the Pisans.

    1. As we've said, once Pisa and Genoa had driven the Saracens from the islands of Sardinia and Corsica, the two powers began to fight over the spoils and over joint rule.

    2. The Genoese opened hostilities with a naval attack on Porto Pisano in 1126.

    3. The bitter rivalry between Genoa and Pisa was finally determined at the Battle of Meloria in 1284, when the Pisans were decisively defeated by the Genoese fleet.

    4. Pisa had been counting on Corsica and Sardinia to develop its western Mediterranean trade. Without these outposts, recovery for Pisa would be difficult.

D. Economic recovery was further hampered by the growing local ambitions of Florence, the Guelf power located upstream from Pisa.

    1. The Florentines needed a port from which to ship their vast production of cloth to northern Europe, and Pisa's location at the mouth of the Arno, Florence's river, made it the obvious target.

   2. Pisa had supported the Tuscan Ghibellines, led by Siena and Florentine exiles, against the Guelf faction, participating in the Battle of Montaperti (1260), at which the Florentines were disastrously defeated.

   3. As a result, the Florentines began not just to covet Pisa as a port but to hate the Pisans as a people.

   4. Pisa was forced to spend its accumulated wealth in landward defense against Florence, rather than in rebuilding its fleets.

III. The Florentine conquest of Pisa was, in many ways, inevitable.

   A. Pisan commerce had already declined. After Meloria, Genoa picked up Pisa's trade routes, and other cities, especially Barcelona, began to serve the markets that the Pisans had hoped to monopolize.

   B. As it had in Genoa, the internal situation in Pisa became chaotic. Complete defeat in war, economic decline, and lack of confidence gave rise to factionalism and political instability.

   C. Ultimately, a great aristocrat of Tuscany—Count Ugolino della Gherardesca—assumed the authority of *capitano del popolo*, although he bore the shame of having fled the Battle of Meloria with his fleet.

   1. Ugolino is perhaps best known from Canto IX of the *Inferno*, in which Dante sustains the myth of Ugolino as the cannibal count.

   2. Initially, Ugolino shared power with the Ghibelline leader in Pisa, who ironically, was the archbishop of Pisa. When tensions arose between the two, Ugolino lost the power struggle and was sentenced to be starved to death with his sons and grandsons.

   3. According to the myth, Ugolino's sons and grandsons requested that he eat them to maintain his strength in the hopes that the *capitano* would be released and could overthrow the archbishop.

4. In 2002, an Italian archaeologist/anthropologist discovered the bones of Ugolino, his children, and his grandchildren and found no evidence of cannibalism.

IV. As happens so often in the history of Italian city-states, a situation that seemed to be insupportable and tragic worsened.

    A. Around 1327, the emperor Louis IV, also known as Louis the Bavarian, crossed the Alps in order to install himself in Rome and to launch a new age of imperial and Ghibelline power.

        1. Despite their Ghibelline allegiance, the Pisans refused Louis admission to the city; they realized that in submitting to Louis, the city would become an enemy of the pope.

        2. Louis besieged the city and, ultimately, starved it into submission. He entered the city and stayed there with his army for two years.

        3. Pisa was finally forced to pay Louis an enormous tribute to induce him to leave. The city was left in such dire economic straits that it had no opportunity to recover from the series of disasters it had survived since 1284 and the Battle of Meloria.

        4. The Pisan government raised taxes, import and export duties, and fees to the point of driving all capital from the city.

        5. The Pisan economy, already damaged, was shattered, and the city fell into an economic decline from which recovery was impossible.

    B. The poverty of the Pisans and the danger of the situation were made clear by 1400.

        1. Giangaleazzo Visconti, the duke of Milan, had united the states in Lombardy and parts of Tuscany under Milanese rule; only Florence stood against him. At the same time, the situation in Pisa was so chaotic that a great noble, Gherardo Appiani, had assumed power.

        2. Appiani established himself as *signori* ("lord") of Pisa, but when Giangaleazzo Visconti and his armies began moving into Tuscany, Pisa realized that it would either have to yield to Giangaleazzo or be besieged and probably destroyed.

   3. Appiani, recognizing in the situation a personal opportunity, sold the city to Giangaleazzo Visconti and kept the proceeds.

C. Once more, the situation then worsened.

   1. In 1402, Giangaleazzo Visconti died unexpectedly. With his death, the Pisans, of course, wanted their independence back, but the heirs of Giangaleazzo had no intention of relinquishing Pisa.

   2. Ultimately, the regents for the young sons of Giangaleazzo sold Pisa to the Florentines.

   3. In 1405, the Florentines took possession of Pisa, having simply bought it, despite the objections of the Pisans themselves.

D. Thereafter, Pisa was integrated into the Florentine territorial state. To some extent, this development benefited Pisa. The Pisans lost their freedom and independence, but they also gained the protection of one of the five great states of Italy.

E. Pisa saw a short period of renewed independence after the French invasions of 1494.

   1. During this period, the Medici were expelled from Florence, the Florentine Republic was resurgent, and the Pisans took the opportunity of this chaos and the support of the French army to renew their independence.

   2. The Florentines were forced to turn Pisa over to the French as a garrisoned town, and when the French left, they permitted Pisa to maintain its independence, despite Florentine objections.

   3. For the Florentines, the recovery of Pisa was the single greatest policy objective. In 1509, after a siege that starved the city, Florence took possession of Pisa once more.

V. The history of Pisa thereafter is part of the Grand Duchy of Tuscany.

A. The Medici rulers of Tuscany, after the establishment of a hereditary duchy under Cosimo I in 1537, treated Pisa remarkably well.

B. Cosimo's ambitions and his desire to be raised to grand ducal status by the pope prompted him to create a new order of knighthood, the Knights of Santo Stefano, a crusading order at sea.

   1. Galleys bearing the Tuscan flag of Florence sailed once more into the Mediterranean and served nobly against the Turks at the Battle of Lepanto in 1571.

   2. Cosimo received his title, and the Pisans reclaimed some measure of honor and respect. Sadly, though, the harbor at Pisa began to silt, and Cosimo had to build a new port at Livorno.

   3. Under Cosimo, the enemies that the Pisans hated most ultimately became their allies in the common Christian war against the Turks.

Essential Reading:

T. Bloomquist and M. Mazzaoui, *The Other Tuscany: Essays in the History of Lucca, Pisa and Siena during the Thirteenth, Fourteenth and Fifteenth Centuries.*

Supplementary Reading:

W. Heywood, *A History of Pisa in the Eleventh and Twelfth Centuries.*

Questions to Consider:

1. The three great maritime cities of Pisa, Genoa, and Venice began with similar opportunities, but by 1380, Venice was dominant. What factors gave Venice an advantage?

2. To this day, there is a popular Genoese saying: "Better a death in the house than a Pisan at the door." Can nations ever reconcile with their past enemies, even after centuries?

Lecture Eight—Transcript
Pisa

Pisa was once one of the great maritime states of Italy. At one point, the Pisani challenged the Venetians and the Genoese for control of the Mediterranean trade. But by the end of the Middle Ages, Genoa and Venice had become triumphant, and Pisa had been left far behind. It's necessary to see what happened, to see how the potential of this great state, also on the Ligurian coast of Italy, resulted in its eclipse by its more powerful, and ultimately victorious, competitors. Pisa was a Roman foundation. It was an ancient city, and it enjoyed an excellent harbor at the mouth of the River Arno in Tuscany. During the Middle Ages, it developed as an important maritime power, as we've seen. It had one of the great maritime fleets of Italy. Both Pisa and Genoa realized that their future to some extent remained together, at least in the initial years, because they dominated the western Mediterranean, the Ligurian coast that faced the islands of Corsica and Sardinia and gave access to the southern coast of France and the coast of Spain, and ultimately to control the pirates and corsairs of the Saracens on the north coast of Africa in what is now Morocco.

The islands of the western Mediterranean, particularly Sardinia and Corsica—but also the Balearic Islands—were dangerous places for Christian shipping. The Saracens, during the Early Middle Ages, had colonized them and used them as the basis to attack Christian shipping, such as it was, in the western Mediterranean. The Pisans and the Genoese cooperated initially in order to drive them out at the request of the pope, but at the same time in their own best interests. They realized that their trade would always be shadowed by the Saracens unless the Saracens were removed from those islands. They had a double commitment: to Christendom to drive the infidel from the Mediterranean Sea; and also for their own economic interest, to make sure that whatever trade there would be was theirs, and it would be safe and protected.

There was originally a close alliance between Pisa and Genoa, and they struggled against the Saracens until, in 1016, they finally drove the Saracens off Sardinia, and they were rewarded jointly by the papacy. The pope saw this alliance as an important one. Rather than seeing the Pisans and Genoese fight one another, it was much better for the papacy and for Christianity that they cooperate against their common enemy of the Islamic powers within the inland sea. The Pisans were given joint control over Corsica in 1077, as with Sardinia. Together, they were supposed to control that seaward route into the southern coast of France and to the coast of Spain.

Although it switched from a Guelf to a Ghibelline alliance, Pisa still remained very close to the papacy. The Ghibelline alliance was a political necessity to some extent, and after 1162 when the Pisans formed themselves into a self-governing commune, they maintained that close relationship with the papacy that allowed them to participate actively in the Crusades, while at the same time allowing their imperial connections to grow. As a consequence, the Pisans did extraordinarily well from the Crusades. Indeed, during the First Crusade, they made great wealth, bringing not only that soil to the Campo Santo to ensure that the Pisans would be first in line when the last trumpet blew, but also bringing the wealth that would allow for the construction of that remarkable complex of ecclesiastical buildings around that Campo Santo.

This was the time of the building of the Cathedral of Pisa, and of the Baptistery, and of course the *campanile* or the bell tower, which today leans the "Tore Pendente," the Leaning Tower of Pisa. They knew at the time that it was beginning to lean, and they actually began to try to correct it so that it would be straighter, but the soil was unsound, and it continued to lean until only recently, when finally the problem was essentially solved.

Another observation is that, besides bringing the soil for the Campo Santo from the Holy Land, the Pisans also brought a form of architectural decoration that ultimately overwhelmed all of Tuscany. The Pisans, when they were in the Levant, saw the attractive Syrian design of alternating white and black or white and dark green marble. This was then applied to that cathedral complex around the Campo Santo. Soon, the other cathedral complexes in the other great states of Italy, such as Florence and Lucca, began to mimic the style. That alternating black and white marble that we see on the facades of the cathedrals of Lucca and churches in Florence reflects that Pisan interest in a style that was essentially Levantine. Not only did the Pisans bring back wealth, soil, and hopes of redemption—they also brought back decorative elements that would influence all of Italy, and all of European culture, for all times.

The next century after the initial success of the first three Crusades saw a decline in Pisan power. Pisa was not ultimately able to compete with the Genoese and the Venetians. The first problem came when it fell out with its original close ally, the Genoese. Pisa had made, to some extent, a mistake. It had made a policy error in not looking to the rich luxury trade of the East—as the Genoese and Venetians had—and trying to establish trading posts that could move those high-volume, high-value luxury goods from the East, such as the silks, spices, and slaves.

Rather, they began looking towards the western Mediterranean, the coast of North Africa, and the southern part of Italy itself. They saw that Sicily, southern Italy, the coast of Spain and North Africa would be much more easily serviced by Pisa. They were shorter routes, and there was rich trade there. Also, the trade in particular to the coast of Spain, and even the south of France, could be protected by the Pisan enclaves on Corsica and Sardinia. There was never the opportunity to reap the enormous profits that the Venetians and the Genoese had by accomplishing that connection with the East. The Pisans were always finding themselves in a secondary market as far as luxury goods were concerned.

Also, this policy had linked the Pisans too closely to the empire. We've seen how the Pisans decided that it was in their best interest to move from a close Guelf alliance—that is, the support of the papacy—to an imperial or Ghibelline alliance. The main reason for this was that the Pisans offered the imperial incursions a fleet. The emperors who decided to come into Italy often needed maritime support, as well as support inland. The Pisans thought that it would be a wise policy to provide that fleet to the emperors, and thereby gain some measure of advantage should the Ghibellines ultimately win in that great battle between Guelf and Ghibelline, papal and imperial, power. In 1137, this policy seemed to actually work, and it seemed to be reinforced by the success that the Pisans had in the shattering and destroying of Amalfi.

The Pisans destroyed Amalfi because they had given their fleet to the Holy Roman Emperor, Lothair II. He wanted to establish imperial power in the south of Italy—power that would be then carefully cultivated by the Hohenstaufen and the Pisans were going to provide the maritime support. Indeed, it initially worked. The removal of Amalfi from the competition of the maritime empires was not just to

Pisa's advantage. Again, there were unexpected consequences. Removing Amalfi meant that the Genoese and the Venetians also had lost a competitor. They could then compete more easily against Pisa, and to some extent more easily against one another. The destruction of Amalfi wasn't only in Pisa's interest. The other is that it cemented once and for all Pisa in the imperial or Ghibelline orbit. It made Pisa a Ghibelline state at a time when the Guelfs were beginning to rise, and also in a place where the Guelfs would ultimately be victorious, Tuscany.

It was the falling out with Genoa, though, the terrible series of wars between Pisa and Genoa, that ultimately sapped the authority, wealth and confidence of the Pisans. Of course, they fell out over the islands of Sardinia and Corsica. As long as the Pisans and the Genoese had a common enemy, as long as they were fighting the Saracens together, they were willing to work in concert. They were, in fact, close allies, and they were able to succeed at whatever they planned. But as soon as the common enemy was removed, once the Saracens were driven from the Balearic Islands, Sardinia, and Corsica, then the Pisans and the Genoese began to fight over the spoils, over their joint rule of these islands, because ultimately their economic and maritime interests were not the same. They were competitors, and to think that they could cooperate in the control of those strategic islands was nothing short of a fantasy.

The Genoese attacked first. They used an opportunity that the Pisans had provided to attack the port of Porto Pisano in 1126. This began the series of wars that ultimately would shatter Pisa, leaving it in a position much dependent upon other powers. This period of bitter rivalry, this hatred between the Genoese and the Pisans—because there is nothing like former friends having fallen out in order to engender hatred—was finally determined at the terrible Battle of Meloria in 1284. At Meloria, the Pisans were decisively defeated by the Genoese fleet. In this defeat, Pisa lost its measure of control over Corsica, and it lost its outposts on Sardinia. The loss of Pisan control over Corsica, and the loss of some of its authority over Sardinia, would be of course a terrible blow because these were the places that the Pisans were counting on for developing their Mediterranean trade. Without them, it would be difficult in the extreme for Pisa to ever recover.

That was bad, but the situation around Pisa and Tuscany was worse. Florence was growing in wealth and power. It was becoming the dominant state in Tuscany, and it was just upriver on the Arno from Pisa. Moreover, Florence was not a mercantile power at all in terms of maritime trade; it was a mercantile power in the production of luxury cloth. The Florentines needed a port through which this cloth could be shipped. The vast amounts of cloth that the Florentines were producing had to be transported across Europe, and the port of Pisa was the obvious place from which to do this. Initially, there was an arrangement whereby Florentine cloth could be shipped, at a price, through Pisa. But it was obvious that Florentine interests, expansionism, and mercantile ambition would ultimately be focused on the seaport at the mouth of the Arno. It was just too natural and too easy.

Pisa also had made another strategic error. Pisa, as a Ghibelline state—and Florence was a Guelf state—had supported Florence's enemies with the exile of the Ghibelline families from Florence, with the Guelf victory, and the support of the Sienese, another Ghibelline state worried about Florentine expansion. The Pisans began to focus on providing military and economic support for the Ghibellines in their attack on Florence and their attempt to overturn the Guelf victory, and the attempt of the Sienese to ensure that they would have a measure of protection from Florentine ambition. The result was the Battle of Montaperti in 1260, a date and a place burned deeply upon the Florentine consciousness because the Florentines were decisively defeated by the Ghibelline armies of Siena, the Florentine Ghibelline exiles, and the Pisans.

As a result of the Pisan support of Florence's Ghibelline enemies at Montaperti, the Florentines began not just to covet Pisa as a port, but to hate the Pisans as people. The hatred was powerful and grew, and Pisa found itself consequently the object of the hatred of two very powerful states: the Genoese—remember a Pisan at the door is worse than a death in the house—and the Florentines, who saw Pisa as a natural supporter of its enemies, as one of the elements that had helped humiliate the Republic of Florence at Montaperti. The Florentines would not forgive Pisa, as the Genoese would never forgive Pisa.

Florence then became Pisa's bitter enemy, and this became known; it became clear. The result was that Pisa was not able to rebuild its fleets after its defeat at Meloria. The defeat at Meloria had shattered the Pisan navy, but rather than use its accumulated wealth and its ability to recover its maritime empire, it had to build landward defense against Florence. Pisa, despite the fact that its past had been at sea and its future hope would be at sea, was in fact turned into a fortress against the Florentines. Pisa was not able to recover, and it was only a matter of time before the power of Florence—that great republic, that powerful state, that enormously wealthy established authority in Tuscany—would claim what it believed was really its.

Florentine conquest of Pisa was in many ways inevitable; the question was when and how. Pisan commerce had already declined dramatically. As soon as the Pisan fleet was shattered at Meloria, the Genoese began to pick up its trade routes, and other cities began to rise in order to serve the markets that the Pisans had hoped to monopolize. Especially, the city of Barcelona arose in order to make sure that the coasts of Spain and France would be served by Barcelona rather than by Pisa, should it ever recover. As with Genoa, the internal situation in Pisa became chaotic. There is nothing like complete defeat in war, economic decline, and lack of confidence to give rise to factionalism and political instability. Pisa suffered almost as much as did the Genoese.

It was impossible to get a consensus because all things seemed to have evaporated and fragmented. Ultimately, despite his embarrassment at Meloria at having fled, a great aristocrat—one of the great landed nobles of Tuscany—Count Ugolino della Gherardesca assumed the authority of *capitano del popolo*. Ugolino is a figure of both myth and history. Ugolino is perhaps best known from Canto XXXIII of the *Inferno*, where Dante maintains the myth of Ugolino as the cannibal count. The story is almost as dramatic as the myth. Count Ugolino assumed power as leader of the popular faction in Pisa. He assumed power as *capitano del popolo*, which was a legitimate office, and he initially shared power with the great Ghibelline leader, who ironically was the Archbishop of Pisa. In Italian politics, nothing can ever be assumed.

The Archbishop of Pisa, as the leader of the Ghibelline faction, worked initially with the Gherardesca, which initially had been a Ghibelline family, but soon tension arose. Ugolino was not anxious to share power with the archbishop, and the archbishop didn't in any way trust Ugolino. Ugolino did bear with him the fact that he had fled the Battle of Meloria with his fleet, resulting in the defeat, and he was then seen as a traitor. It was believed that he had fled because he was working in his own interest rather than the interest of the Pisan people, and there may indeed be some measure of truth to it. Usually it's unwise to take on an archbishop, even a Ghibelline one. This was proved when Ugolino lost the power struggle with the Archbishop of Pisa. Ugolino was sentenced to be starved to death. He, his sons, and his grandsons were locked in a tower and deprived of food until they were dead.

This begins the famous myth of Ugolino and the story from Dante: that ninth pit, the pit of the traitors. By tradition, Ugolino stayed alive—and again by tradition, at the request of his sons and grandsons that he eat them in order to maintain his strength so that he may be one day released when his supporters could overthrow the archbishop. As long as Ugolino remained alive, the Gherardesca could become resurgent. The story of Ugolino eating his children and grandchildren became part of Italian myth, very strongly supported by those miraculous 30 lines of Dante—30 lines that the English poet and Italian resident Walter Savage Landor described as the 30 most powerful lines ever written in poetry.

Ugolino did die in that tower, and he also was not a cannibal. As an aside, in 2002, an Italian archaeologist/anthropologist discovered the bones of Ugolino, his children, and grandchildren. They were determined, because the Gherardesca remains a powerful and influential family to this day in Tuscany, and the DNA proved that this was almost certainly the resting place of the cannibal count, his children, and grandchildren. Tests were done upon the skeletons, and there's no evidence of cannibalism. What convinced the anthropologist completely is that there is no indication that Ugolino had any access to meat for at least 30 days before his death. His children and grandchildren, it seems, died intact. The story of Ugolino is not only dramatic, but it is reflective—it's almost a parable; it's metaphorical—of the chaos and terrible circumstances within the city of Pisa.

As in so many things in the Italian city-states, what seems to be insupportable and tragic can actually get worse. In the 14th century, the Emperor Louis IV, the Bavarian, crossed the Alps in order to install himself in Rome and to lead a new age of imperial and Ghibelline power. This was the same Louis the Bavarian that inspired Cola di Rienzo in Rome. This was the Louis that had brought about so much political theory and hope of a new regime that would bring some measure of quiet and stability to the Italian Peninsula. Of course, he really was nothing short of just another Holy Roman Emperor entering Italy for his own advantage.

Pisa tried to hold out against the emperor despite their Ghibelline allegiance because the Pisans realized that there would be a particular danger in submitting to Louis. Louis was the enemy of the pope, and to open the gates of the city to Louis would mean that the pope would then be an enemy of the Republic of Pisa. Therefore, in 1327 the Pisans refused Louis admission. Louis, though, decided he was going to take the city anyway, and he besieged it and ultimately starved it into submission. The gates were opened, and Louis entered the city and stayed there with his army for two years. He finally left, but he had to be bribed to leave, and the bribe was enormous. The amount of money that had to be paid to Louis essentially bankrupted Pisa and left the city in such economic straits that it had no opportunity to recover at all from the series of disasters that it had survived since 1284, since the Battle of Meloria.

Consequently, they had to get money quickly in order just to sustain some measure of government and civil policy. They did what so many governments do in moments of crisis; they raised taxes, import and export duties, and fees to the point that there was an enormous flight of capital from Pisa. The attempt by the state to raise money made the situation worse by driving all of the money out of the city. The greatest loss was the Florentine merchants. The Florentine merchants hated the Pisans anyway—they were hostile—but in many ways they had no choice if they wanted to ship by sea, since the closest and most navigable port for the Florentines was Pisa because they could ship, at least most of the year, down the Arno. With the new fees and duties imposed, the Florentine merchants simply left and no longer shipped their cloth through Pisa. The Pisan economy, already damaged, was totally shattered, and the city fell into an economic decline that really was impossible to recover from.

The poverty of the Pisans and the dangerous situation was made clear by 1400. Hereto, the issue of geopolitics—that is, the larger Italian picture—begins to play out in the Pisan world as it had played out in the Genoese world. Giangaleazzo Visconti, the Duke of Milan, had a policy to unite all of Italy under Milanese rule, and he was almost successful. He united not only the Milanese and not only the states in Lombardy, but he moved into Tuscany, and only Florence stood against him. It was clear, and it was generally believed, that the Visconti would be ultimately victorious. The situation in Pisa was so chaotic that a great noble, Gherardo Appiani, had assumed power.

He established himself as *signori* of Pisa, as the lord of the city. But there wasn't much to be lord of, and when Giangaleazzo Visconti and his armies began moving into Tuscany, Pisa realized it would either have to yield to Giangaleazzo or be besieged and probably destroyed. Appiani, realizing that this was at least a personal opportunity, and one that he was willing to take, sold the city to Giangaleazzo Visconti. As lord of the city, this was, I suppose, his right. The Pisans, although they objected terribly, had no choice. Giangaleazzo Visconti bought Pisa in 1400, and Appiani walked away with the cash, and the Milanese ruled the Republic of Pisa.

The situation was bad, but once more it got worse. In 1402, Giangaleazzo Visconti died quickly and unexpectedly, probably of soldier's fever, as he was readying his armies for the final conquest of Florence, which would have united all of north central Italy under his rule. With the death of Giangaleazzo Visconti, the ruler of Pisa, it was very difficult to know what to do. The Pisans, of course, wanted their independence back, but the heirs of Giangaleazzo had no intention of giving Pisa back. Ultimately, they realized that Appiani had provided a very, very nice model. The regents for the young sons of Giangaleazzo sold Pisa to the Florentines. The Florentines wanted it; the Florentines had the money, and the Pisans really had no authority to reject this decision. They had nothing to do about it whatsoever. There was nothing to be done. The Visconti sold Pisa to its archenemy, Florence. In 1405, the Florentines took possession of Pisa, having simply bought it, despite the objections of the Pisans themselves.

Thereafter, Pisa became part of Florentine territory and was integrated into the Florentine territorial state. To some extent, it benefited Pisa. The Pisans had lost their freedom and their independence, but they had also gained the protection of one of the five great states of Italy, and a state that was economically powerful—one that was growing in wealth and influence. There was a short period of renewed independence after the French invasions of 1494. During this period, the Medici were expelled from Florence, the Florentine Republic was resurgent, and the Pisans took the opportunity of this chaos and the support of the French army to renew their independence.

The French garrisoned the city because the Florentines were forced, in turn, to turn the city over to the French as a garrisoned town. But when the French left, they permitted the Pisans to maintain their independence despite, again, Florentine objections. The Florentines at that point were in a moment of chaos themselves, and the Pisans seemed to have regained their ancient independence once more. But of course, this could not last. The Florentines saw the recovery of Pisa as the single greatest objective of their policy, and everything was directed towards it. In 1509, after a siege that starved the city to death, the gates were opened and Florence took possession of Pisa. Pisa would be part of the Florentine territorial state until its extinction.

The history of Pisa thereafter is part of the Grand Duchy of Tuscany. The Medici rulers of the Grand Duchy, after the establishment of a hereditary duchy under Cosimo I in 1537, treated Pisa remarkably well. Indeed, one of the ironies is that Pisa benefited so much from Florentine rule that it's odd that the Pisans should maintain this antipathy towards their governors, the Florentines. Cosimo I needed a seaport, and Pisa provided one. Cosimo also wanted a great university because Florence didn't have one, and Pisa was the university that had served Tuscany from medieval times. The university benefited with the greatest professors, including Galileo Galilei, teaching there and lecturing to students from all over Europe.

Cosimo also had ambitions in the Mediterranean. He wanted not only to be seen as a Christian prince, but he wanted the title of Grand Duke of Tuscany. To get this, he had to honor the pope because it was a title in the pope's gift. In order to do this, he created a new order of knighthood, the Knights of Santo Stefano, a crusading order, but a crusading order at sea. This crusading order resulted in the creation of galleys once more. Great galleys bearing the Tuscan flag of Florence sailed once more into the Mediterranean and served nobly at the Battle of Lepanto in 1571. Cosimo got his title of Grand Duke of Tuscany, and the Pisans got some measure of honor and respect back, and galleys once more sailed from the port. Sadly, though, the harbor began to silt, and Cosimo had to build a new port at Livorno, which the English strangely call Leghorn.

Cosimo had restored some measure of dignity to the city. Cosimo always showed Pisa some measure of privilege, and Pisa had reentered not only the Italian, but the European, fraternity of nations as one of the contributors to the great Christian victory against the Turks at Lepanto. The irony was that the enemies that the Pisans hated the most ultimately became their allies and friends once more in the common Christian war against the Turks, solidified by their participation at Lepanto and recognized by papal insignia and Medici privilege.

Lecture Nine
Christians vs. Turks in the Mediterranean

Scope:

Although the period of the Crusades generally gave Christian Europe the advantage over the Saracens, the rise of the Ottoman Turks changed this situation dramatically, the fall of Constantinople in 1453 heralding a period of relentless Turkish expansion. This threat stimulated the voyages of discovery begun by the Portuguese under Prince Henry the Navigator: His ambition to chart Africa was connected to his intention of attacking the Islamic states from behind. Similarly, the desire to avoid the dangers of the Mediterranean impelled the circumnavigation of the Cape of Good Hope by Vasco da Gama in 1497–1498. This had the dramatic effect of shifting the economic center of Europe from the Mediterranean to the Atlantic seaboard. By 1550, the Ottoman Empire had trebled its territory, controlling an arc around the Mediterranean from the Balkans to Gibraltar. It was only with the great Christian victory in 1571 at Lepanto that the Turks were halted. But despite Lepanto, the economic advantage of Italy, a fact from ancient times, was superseded by the rise of the Ottomans, and the Italian city-states collectively were to confront a long period of economic decline.

Outline

I. The maritime powers of Italy all had to confront the resurgence of Islam under the Turkish Empire. Indeed, after the second half of the 15th century, the Mediterranean became the battleground between East and West, between Christianity and Islam.

   A. The period of the Crusades had given the Christians an advantage over the Saracens, despite the fact that the Latin Kingdom of Jerusalem had not lasted long and the Saracens had recovered territory taken from them in the First Crusade.

   B. As we've seen, the Pisans and the Genoese had succeeded in driving the Saracens from Corsica and Sardinia. But Islamic pirates and fleets continued to prey upon Christian ships in the Mediterranean, and Christian settlements were endangered by Saracen raids.

C. The period of the Crusades and the growing power of Venice, Pisa, Genoa, and Amalfi gave the Europeans an opportunity to try to curb the threat of the Saracens.

    1. The maritime might of these collective forces, combined with a Crusader mentality, was sufficient to ensure that Christianity would play an important role in the Mediterranean, despite the growth of Islamic power.

    2. Moreover, the Saracen kingdoms were divided, unable to come together to drive the Christians from the inland sea.

II. The rise of the Ottoman Turks changed this situation dramatically.

    A. The fall of Constantinople to the Turks in 1453 and the consequent elimination of the Byzantine Empire permitted Ottoman expansion into and around the Mediterranean.

        1. The Turkish assault on the Balkans, for example, had begun decades before Constantinople fell.

        2. Serbia became a vassal state of the Turkish Empire after the Battle of Kosovo in 1389, with the entire territory becoming a province of the Turkish Empire in 1459.

        3. In 1396, the Turks defeated the Bulgarians, and again, that territory became a Turkish province.

        4. The Turks assaulted both the Venetians and the Genoese, and with the fall of Caffa in 1475, the Genoese Empire was destined to be destroyed by Turkish expansion and Venetian victory.

        5. The final humiliation came when the Turks took Otranto in Italy in 1480, holding the city for a year before abandoning it.

        6. The triumphant Turks then sent their seemingly invincible armies against their Islamic neighbors, overcoming Persia in 1514, Syria in 1516, and Egypt in 1517.

    B. With an arc of Turkish control now inscribed around the Mediterranean, the Sultan Selim I realized that he had a power base from which to expand his interests in Europe.

1. He conquered Belgrade in 1521, using it as a base of operations for incursions deeper into the European heartland.

2. The same year, Selim's fleet took the island of Rhodes from the crusading order of the Knights of St. John of Jerusalem.

3. By the 1520s, it seemed as if the Mediterranean would become a Turkish lake.

III. This threat stimulated the European voyages of discovery.

    A. The rise of the Turks had weakened the Venetian monopoly on long-distance trade and had driven the rulers of states on the Atlantic seaboard to search for other means of acquiring Eastern luxury goods.

        1. The activities of Prince Henry the Navigator, Bartholomew Diaz, and Vasco da Gama had proved that Africa could be circumnavigated and that it was possible to sail from Lisbon or the coast of Spain directly to the markets of India and China.

        2. Thus, the luxury goods that the Venetians and Genoese had sold at such enormous profit to their fellow Europeans now became the monopoly of those states that enjoyed harbors well away from Turkish power.

        3. The decline of the Italian economy was inevitable, and the decline of European shipping and power in the Mediterranean was abrupt.

    B. The ambitions of the Turks not only threatened the immediate powers of Italy but also changed the nature of policy in other states that bordered the Mediterranean, particularly Spain.

        1. The dynastic union of Ferdinand of Aragon and Isabella of Castile in 1479 created a new state, linked by religion.

        2. Spain became a Crusader kingdom, with Ferdinand and Isabella directing their armies against the Moorish kingdom of Granada.

        3. Granada had shared the Iberian Peninsula with the Spanish and Portuguese kingdoms since the 7th and 8th centuries. Because of the success of the Turks and the

Saracens, however, the existence of Granada was now seen as a danger to the European economy and to Christendom.

4. The expulsion of the Moors in 1492 and the expulsion and forced conversion of the Jews came about as a desire to win battles for Christianity when it seemed as though God had abandoned Christendom and given favor to the infidels.

5. The creation of the kingdom of Spain introduced a new power in the Mediterranean that would ultimately prove to be dangerous to the Italian Peninsula. When Spain was inherited by the House of Habsburg in 1517, the freedom of Italy would be compromised.

C. The economic center of Europe had shifted, from the Mediterranean to the Atlantic seacoast, and this shift complicated the relationship between Christians and Turks.

1. The Turkish Empire had become the most powerful state in the Western world by the middle of the 15th century.

2. By the middle of the 16th century, the Islamic power of Turkey controlled a region that spread from the Balkans around the eastern Mediterranean into the Straits of Gibraltar. This territory served as a base of power, authority, and opposition to the European economy and to European autonomy in the Mediterranean.

IV. The most powerful state in Europe faced one great opponent—Christendom—but Christendom was not united. The Turks, by force of arms, had largely united the territory under their rule. The Christians were fighting on several fronts and in the interest of individual principalities, city-states, or dynastic monarchies.

A. By 1526, the Turkish army broke out of the Balkans. An army of volunteers and soldiers from most Christian nations was raised to stop it, led by the king of Hungary. In 1526, these Christian forces were slaughtered by the Turks at the Battle of Mohacs.

B. There was now nothing to stop the Turks from crossing the Hungarian plain and besieging the imperial capitals, specifically, Vienna. The siege was unsuccessful, but Europe was in turmoil.

C. The Turks next turned to the fortified trading posts established by the Venetians and Genoese. One by one, these began to fall, including the Venetian outposts of Crete and Cyprus and Genoa's center at Caffa on the Black Sea.

D. The Turks also commissioned Barbary pirates as admirals of the Turkish fleet, giving them full permission to prey on Christian shipping.

V. Circumstances for the Christian nations seemed to worsen.

A. In 1560, King Philip II of Spain, the son of the emperor Charles V, collected a great fleet to attack the coast of North Africa. This force was surprised and destroyed by the Turkish fleet at Djerba.

B. Just a decade later, Cyprus, perhaps the most important of all the Christian islands in the Mediterranean, fell to the Turks.

C. Europe had lost not only trading posts but also staging posts, bases from which Christian shipping could be protected and fleets could be assembled to attack the Turks.

VI. At this moment of almost complete desperation, an event took place that allowed Christians to believe that perhaps the Turks were not invincible.

A. The siege of Malta (1565–1566) is, of course, one of the great acts of heroism in Western history. The island had been given to the knights of St. John of Jerusalem by the emperor Charles V after the knights were driven from Rhodes.

B. The crusading knights of the Order of St. John of Jerusalem volunteered their lives to further the goals of Christianity everywhere. At Malta, these knights now found themselves facing one of the greatest invasion forces of all time.

C. The sultan had planned to conquer Malta because of its strategic location in the middle of the Mediterranean, south of the coast of Sicily. Thus, Malta protected not just the Mediterranean but also the southern coast of Italy and the island of Sicily. Had it fallen, Europe would have found itself in an extremely dangerous position.

D. Altogether, there were about 6,000 defenders on the island, facing at least 30,000 Turkish troops.

1. Fortunately, the Grand Master Jean de la Valette knew that the assault was coming and had wisely fortified parts of the island. When the assault came, it was brutal, but the knights held out and ultimately succeeded in turning back the Turks.

2. This victory gave a renewed confidence to Europe, proving that the Turks could be defeated. A few years later, this was proved again at the Battle of Lepanto.

E. Lepanto was the opportunity for Christianity to function together as a military unit for the first time since the success of the First Crusade.

1. Under the command of Don John of Austria, the illegitimate son of the emperor Charles V and the half-brother of King Philip of Spain, a huge multinational fleet was assembled.

2. This fleet routed the Turks off the coast of Greece at Lepanto. The Turks lost all but 30 of their ships and about 30,000 men.

3. The Christians could have gone on to assault Constantinople, but the commanders fell out among themselves, giving the Turks the chance to reconstruct a fleet that would again challenge Christendom.

F. Nonetheless, Lepanto helped the Europeans regain some of their confidence. In addition, the world of the new Europe and the new Mediterranean was, to some extent, foretold at Lepanto.

1. The House of Habsburg would now have hegemonic power in the peninsula, as it did on the continent.

2. Lepanto, one of the most decisive battles of all time, protected Europe from a much more aggressive Turkish Empire.

3. Nevertheless, Turkish control of the Mediterranean would, to a degree, remain, and as long as that was true, Christians would have to fight to maintain trade, the southern borders of Europe would always be at risk, and the ability of Christendom to withstand Islamic Turkish advance would always be in question.

Essential Reading:

E. Bradford, *The Great Siege: Malta, 1565*.

Supplementary Reading:

A. Konstan and T. Bryan, *Lepanto, 1571: The Greatest Naval Battle of the Renaissance*.

Questions to Consider:

1. Does the struggle between the Turks and Christians in the 15th and 16th centuries elucidate the current theory of a clash of civilizations?

2. The discovery of America was an unintended consequence of the need to avoid the Mediterranean. Can you identify other significant unintended consequences of these voyages?

Lecture Nine—Transcript
Christians vs. Turks in the Mediterranean

The maritime powers of Italy all had to confront the resurgence of Islam under the Turkish Empire. Indeed, after the second half of the 15th century, the Mediterranean became the battleground between East and West, between the Christians and Islam, between the Turks and Europeans. What developed was a dramatic moment in which not only was the character of Europe to some degree defined, but also the sense of other identified. The period of the Crusades had given the Christians a good deal of advantage over the Saracens, despite the Latin kingdom of Jerusalem lasting not terribly long and the Saracens being able to recover the territory that the First Crusade had taken from them.

After all, the Christian maritime powers had gained enormously by the adventure of the Crusades. They had fought against the Saracens before, and they would fight against them afterwards. The Pisans and the Genoese had succeeded, as we've seen, in driving the Saracens from the Balearic Islands, from Corsica and from Sardinia. But Islamic pirates and fleets still continued to prey upon Christian ships in the western Mediterranean, particularly around the coast of North Africa and in the eastern Mediterranean as well. Christian settlements were endangered by Saracen raids, including in the Italian Peninsula. Nowhere was safe from those Saracen raiders who attacked, plundered, and took what they wanted—not only objects of wealth, but also people, young men to become the galley slaves and women to inhabit the *seraglio*.

The period of the Crusades and the growing power of Venice, Pisa, Genoa, and Amalfi gave the Europeans an opportunity to try to, if not reverse this power of the Saracens, at least control it and contain it. The maritime might of these collective forces was sufficient in order to ensure that Christianity would at least play an important role in the Mediterranean despite the growing Islamic power—not only the power of the Saracens, but also the power of the Turks, which was becoming stronger almost each year. Moreover, there was the crusader mentality, and this can't be discounted. Europeans, with the coming of the Crusades, saw the expansion of Europe into the Levant, and areas previously controlled by Islamic peoples, as a natural extension of God's will. They were ideologically driven. They believed that God was on their side, and this provided

Christendom with a good deal of confidence in the struggle between East and West. The other reality was that the Saracen kingdoms were divided. They had no singular policy. With the exception of the great leader Saladin and the reconquest of Jerusalem, there was no leader able to bring them all together into a singular force that could have driven the Christians from the inland sea.

The motive of most of the Saracen fleets was to raid and plunder, to act through piracy rather than any kind of established coherent policy of conquest and expansion. The rise of the Ottoman Turks changed all of this. Well before the conquest of Constantinople in 1453, which ended once and for all the great Byzantine Empire, the Turks had begun to spread farther and farther, more and more westward, into the Mediterranean. The Turkish assault on the Balkans, for example, had begun decades before Constantinople fell. Serbia became a vassal state of the Turkish Empire after the Battle of Kosovo in 1389, a place so burned on the consciousness of Serbians that they today can't imagine Serbia without Kosovo and the implications that had for contemporary European politics. However, the entire kingdom fell by 1459, becoming but another province of the Turkish Empire.

In 1396, the Turks defeated the Bulgarians, and with the defeat of the Bulgarians, that entire territory fell again into a Turkish province, controlled by the Turks and able to put a deeper beachhead into the European continent itself. The Turks also attacked the trading posts that the Europeans had established. The Turks assaulted not only the Venetians, but also the Genoese, and with the fall of Caffa in 1475, the Genoese Empire was, in fact, destined to be destroyed by Turkish expansion and Venetian victory. The final humiliation came—and to some extent, the greatest shock to the Christian mentality—when the Turks took the city of Otranto on the Cape of Otranto in Italy itself. That cape that sticks into the Adriatic was conquered by a Turkish fleet, and the Turks held it for a year, slaughtering all the men, women, and children who had taken refuge in its cathedral, and establishing a sense of Turkish violence; a fear of the Turks that was not only religious, but real and physical given the activities of the Turks in Otranto and other places.

The triumphant Turks seemed to be invincible. Their power seemed to be overwhelming. But a change in policy in the sacred court, in the court of the Turkish sultan himself, made the provinces of

Europe a little bit safer, made the hopes of Europe a little bit more secure. The change in policy was to turn the Turkish armies not against Europe, not working from the Turkish provinces in the Balkan, but first to work towards the conquest of fellow Islamic states in the Near and Middle East. The invincible armies were then turned not against Christians, but against, in 1514, the Persians, who were conquered when the shah was defeated. In 1516, the Syrians were conquered, and Syria became a province of the Turkish Empire, as did Egypt in 1517.

By 1517—the year of Luther's revolt, we must remember—the Turks had become triumphant and had inscribed an arc around the Mediterranean, controlling not just the states that one associates most closely with the Turkish Empire, but also increasing its control over the coast of North Africa and setting deeper and deeper roots into the Balkans—that is, in the continent of Europe itself. The Sultan Selim II [*sic* I] realized that this was an opportunity, and he now had a power base in order to expand his interests in Europe and his conquest of the Christian forces in the European continent. He conquered Belgrade in 1521, using it as a base of operations for further incursions deeper and deeper into the European heartland. The same year, the fleets of the Turks, under Selim's admiral, took the island of Rhodes from the Knights of St. John of Jerusalem, that crusading order that had been given the island to protect Christian shipping, and to be a vanguard of Christian defense. It seemed, by the time we reach the 1520s, that the Mediterranean would become a Turkish lake, and that the Turks would control all elements of not only trade, but of power and authority around that sea.

It was this threat, this fear, that had given rise to the voyages of discovery. We've already discussed how the circumstances of the rise of the Turks had weakened the Venetian monopoly on long-distance trade, and the enormous profits that that generated. We've seen how the power of the Turks had driven the rulers of the states on the Atlantic seaboard to search for other means of reaching the riches, spices, silks, and other luxury goods of the East. It was because of Prince Henry the Navigator, the school that he founded, and the activities of the Portuguese under Bartholomew Diaz and Vasco da Gama that not only proved that Africa had an end, but that you could sail from Lisbon or the coast of Spain directly to the markets of India and China. Thereby, the spices and luxury goods that the Venetians and the Genoese had monopolized and sold at such enormous profit to their fellow Europeans, now became largely the monopoly of those states that enjoyed harbors well away from Turkish power, outside the Straits of Gibraltar on the Atlantic coast.

We've seen the consequence for Venice: Spices to be purchased at 20 percent in Lisbon what they cost in Venice. The decline of the Italian economy was inevitable, and the decline of European shipping and power in the Mediterranean was abrupt and rapid. The ambitions of the Turks not only threatened not just the immediate powers of Italy—the powers that had previously been almost the policemen and the economic engines of Mediterranean commerce—but also began to change the nature of policy in other states that bordered the Mediterranean. The best example is probably that of Spain. The dynastic union of the crowns of Ferdinand of Aragon and Isabella of Castile created a dynastic union that would give rise to the kingdom of Spain. This dynastic union in 1479 created a new state—one that was linked not by law or history, but rather by religion. Indeed, the crusading mentality that had developed in the Mediterranean against the Saracens and the Turks was used to forge links where there had been none before.

The kingdom of Spain became, in many ways, a crusader kingdom. It was for this reason that the new state of Ferdinand and Isabella directed their united armies against the kingdom of Granada. Granada had shared the Iberian Peninsula with the Spanish and Portuguese kingdoms from the time of the Moorish incursions into the Spanish Peninsula in the early 8th century. This period of Islamic rule in part of Europe was largely part of the landscape by the 15th century. But also, because of the success of the Turks and the Saracens, it was seen as not only against God's plan, but also as a real danger to European autonomy, and indeed to Christendom itself. The Europeans saw no difference between the Moorish kingdom of Granada and the Turks. They saw them just as infidels. They believed that they were working together in favor of their religion and against Christianity. Not only was it good policy in uniting their disparate kingdoms, but also it was a Christian discipline, a Christian necessity, for Ferdinand and Isabella to turn their forces against the Moors and drive Islam out of Europe.

The expulsion of the Moors in 1492 in that great European Crusade, and the expulsion and forced conversion of the Jews, resulted not from simple hatred, fear, or a sense of exceptionalism, although all of these things were there. It came about as policy, necessity, and a desire to win battles for Christianity when it seemed as though God had abandoned Christendom and had given favor to the Turks, to the infidels. The creation of the kingdom of Spain introduced a new power into the Mediterranean, one that ultimately would be proved not just as useful to the continent, but also as dangerous to the Italian Peninsula. When Spain was inherited by the House of Habsburg, when Charles of Habsburg became King of Spain in 1517, the Habsburg power united, and with their interests in the Mediterranean, the freedom of Italy would certainly be compromised.

Nevertheless, we have to realize the decline of the Mediterranean trade, the decline of the cities of the Italian Peninsula in serving that trade, the long-term decline of the wealth of Italy—and to some extent even the independence and the autonomy of the Italian states—came about largely because of the victory of the Turks and the spread of Turkish power into the inland sea. Now the economic center had shifted, almost for the first time in recorded European history, from the Mediterranean—that *Media Terra*, that center of the earth—to the Atlantic seacoast. No longer were trade and control of the Mediterranean the keys to European power. Now that power had shifted to those seaports and nations that controlled the Atlantic seaboard. These new nations—these powerful new states, united dynastically, ambitious and filled with that crusading zeal—would challenge the Italians for supremacy, and ultimately they would win.

This complicated the situation in the Mediterranean, and it complicated the relationship between Christians and Turks. The Turkish Empire, after all—and this is something that we tend to forget in the West—had become the most powerful state in the Western world by the middle of the 15th century. With the conquest of Constantinople, and in particular by the middle of the 16th century and the expansion of the Turks into Europe, the Islamic power of Turkey controlled an arc that spread from the Balkans right around the eastern Mediterranean, the southern sea coast of the Mediterranean, right into the Straits of Gibraltar. This vast arc was a base of power, authority, and opposition to the European economy and to the European autonomy in the Mediterranean.

©2007 The Teaching Company.

The most powerful state in Europe, then, faced one great opponent, and that was Christendom; but Christendom was not united. The Turks, by force of arms, had largely united the territory under their rule. The Christians were fighting on several fronts with several policies, and not necessarily in their own collective interest, but rather in the interest of individual principalities, individual city-states, or individual dynastic monarchies. By 1526, the Turkish army broke out of the Balkans. This was the initial plan of fortifying and supporting the Balkan incursions that had begun in the 15th century. A Christian army was raised to stop it, an army that consisted of volunteers and soldiers sent by most Christian nations—and a large amount of money sent by the pope to hire mercenaries to add to the number of fighting men—led by the King of Hungary and the Hungarian nobility, who would be on the frontline of this expansion of Islam, resulted in 1526 in the Battle of Mohacs. This, too, was a dramatic moment in European history when the Christians were annihilated by the Turks.

The King of Hungary, King Louis—who was born too soon, king too soon, and died too soon—and the flower of his nobility lay dead and bleeding in a field. With the destruction of the Christian army at Mohacs, there was nothing to stop the Turks from crossing the flat Hungarian plain and besieging the imperial capitals, and that is precisely what they did. The Turkish army broke out of the Balkans, marched over the dead of Mohacs, and in 1529 besieged the city of Vienna. The imperial capital of Vienna in central Europe, the key to the West, was in fact threatened by the Turks. It was really only the impossibility of sustaining such long supply routes in the 16th century that the city did not fall. The siege was unsuccessful, but to say that Europeans were frightened, that Europeans felt that the Turks were invincible and somehow God was punishing them, was an understatement. Europe was in turmoil. The Protestant Reformation had broken out, and Catholics blamed it for the fault. The Protestants blamed the Catholics and their impure method of living, and all kinds of personal assaults and challenges were made.

The reality was that Europe was not united against the Turks, and the Turks were. Moreover, the Turks not only focused on the European continent, they focused on the fortified trading posts that the Venetians and the Genoese had lovingly established, supported, and protected almost from the beginnings of their maritime empires. One by one, they began to fall, including those jewels in the Venetian Stato da Mar. Crete and Cyprus became Turkish islands. The Genoese saw Caffa fall to the Turks in the Black Sea. If that were not bad enough, the Turks commissioned Barbary pirates to be admirals of the Turkish fleet, giving them full permission to prey upon Christian shipping, to engage in battle. Christians found themselves not only fighting the organized galleys of the Turkish navy, but also the large numbers of corsairs working out of North Africa and the coast of Albania.

The situation did appear to be desperate, but once more it seemed to be getting worse. Rather than the intervention, the belief that God would somehow come and salvage the Christian nation, the circumstance seemed to get more and more desperate. In 1560, King Philip II of Spain, the son of the Emperor Charles V, collected a great fleet—a fleet of hundreds of galleys, the point of which was to attack the coast of North Africa. In 1560, that fleet was surprised by the Turkish fleet at Djerba, and the fleet of Philip II was destroyed. Half of the ships were captured or sunk, and Philip found himself without a fleet to protect Christian interests in the eastern Mediterranean. Charles V had seen himself very much as a protector of a united Europe, as the maintainer of Christendom. Now his son saw himself defeated by the Turks and the great fleet that he had collected destroyed by a Turkish navy.

Again, it got worse. In 1560, the fleet at Djerba was destroyed, and just a decade later Cyprus fell to the Turks. The fall of Cyprus was one of those psychological moments. Cyprus was perhaps the most important of all of the Christian islands in the Mediterranean, inasmuch as it had been part of Venetian territory, and that the last Lusignan King of Cyprus, the descendants of the Latin kings of Jerusalem, the crusader dynasty that had so represented Christina power in the East, fell to the Turks. The island that had been given to Venice by Caterina Cornaro, the widow of the last Lusignan King of Cyprus, was now a Turkish province. With the loss of Cyprus, the Venetians really felt they were exposed. With the loss of Cyprus, Christianity was exposed to Turkish attack and Turkish assault.

Not only had Europe lost trading posts, but also staging posts, places from which they could protect Christian shipping and assemble fleets in order to attack the Turks. With these gone and missing, it meant that the sail would have to be longer. The voyages to meet the Turks, to stop them, to protect or patrol the Mediterranean, would be long voyages indeed, without any opportunity to stop to be revictualed, to have the ships repaired, or to replace those men who had been killed or were sick. At this moment of almost complete desperation, there was an intervention. There was an opportunity provided that allowed Christians to believe that maybe God was still with them, that maybe the Turks could be stopped. Up to that point, the Turks had been essentially invincible. There had been no major defeat of the Turks under any circumstances. They had swept all Christian fleets before them, and they had swept Christian armies on land.

Then there was the siege of Malta of 1565–1566. The great siege of Malta is, of course, one of the great acts of heroism in all of Western history. The island was given to the Knights of St. John of Jerusalem by the Emperor Charles V once the knights were driven from Rhodes. The Order of St. John of Jerusalem was a crusading order founded during the period of the Crusades and dedicated to the protection of Christians everywhere, but particularly Christians in the Holy Land and Christian Crusaders. It was an odd place; it was an odd bunch because they were knights, but they were celibate. They had to be noble by birth. They couldn't earn a place; they had to be born into it. This order of celibate knights, carefully trained and chosen, who had volunteered their lives in order to further the goals of Christianity and to protect Christianity everywhere, now found themselves facing one of the great invasion forces of all time.

The sultan had planned to conquer Malta because of its strategic importance. Malta and its satellite island of Gozo are in the middle of the Mediterranean, south of the coast of Sicily. Therefore, Malta protected not just the Mediterranean, but also the southern coast of Italy and the island of Sicily. Had it fallen, it would have been an extremely dangerous position for Europe to find itself in. There were only a few hundred knights, 600 or 700. There were some mercenary soldiers, some Maltese who had volunteered or joined, but all together there were about 6,000 defenders on the island. The Turkish fleet and the Turkish army represented at least 200 galleys and at least 30,000 troops. These 30,000 soldiers besieged the island.

Fortunately, the Grand Master, Jean de la Valette, knew that the assault was coming, and it was only a matter of time before the Turks would turn against Malta. He had wisely fortified parts of the island. He had built the great fortresses of St. Elmo and St. George, and he awaited their assault. When it came, it was brutal, but they held out. The Turks did not succeed in driving the Knights Hospitaller of St. John of Jerusalem from the island, but rather it was the Turks who were ultimately driven out. This victory, this great moment, this final turning of the tide, gave a renewed confidence to Europe. It indicated that the Turks could be defeated, that the Christians could withstand the Turkish advance. A few years later, this was proved at the Battle of Lepanto.

Lepanto was, again, a dramatic moment. It was the opportunity for Christianity to function together as a military unit for the first time almost since the success of the First Crusade. Under the command of the illegitimate son of the Emperor Charles V and the half-brother of King Philip of Spain, Don John of Austria, a huge multinational fleet provided by Venice, Spain, Pisa, and Genoa—by almost all Christian seafaring people—put together an enormous flotilla that also was armed with tens of thousands of soldiers trained to fight at sea, and particularly well-trained Spanish mercenaries and veterans. The two fleets met off the coast of Greece at Lepanto, and it was a complete and total rout. The Turks hadn't provided as many soldiers, and as a consequence, when the ships came close and the battle became almost hand-to-hand—and when the ships came close enough for the Christians to use their much more effective canon against the Turks' use of arrows and bows—the Turks were defeated.

The defeat was devastating. The Turks lost all but 30 of their ships, and they lost about 30,000 men. The men and ships that they lost were the most experienced and the best that they had. Turkish power in the Mediterranean was then temporarily completely obliterated. The Christians had an opportunity that they, of course, lost. They had an opportunity to work together once more and to actually assault Constantinople itself, to move the fleet into the Dardanelles to blockade the capital or the ports. But once more, the Christian commanders fell out amongst themselves. They couldn't determine a policy on which to act, and the result was that the Turks were able to rebuild, to very quickly use the resources of their great empire and reconstruct a fleet that would again challenge Christendom.

The important thing about Lepanto, though, is that it happened at all. Lepanto provided an element of confidence that the Europeans had lacked. The Europeans seemed to be always being defeated by a people they believed to be infidel. They were beginning to think that

God had left them, but Lepanto and the siege of Malta had disproved that. In those 10 years, Christianity had regained some of its confidence, its aggressive nature, and its crusading spirit. Of course, the fleets that fought were under Spanish Habsburg rule. The fleets that fought the Turks were not controlled by the city-states of Italy, even though most of the ships were provided by them, with Venice providing the largest number of galleys.

The world of the new Europe and the new Mediterranean was, to some extent, foretold at Lepanto. The Austrians were in control. The House of Habsburg was the house that was going to be the hegemonic power in the Peninsula, as it would be on the continent. The Mediterranean might not be a Turkish lake as a consequence of Lepanto, but to some extent it would have to be shared with the House of Habsburg and the Turks. Lepanto was perhaps the single most important naval victory since the Battle of Actium in 31 B.C., when Augustus defeated the fleets of Marc Antony and Cleopatra. It was one of the decisive battles of all time, and it did perhaps protect Europe from a much more aggressive Turkish Empire that might have, in fact, besieged not only Vienna, but moved farther into Europe to actually challenge the European heartland itself.

Nevertheless, the reality of the future became clearer. The Turkish control of the Mediterranean would, to a degree, remain. The Christians would be there to some extent on sufferance, and there would never be peace. As long as the Turks controlled the Mediterranean, the Christians would have to fight them for whatever commerce or trade they hoped to achieve. As long as the Turks controlled the Mediterranean, the southern borders of Europe would always be at risk. The ability of Christendom to withstand Islamic Turkish advance would always be in jeopardy.

Lecture Ten
Rome—Papal Authority

Scope:

The story of Rome is, in essence, the story of its popes: They influenced the city not only through their responsibilities for international events, such as the Crusades, but also through the force of their own personalities. Like most Italian city-states in the Middle Ages, Rome was riven by the feuding of violent factions. In 1305, the pope sought protection outside the city in the papal territory of Avignon. This initiated a lengthy period known as the *Babylonian Captivity*, followed immediately by the *Great Schism*, which saw the reign of competing popes in Rome and Avignon. Ultimately, an international church council elected Martin V (1417–1431) as the only pope, on condition that he recognize conciliar authority. Of course, Martin had no intention of submitting once he had established himself. But his first concerns were to secure financial stability for the Church and to restore Rome to a splendor befitting the papacy. Indeed, it was a response to the fiscal, military, and political exigencies of Rome after the restoration that changed the nature of papal government and made the papacy a more aggressive participant in Italian political life.

Outline

I. Rome had a dual function during the Middle Ages and Renaissance as both a secular and a religious kingdom.

    A. In one sense, Rome was an Italian city-state like any other, ruled by a prince who also happened to be the pope.

        1. Rome had political ambitions to expand at the expense of its neighbors, to consolidate territory, and to protect the papacy.

        2. It functioned not exactly as a secular power but as a state in which the operations of secular authority were just as visible as they were in any other the Italian jurisdictions.

B. Rome's other great role was as the spiritual center of European Catholic Christianity.

    1. By the Middle Ages, the primacy of the bishop of Rome was recognized throughout Western Christendom.

    2. This assumption of power was, in part, the cause of the schism with the Eastern, or Orthodox, Church in 1054.

    3. The pope's absolute authority was attested by such evidence as the Donation of Constantine. This document, later identified as a forgery, purported to be a grant of the Western Roman Empire to Pope Silvester by Constantine the Great.

C. However, conflict with the Holy Roman Empire divided Catholic Europe into the two camps of Guelf and Ghibelline, each recognizing a different source of sovereignty and authority.

    1. The popes initially emerged as the victors in this conflict, symbolized by the humiliation of the emperor Henry IV by Pope Gregory VII at Canossa in 1077.

    2. The ambitions on the part of the pope reached their apogee by the early 13th century with the election of Pope Innocent III (d. 1216), whose claims of universal dominion and both secular and religious authority were almost universally accepted.

D. Events in some of the secular states of the Italian Peninsula assisted in translating the pope's claims of universal authority into reality.

    1. Urban II's call for the Crusades at Clermont in 1095 illustrated the pope's ability to harness the forces of Europe to accomplish a significant goal from the perspective of the West and the Church.

    2. The marshaling of aid for the patriarch of Constantinople implied the pope's authority and power above the patriarch.

    3. The flood of capital into Rome to support the Crusaders filled the papal coffers and necessitated the creation of the papal *camera*, or finance ministry, to manage the money.

4. As a corollary, the sacred *Rota*, the highest court of appeal in canon or Church law, was established to ensure that the center of decision-making would be in Rome at the court of the pope.

II. The belief that the popes were the secular and spiritual authority in the West was challenged by the *Babylonian Captivity*, a crisis that divided the Church and threw the position of the pope and the ambitions of papal government into confusion.

A. Like most Italian cities in the Middle Ages, Rome was riven by faction.

1. Powerful noble families saw the papacy and the high offices of the Church as prizes to be added to their already significant authority.

2. These nobles had fortified palaces in the city, and they fought what amounted to civil wars within the walls, creating chaos in Rome.

3. Consequently, in 1305, the pope sought protection outside the city in Avignon, a small papal enclave attached to France.

B. Avignon was closely associated with French culture, and with the pope's move there, the idea of the papacy as a French institution rather than a Roman one gained strength. This idea was reinforced as one pope died and another pope was elected in Avignon.

C. The papacy remained in Avignon until 1377. The division between the see of St. Peter in Rome and the successor to St. Peter at Avignon was such that the very nature of the Church and the complex and abstract concepts of sovereignty were thrown into question.

1. Many saints, particularly females, such as St. Bridget of Sweden and St. Catherine of Siena, argued that the pope must return to Rome or the authority of the papacy would diminish.

2. This theory was reinforced by the belief of France's enemies that the papacy had become nothing but a pawn of the French king. The English and their allies in the Hundred Years War saw the papacy as choosing sides rather than offering the evenhanded support that should be given to all Christian princes.

III. International pressure was such that in 1377, Gregory XI decided to return the papacy to Rome.

A. Rome had been the administrative center for a multinational ecclesiastical organization, but in the 70 years since that organization had been removed from the city, Rome had become depopulated and impoverished.

B. A year after his return and before he was able to reestablish a centralized papacy in Rome, Gregory died. The people of Rome rioted, demanding that an Italian be chosen as his successor, despite the fact that the curia was dominated by French cardinals.

C. The cardinals chose an Italian, the elderly archbishop of Bari, who took the name Urban VI. Urban sought to reconnect the papacy with Rome and to strengthen the moral authority of the papacy, which many believed had been weakened by a life of luxury in Avignon.

D. When Urban VI tried to impose canonical living on the French cardinals, they assembled outside the city and declared Urban deposed, arguing that he had been elected under duress. In his place, a French cardinal was elected, and the papacy was returned to Avignon. Urban then excommunicated the cardinals and the French pope.

E. Thus began the Great Schism, a scandal that saw two churches and two popes, both exercising *plenitudo potestatis*, the ultimate binding power on heaven and Earth; each excommunicating the other; and each calling the other the Antichrist.

  1. Both the pope in Rome and the pope in Avignon declared his superiority to the other, and all of Europe lined up behind one or the other.

  2. The French and their allies supported the pope in Avignon; the English and their allies supported the pope in Rome. This division was believed to endanger the spiritual hopes of European citizens, leading them to perdition rather than to salvation.

  3. The schism also resulted in the growth of heterodox groups, especially those that favored a more direct relationship between the individual believer and God.

For example, in Bohemia, the Hussite movement challenged both the authority of the Church and the position of the German bishops, who had traditionally controlled the administrative and physical structure of the ecclesiastical establishment. This challenge was dangerous from the point of view of the emperor.

4. Questions arose concerning both the political and the religious state of Europe: Where did sovereignty reside? Should there be a union of Church and state? And with two authorities to decide these issues, which one should be accepted?

IV. Finally, the Holy Roman Emperor, Sigismund, was forced to intervene.

A. An earlier attempt to end the schism had worsened the situation. In 1409, a group of cardinals from the two colleges—one in Rome and one in Avignon—had elected a third pope and declared the other two to be deposed. Of course, neither standing pope recognized the legitimacy of this decision, with the absurd result that there were now three popes.

B. In 1417, Sigismund called a Church council to meet at the city of Constance. There was precedent for the emperor calling a council, as the early councils of the Church, such as Nicea (325) had been summoned by Constantine.

C. The council was to address two pressing issues: the Hussite revolt in Bohemia and the division in the Church.

1. The Hussite problem was solved quickly: John Hus and two of his leading followers were invited to Constance to explain their case under a guarantee of safe conduct. Once they arrived in Constance, they were arrested, tried, and burned as heretics.

2. That problem taken care of, the Council of Constance ultimately reached a set of conclusions that ended the schism and established a singular papacy. The three standing popes were declared deposed and a single pope was elected in their place. This was Oddone Colonna, who took the name Martin V (1417–1431).

3. In 1420, Martin returned to Rome, reuniting the bishop with his see and recreating a singular papacy.

V. The principle that had elected Martin was a dangerous one for the papacy: the idea that the Church, acting collectively through a council, had more authority than the pope.

   A. According to this principle, known as *conciliarism*, the Church was a collective entity in which the faithful participated through their representatives—the bishops, archbishops, and so on. Conciliarism, then, had ended the schism.

   B. Under the terms of his election, Martin V was required to sign and promulgate bulls, such as *Frequens* ("often"), that recognized the authority of councils over popes and called for the convening of regular councils to monitor papal actions.

   C. Of course, Martin had no intent of obeying these requirements. He believed that once the situation calmed down, the idea would be largely forgotten. Neither did the council enforce its authority aggressively during Martin's pontificate.

   D. Further, Martin faced significant problems that rendered trivial the abstract concept of sovereignty within the Church. The pope had to rebuild the papal administration, the system for collecting papal taxes, and the churches and palaces of Rome. Martin was a skilled administrator and succeeded well at these tasks.

   E. By the time of Martin's death in 1431, the pope paid lip service to the idea of conciliarism but was essentially left to act freely. At the same time, the power and structure of conciliarism was generally believed to be the new operating principle of the Church. Thus, a new conflict was established between papal monarchy and conciliar authority.

   F. This conflict would be reflected in many ways in the coming decades.

      1. It would be seen in the tension between the papacy and the collective body of the Church and in the ambitions of secular princes who saw conciliarism as an instrument to weaken the authority and sovereign claims of papal power.

2. The conflict was also seen in the states of the Church itself: If the pope was not an absolute monarch in terms of ecclesiastical authority within the Church, was he an absolute monarch in terms of secular authority?

3. The confusion of jurisdictions that we've seen operating so often in the Church, and even in secular powers, was brought into relief. The history of Rome, the history of the Church, and the history of the states of Italy came together over these issues of sovereignty and the exercise of authority in the Church and state.

Essential Reading:

C. L. Stinger, *The Renaissance in Rome.*

Supplementary Reading:

G. Mollat, *The Popes at Avignon: 1305–1378.*

Questions to Consider:

1. Why was the residence of the pope in Avignon so disastrous for the city of Rome?

2. Can you explain why so many successful and attractive heretical groups developed in Europe during the period of the Great Schism?

Lecture Ten—Transcript
Rome—Papal Authority

Rome had a dual function during the period of the Middle Ages and Renaissance. Indeed, Rome functioned as both a secular and a religious center. On the one hand, it was an Italian city-state like any other. It was ruled by a prince who also happened to be the pope. It had political ambitions to expand at the expense of its neighbors, consolidate territory, and ensure that the role of the papacy would be protected by a large state that would ensure that the freedom of the pope to act in religious matters would always be sustained. Consequently, it acted like any other Italian state. It functioned as not exactly a secular power, but a state in which the operations of secular authority could be seen to be just as visible as with any other of the Italian jurisdictions.

But like any principality in Italy, the story of the papacy, and the story of the Church itself, is very much the story of the popes—those successors to St. Peter who ruled in that role of priest-king, both monarch and head of an ecclesiastical organization that stretched back to the first bishop in the 1st century A.D. Consequently, their personalities and the international events that were determined by those personalities, and which in turn determined them, must be looked at in some detail because Rome's center was, in many ways, the center of a spiritual authority and a spiritual power—that is, the Western Latin Church. By the Middle Ages, it was generally recognized that the bishop of Rome was, in fact, the leading cleric. It was a recognition of primacy on the part of a singular bishop who had the authority to largely do and undo things in the Church according to the requirements of Rome and his own desires.

These assumptions of power and authority had already caused some measure of difficulty and schism. By 1054, the Eastern Orthodox Church had broken away from the unitary Christian confession, and it started its own ecclesiastical organization centered around the patriarch of Constantinople. Evidence that the pope really did have an absolute priest-king role, an absolute authority that stretched beyond the simple practice of religion, was determined by things like the donation of Constantine. We know now—in fact, by the 1450s it was known as the result of the work of Lorenzo Valla—that this was an 8th-century forgery. But nevertheless, this document that purported to be the gift of the Western Roman Empire to Pope

Silvester by that first Christian emperor, Constantine the Great, gave some measure of evidence and a good deal of authority to the belief that the pope could bind both on earth and in heaven.

However, the conflict with the Holy Roman Empire, that secular memory of Roman *imperium* in the West, caused a good deal of division as well. In fact, Catholic Europe divided into two camps, each recognizing a different source of sovereignty—and, to some extent, a different source of authority. On the papal side, there was the Guelf faction, and on the imperial side the Ghibelline faction. From the initial struggle between pope and emperor, the popes emerged victorious—inasmuch as the emperor Henry IV was humiliated by Pope Gregory VII, known as Hildebrand, at the castle of Canossa in 1077. From that, it seemed as though the papal position would be dominant, and the imperial position would always be one of secondary desire.

These ambitions on the part of the pope reached their apogee by the time we reach the early 13th century with the election of Pope Innocent III. Especially by the beginning of the 13th century, we see Innocent III's claim of having universal dominion and both secular and religious authority being almost universally accepted. The idea that the pope could not just bind on earth and heaven, but the desires, decrees, and ambitions of the pope could be seen as part of the requirement of universal politics and religion, had reached a stage that even the earliest popes could only dream of. As in so many things in the Italian Peninsula, many of the events that seemed to be crystallized by a particular papacy or political moment really had much deeper roots, and the causes were much more complex. It wasn't just the claims of Innocent III to having full and universal authority that resulted in the papacy being recognized as the sovereign power in the West. It really had been a series of events that we've already seen operating in some of the secular states of the Italian Peninsula.

The Crusades, once more, must be investigated as one of the sources for papal power. It was, after all, a pope who called the Crusades. Urban II's sermon at Clermont to the French nobility and clergy did crystallize a moment, did set an example of the pope being able to bring together and harness the forces of Europe in order to accomplish, in fact, a great thing from the perspective of the West and the Church. The Crusades gave the papacy a spiritual authority that was real because it actually engendered action. People did what the pope said. Those cries of *"Deus vult"* could almost be reflected in the parallel cry of *"Papa vult."* The idea of the pope wanting to do something, and all of Europe rallying behind this spiritual leader, was reflected in a moment that really changed the character of European history. Urban made a contribution that went beyond his being head of the Church. In fact, he became a spokesman for what really was a Europe-wide venture.

Moreover, it was a very wise political move on the part of the papacy because the initial reason for the Crusades being called was to provide assistance to the Byzantine emperor in Constantinople. For the pope to do this, to rally Western Latin Christendom in order to save the Eastern Orthodox Church so soon after that schism had divided East and West was a very, very clear indication that the pope did have primacy, and that the pope was the force that really had to be reckoned with rather than the patriarch in Constantinople, who seemed to be incapable of doing this. The amount of money collected across Europe, the desire of the faithful of all classes to contribute to this great Christian adventure of the Crusades, also aided the papal position not just in terms of politics and fervent desire, but in terms of income.

The flood of capital that came into Rome from those knights, nobles, and simple people who themselves felt they were too old or unable to go on crusade, but wanted to make some kind of personal contribution to this event, resulted in the papal *camera* not only becoming richer, but almost being formed in the state that would give it its character during most of the Middle Ages. When we think of the word "camera," in Latin it means room, and it often, in medieval Latin, refers to a bedroom. The camera was the most secure place in a papal palace. In fact, the camera was the most secure place in any princely palace because it was there that the royal or papal bed was kept. It was there that the pope or the prince was most in danger because it was there that he slept. It was underneath the bed of the pope or the prince that the treasures were kept because it was the most secure place that the treasure could be sustained and protected.

The papal finance ministry, the camera, grew enormously not only in size, but in sophistication, in order to manage the huge amounts of money that were flowing into Rome from the faithful. Once you have large amounts of money being delivered to a particular place for a particular purpose, and being accounted for, as in all things, the law follows trade. The sacred *Rota*, or the highest court of appeal in canon law or Church law, was established soon after to make sure that not only in financial terms, but also in legal terms, the center of decision-making would be in Rome at the court of the pope.

This happy situation from the point of popes in the Middle Ages—that is, belief that they were the secular and spiritual authority in the West—was greatly challenged by a crisis that divided the Church and threw the whole position of the pope, and the very ambitions of papal government, into a great deal of confusion. This was the *Babylonian Captivity*, given its name from the servitude of the Israelites in Babylon. It was more than a crisis in the Church; it divided it dangerously to the point that the nature of the papacy was forced to change.

Like most Italian cities in the Middle Ages, Rome was riven by faction. The great noble families saw the Church and the papacy as prizes to be added to their already significant authority. They had fortified palaces in the city. They fought what amounted to civil wars within the walls, and it made Rome a very dangerous place—a place that was always being threatened by the secular and private powers of individuals who saw their own ambition as more important than the collective desire of the community in which they lived. In order to escape this, and initially in order to ensure that the Church would be free from this kind of danger, popes decided that they had to find some mechanism to ensure that the papacy would be protected and could operate free of any kind of coercion. In 1305, this drove the pope to seek refuge in a small papal enclave attached to the kingdom of France.

Avignon was not part of France; it was the papal fief. But nevertheless, it was very closely associated with French culture, and it was also a very long way away from Rome. Once the pope moved there in 1305, the idea of the papacy being no longer a Roman institution, but increasingly a French institution, was generally observed. This was reinforced as one pope died and another pope was elected—not in Rome, not in conclave in the city of St. Peter, but in Avignon, a place that seemed to be not just a papal fortress, but a purely political place in which the pope was free from all kinds of coercion, both secular and religious.

It was initially believed that this was only a temporary situation, but it lasted until 1377. The division between the See of St. Peter in Rome and the successor to St. Peter as the pope in the Middle Ages at Avignon was such that the very nature of the Church and these very complex and abstract concepts of sovereignty were thrown into great relief. There had to be a solution to this problem, and many saints—many of whom were female saints like St. Bridget of Sweden or St. Catherine of Siena—argued that the pope must return, that the bishop must be reunited with his flock, or the authority of the papacy would somehow diminish, and the papacy would be seen as a plaything of the King of France and no longer a source of universal dominion. This was reinforced by the actual belief of France's enemies that the papacy had become nothing but a pawn of the French king. It was the period of the Hundred Years War, so the English and their allies saw the papacy as really choosing sides, supporting the French as opposed to giving the evenhanded support that should be given to all Christian princes.

Consequently, in 1377, the decision was taken by Pope Gregory XI to return to Rome, to abandon Avignon and his beautiful palace that the popes had built for themselves, and to return to a city that in the previous 70 years had become largely depopulated. Rome was a company town. Rome produced nothing; it had no industry. It wasn't a center of trade or commerce. It was an administrative center for the Roman Church. That huge multinational ecclesiastical organization that stretched all across Europe had as its headquarters a city that had not only imperial memories, but had the practical recognition of being the administrative center of the most complex institution that existed at the time. Remove that institution, and the city then becomes much less. It became not just depopulated, but impoverished. It had shrunk to a city of between 17,000 and 20,000 people; whereas at the time of Constantine the Great in the 4th century, it had well over a million. It was a poor place, and the pope needed to return to something that was much greater not only in authority, but also much greater in its physical attributes, to reflect the glory of the papacy.

In 1377, the pope returned, and Gregory XI made one of those sad decisions that popes often make, and the following year he died. He died at a time when he had not yet reestablished, reaffirmed, and reconstituted a centralized papacy in the city of St. Peter. But the people of Rome realized the dangers. Knowing what had happened during those previous 70 years when the city had shrunk and become impoverished, they rioted around the room in which the papal conclave was being held, and they demanded that an Italian be chosen. There were far more French cardinals than there were Italian cardinals. The fear that another Frenchman would be elected pope, and that he would return to Avignon, was great. The cardinals in conclave listened to the crowds outside and did choose an Italian, the elderly archbishop of Bari, who took the name of Urban VI.

Urban VI was a man of great strength of character. He also was a man of significant piety. On the one hand, he wanted to ensure that the papacy would be reconnected with Rome and its traditions; on the other hand, he wanted to revitalize the Church. There was a general sense, which we can see in authors such as Petrarch, that the moral authority of the papacy had been weakened by the position that the papacy had enjoyed in Avignon—that it was a place of luxury and easy living. It was a place where cardinals thought more of their own ambition and wealth than of the wellbeing of the faithful. Urban VI had decided to change this, and so he tried to impose canonical living on those luxury-loving French cardinals.

The French cardinals were not happy, and so they stole from the city of Rome to a papal fortress. They declared that the election of Urban had been done under threat. Consequently, it was not the act of the Holy Spirit working collectively through the conclave, but rather the fear of the Roman populace that resulted in Urban's election; therefore, Urban's election was invalid. They declared the pope deposed and an anti-pope. They elected one of their own members as the new pope. Of course, that new pope returned to Avignon and asked that Urban either resign or be deposed. Of course, when Urban heard this, he had no intention whatsoever of resigning, and he would not recognize the authority of the cardinals. In fact, he excommunicated them and the pope that they had elected and declared them to be outside the Church.

We now have the difficult situation, beginning in 1378, of the *Great Schism*. Two churches, two popes, both exercising that authority that was the *plenitudo potestatis*, that ultimate power to bind on heaven and earth—each excommunicating the other, each calling the other the Antichrist. This scandal was to divide Christendom and endanger the very essence of what was the Roman Church. The problem was not easily solved. Both the pope in Rome and the pope in Avignon declared their superiority to the other, and all of Europe divided behind one or the other. The alliance system of the political world of Europe reflected this new alliance system of the spiritual world of Europe.

The French and their allies supported the pope in Avignon; the English and their allies supported the pope in Rome. With this division, there was a division in Europe that wasn't just endangering the physical lives and the secular ambitions of the citizens of the continent, but was believed to be endangering their spiritual hopes, leading them perhaps to perdition rather than to salvation. Which one would Europeans follow? Which was the true pope? Which one was the Antichrist? It was impossible for the simple faithful to know, and the division of the Church then became profound and extremely dangerous, and a heavy psychological burden that all Christians in the West were forced to deal with.

Moreover, the Great Schism, with two popes and no singular force of authority to exercise singular power and impose a singular view of the faith, resulted in heterodox groups growing. This resulted not just from the lack of authority to impose unity, but also from that confusion that we've talked about, that spiritual fear on the part of the faithful about how they were going to achieve salvation not knowing whether the pope in Rome or the pope in Avignon was the real pope or the Antichrist. Heterodox groups, especially those who saw the more direct relationship between the individual believer and God—trying to get around or avoid the institutional structure of the Church itself and the position of priest to mediate between God and man—began to grow in large numbers. In particular, they began to grow in those fringes of Europe where the ecclesiastical control was, to some extent, weakest and where the fear was most widely felt.

In particular, in the kingdom of Bohemia—one of the kingdoms attached to the imperial crown—the movement of John Hus and his Hussites began to challenge not just the authority of the Church, but more dangerously from a perspective of the Holy Roman Emperor, the position of the German bishops that had traditionally been in control of the administrative and physical structure of the Bohemian ecclesiastical establishment. The emperor now found himself in a position where he had to act. The German bishops were being challenged by the Bohemian Hussites. Many heterodox groups were growing to challenge not just the religious state of Europe, but also the political state of Europe; there were questions about where sovereignty resided. Should there be a union of Church and state? Someone had to ultimately decide those difficult issues—but with two sources of decision, which one was going to be accepted?

The emperor realized that something had to be done, and quickly, so he called a council of the Church. This was not the first attempt to end the Schism. The first attempt to end the Schism had actually made the situation much, much worse. In 1409, a group of cardinals from the two colleges—the one in Rome and the one in Avignon— tried to solve the problem by meeting in the Italian city of Pisa, electing a pope, and declaring the other two to be deposed and anti-popes. But of course, what happened was that the pope elected at Pisa became a third pope. You had, after 1409, the totally absurd situation of three popes: one moving around central Europe, one in Rome, and one in Avignon—all claiming the *plenitudo potestatis*, all claiming to be the successor of St. Peter and the successor of Constantine.

The emperor, in calling the council, had a very, very difficult issue to address. He also had a political position that had to be taken into account. The councils of the Church had, from the early days of the Church, been largely separated from secular power. However, the early Church had followed the leadership of the Christian emperors. In particular, the great Church councils that had largely defined the faith, like Nicea in 325, had been called by the Emperor Constantine. So there was precedent, and there was the belief that the emperor had the authority to actually heal the Schism in the Church. In 1417, the Emperor Sigismund called a council to meet at the city of Constance, and it did. It was one of the great councils of the Church, and it addressed the two most pressing issues. The one that needed to addressed immediately by the emperor was the Hussite revolt in Bohemia. The other, which affected everybody equally, was the division in the Church.

The Hussite problem was solved very, very quickly, and in an extraordinarily reprehensible way. John Hus and two of his leading followers were invited to Constance in order to explain their case. They were given an absolute safe conduct by the emperor. But when they were in Constance, they were not only arrested, they were tried and burned as heretics. This, of course, didn't end the Hussite revolt.

In fact, in many ways it gave it new strength because it indicated that the emperor was willing to act outside the law and outside the general provisions of safe conduct, which was seen as almost a sacred responsibility once granted.

Regardless of that problem, the other had to be addressed immediately and once and for all. The Great Council of Constance ultimately reached a set of conclusions that ended the Schism and established a singular papacy. The pope that had been elected in succession to the Council of Pisa participated in his own dethronement by essentially resigning in exchange for a large pension and a good deal of honor. The pope in Rome and the pope in Avignon were both deposed by the council, and a single pope was elected in their place. They chose well. The pope elected was a great Roman noble from the family of Colonna, Oddone Colonna, who took the name of Martin V. From 1417, then, the Schism was over. There was one pope, and that pope was determined to return to Rome. He couldn't immediately because of the state the city was in. It was not just depopulated, but the great churches, and even the papal Lateran Palace, were uninhabitable. It wasn't until 1420 that Martin was able to return to Rome and reunite the bishop with his See, to recreate a single papacy in the capital of both the Western Latin Church and the capital of the great empire that had united the Western, and much of the Eastern, world.

The principle that had elected Martin was a dangerous one for the papacy. It was an idea that had very deep roots in the Church, and it had almost an ideological argument behind it that had stretched deeply from the time of the Babylonian Captivity and built upon other medieval precedents. This was the idea that the Church, acting collectively through a council, had more authority than the pope. In other words, the Church was not a divine theocracy. It wasn't a divine monarchy where the pope was omnipotent and acted as Christ's vicar on earth in all things. This argument, known as *conciliarism*, was that the Church was a collective entity in which the faithful all participated through their representatives—through the bishops, archbishops, and those high ecclesiastics who spoke for the faithful in all things.

Conciliarism, then, had ended the Schism, and it was the only thing that could. None of the popes would willingly resign, so there had to be a force greater than the pope in order to impose unity once more on the Church. The council did exactly that, and Martin V was required to recognize this as part of the terms of his election. He had to issue decrees such as *Frequens*, which in Latin just means "often." It meant that the council was to be called often in order to review the activities of the pope, and that the pope was accountable to the council—the council representing the body of the faithful, and the pope—to some extent—being the chief executive officer of this corporate entity known as the Roman Church.

Martin, of course, had no real intent in obeying this. Martin's belief was that once things calmed down a little bit, the idea would be largely forgotten. He in no way decided to address it, and he couldn't; neither did the council want to address it in a very aggressive way during his pontificate. After all, the Church had just been cleansed of its division. The Church had just been healed, and to open a wound by assaulting the position of the pope that had just been elected in order to achieve this reunion of the faithful would have been a dangerous, suicidal thing to do. During Martin's pontificate, there was no real sense of allowing the idea of conciliarism to come into conflict with the papacy.

Moreover, Martin had problems that were so huge that the idea of addressing this abstract concept of sovereignty within the Church would just be unnecessary. He had to rebuild the papal administration, rebuild the machinery of the collecting of papal taxes, rebuild the churches and palaces of Rome so that the faithful and the pilgrims could come and worship—and so that the pope could live in appropriate grandeur, reflecting the authority of the Vicar of Christ on earth. The basic policy of Martin was to try to put the Church back together again. He was a very skilled administrator, and he succeeded extraordinarily well. Similarly, the faithful didn't want to impose any sense of fear on his part. There was no desire to address the issue so that the pope would feel that he couldn't act in these decisive and appropriate ways in order to heal the Church. One side left the other alone, and Martin was then able not to reestablish the idea of papal monarchy—because, after all, he had agreed to this limitation through conciliarism—but he was allowed to act relatively independently.

Consequently, by the time of Martin's death in the 1430s, we have a curious situation. We have a pope that acted very much independently, that paid lip service to the idea of conciliarism, but one that was essentially left to act freely. On the other hand, you have the memory, the power, and the structure of conciliarism that had been put in place in Constance, a structure that was very much there, still remembered, and generally believed to be the new operative principle of the Church. By the time of Martin's death in 1431, what we see is the bishop of Rome reestablished in the city, the beginnings of the rebuilding of the city, and its restructuring according to not only ecclesiastical, but imperial, memories. But you also have built in this conflict between the idea of papal monarchy and conciliar authority.

This conflict was to be reflected in many ways in the coming decades. It was not only to be reflected in tension between the papacy and the collective body of the Church, but it was to be worked out as well in the ambitions of secular princes who saw conciliarism as an instrument to weaken the authority and the sovereign claims of papal power. It also worked out, of course, in the states of the Church itself. If the pope is not an absolute monarch in terms of ecclesiastical authority within the Church, is he an absolute monarch in terms of the secular authority of the prince who rules that large state in the center of Italy? The confusion of jurisdictions that we've seen operating so often in the Church, and even in secular powers, was brought into relief. The history of Rome, the history of the Church, and the history of the states of Italy are all brought together over these issues of sovereignty and power and the exercise of authority within the Church and the state.

Lecture Eleven
Papal Ambition

Scope:

Because the papacy determined both the policy and the character that was Rome, there was little consistency in its conduct: The ambitions and weaknesses of individual popes had a determining influence on the perception and function of the city itself. Martin's successors were equally prey to the larger international situation; Pius II (1458–1464) was particularly affected because his papacy was dominated by the great tragedy of the conquest of Constantinople. But Pius's immediate successors were self-indulgent men, more interested in promoting their own personal interests than those of the Church. This was particularly true of the Borgia pope Alexander VI (1492–1503). Morally and spiritually corrupt, he directed his administrative skills toward his dream of creating a wealthy Borgia kingdom in Italy. Alexander was succeeded by Pope Julius II (1503–1513), who had all the single-minded energy and imagination of the Borgias but a greater commitment to the Church and culture in Rome. Julius's successors, however, were increasingly vulnerable to events in Europe, particularly the Protestant revolt and the rivalry between Emperor Charles V and Francis I of France. The horrific result was the sack of Rome in 1527. Once peace returned, attempts were made to restore the authority of the pope and the dignity of the city, but little was accomplished until the election of Paul III (1534–1549). He summoned the Council of Trent, which reinforced the ideal of an imperial papacy. Rome became an imperial capital, and the Church survived—indeed, thrived.

Outline

I. The tension between conciliarism and papal monarchy came into high relief with the election of Martin V's successor, Eugene IV (1431–1447).

   A. Eugene lacked the diplomatic skills necessary to address these diametrically opposed principles and ran into difficulty almost from the beginning of his career.

B. Many of the princes of Europe saw the tension between conciliarism and papal monarchy as an opportunity to reassert their authority over the jurisdiction of the Church. Indeed, one prince realized that the Church could be brought under secular control if the schism could be sustained or if conciliarism could be enforced to weaken the papacy.

C. A council was called to depose Eugene, and an anti-pope, Felix V (1439–1449), was elected on the basis of conciliar theory. Once more, the Church was divided, with both Felix and Eugene standing as popes.

D. With Eugene's death in 1447, Nicholas V Parentucelli (1447–1455) was elected, who succeeded in restoring the dignity of the Holy See and was able to end the schism that seemed to be growing once more.

    1. The anti-pope, Felix V, was convinced to resign, and the issue of conciliarism didn't arise, largely because of Nicholas's irenic quality and his desire to do good.

    2. Nicholas was one of the great Renaissance popes and is credited with bringing the Florentine Renaissance to the Holy City.

    3. Nicholas also moved the headquarters of the Church from St. John Lateran to the Vatican, next to the Basilica of St. Peter, in recognition of the burial place of the first pope and the apostle on whom Christ had decided to build his Church.

    4. The idea of connecting the papacy with the apostolic succession and with Christ's charge to Peter belonged to Nicholas. In many ways, this connection addressed the conciliar issue head on without seeming to have addressed it at all.

    5. Nicholas had three ambitions when he became pope: to be a good man, to restore learning, and to rebuild Rome. In all three goals, he was largely successful.

II. Nicholas was succeeded by a series of lesser men who contributed little to the glory of Rome or Christianity.

A. Of these, the best known and, to some extent, one of the saddest examples was Pius II (1458–1464).

1. Pius had been a conciliarist, as well as a great Humanist and scholar, a diplomat, and a man of substance.
2. When Pius was elected pope, all those ideals evaporated; he came to see papal monarchy as much more appropriate to his new role.
3. His pontificate was dedicated to leading a crusade to reconquer Constantinople, which had been lost to the Turks in 1453.
4. In 1464, just as the fleets of the participating states arrived at the coastal city of Ancona to carry the crusaders to the Bosphorus, Pius died. The fleets went home, and no crusade was mounted.

B. The successors of Pius saw the Church as an instrument for their own advantage and that of their families. The prime example here is Sixtus IV Della Rovere (1471–1484).
1. Sixtus was a learned man who had all the makings of a great pope, but he used the authority of the papacy to benefit his own family.
2. Sixtus made significant contributions to Rome, constructing the first bridge across the Tiber since antiquity, enlarging the Vatican Library, and building the Sistine Chapel.
3. Unfortunately, Sixtus was attracted by the opportunity to establish a princely line in the papacy. Because he wanted to give his nephew a state on the borders of Tuscany, for example, Sixtus supported the Pazzi conspiracy, which saw the attempted assassination of Lorenzo de'Medici and the successful attempt on Lorenzo's brother.
4. This policy of nepotism reflected not so much the weakness in character of a man but the tension and internal contradiction in an office that was at once spiritual and secular.

C. Innocent VIII (1484–1492) was ambitious for his family but not in the same way as Sixtus.
1. Innocent had a number of children, all of whom he recognized. He was immensely rich personally and was more interested in living well himself than in dispossessing others.

2. It was with Innocent that the moral position of the papacy began to decline dramatically.

III. If Innocent VIII began the moral slide of the papacy, it was accelerated by Alexander VI Borgia (1492–1503).

A. Alexander VI's wealth had allowed him, in effect, to purchase the papacy. He had a long-time mistress, known as the "queen of Rome," and four children, who were often entertained in the papal palace.

B. Alexander sought to use the papacy as a platform on which to build a Borgia kingdom out of the states of the Church. His eldest son, Juan, was to be the initial instrument of this policy, but he was found murdered, almost certainly assassinated by his brother Cesare.

C. Cesare Borgia (1475/76–1507), one of the psychopaths of history, became Alexander's instrument for creating a Borgia kingdom. With the death of Alexander in 1503, however, while Cesare himself was ill with malaria, Borgia power collapsed.

D. The elective nature of the papacy indicated why individual papal policy could not be sustained over long periods of time.

IV. An elderly nephew of Pius II reigned briefly following the death of Alexander VI. The papal throne then fell to the Borgias' worst enemy, Cardinal Della Rovere, who took the name Julius II (1503–1513).

A. Julius II had no intention of sustaining Borgia policy, nor was he guilty of nepotism, although he was ambitious for the papacy and the Church, more as a political entity than a spiritual one.

B. Julius II stressed the secular role of the papacy, seeing himself as an emperor and a prince. His ambition was to destroy the power of the great Roman families, which he succeeded in doing, and to unite the Papal States so that they could be passed down to succeeding popes.

C. Julius II was successful to a degree, although he came into conflict with other powers that challenged the Italians for rule of their own nation, including the French and the Habsburgs.

D. Julius II was a remarkable man, a great patron of art and culture, a soldier who loved battle and warfare, and a skilled administrator. He brought in Michelangelo to paint the ceiling of the Sistine Chapel and commissioned Raphael to paint the papal apartments. When Julius died in 1513, neither of these projects was completed.

V. Julius was succeeded by another pope who saw the advantage of patronage as a means of achieving grandeur for the papacy and immortality for the man who served as pope. This was the second son of Lorenzo de'Medici, Giovanni, who took the title Leo X (1513–1521).

A. Leo, elected when he was only 37, was highly educated and cultivated, and his ambitions for the papacy were essentially good. He was, however, limited by his own personality. He intended to enjoy the papacy, and did so, in ways from which we still benefit today.

1. Leo continued Raphael's work in the papal apartments, expanded the Sistine Choir, and had Raphael make the tapestries that are still hung for high liturgical events in the Sistine Chapel.

2. The Protestant Reformation that began with Martin Luther during Leo's reign, however, would ultimately split the Church forever.

B. The Reformation was, to some extent, an unintended consequence of events that can be traced back to the Babylonian Captivity. The Reformation was also a response to the creation of dynastic territorial monarchies in Europe.

1. We've already seen princes playing papal authority against royal authority and setting their own ability to rule their territories against the traditions of an independent ecclesiastical jurisdiction.

2. The Pragmatic Sanction of Bourges in 1438, which resulted in the French king gaining control over the Church, and similar actions were part of a process that reached completion and was fulfilled by Martin Luther.

C. Leo underestimated the Lutheran revolt, misreading it as an argument among monks rather than an assault on the idea of papal monarchy and the concept of a singular Church ruled by a priest-king.

D. The political divisions in the German empire and the hostility to the ambitions of the emperor, Charles V, prompted German princes to fulfill their ambitions of taking possession of the property of the Church and of the jurisdiction of canon law and ecclesiastical authority.

E. Leo was not a successful pope, but the crisis didn't truly arrive until after his death, when the events that would change Europe so dramatically became focused on the Italian Peninsula.

VI. The cousin of Leo X, Clement VII de'Medici (1523–1534), had to face the crisis.

    A. In 1525, the French king, Francis I, was humiliated and captured at the Battle of Pavia by the Holy Roman Emperor, Charles V of Habsburg. Afterward, Charles allowed his army in the peninsula to languish.

    B. The leader of this force, the constable of Bourbon, was unable to control the soldiers. The army ravaged its way through the peninsula until it ultimately, in the spring of 1527, stood before the gates of Rome. The gates and the wall were breached, and the city was sacked over the next eight months in the most horrific way imaginable.

        1. The sack of Rome destroyed the Renaissance Humanist belief in human dignity and the idea of the pope as omnipotent on Earth and in heaven. Clement VII was forced to flee from the Vatican Palace to seek protection in Castel Sant'Angelo.

        2. The sack of Rome was seen by the Lutherans as God's righteous anger, the chastisement of the Antichrist. It was seen by Catholics as evidence that God had somehow abandoned Europe.

        3. The sack took place at a time when Christendom was threatened by Turks; it appeared that the apocalypse was at hand.

C. Of course, there was no apocalypse; indeed, this crisis brought forth the ability of the papacy to restructure and redefine itself. In 1534, a new pope was elected, Paul III Farnese (1534–1549), who called the Council of Trent to restructure and revitalize the Church.

    1. The council met between 1545 and 1563, and it specifically addressed the issues that the Protestants had used to assault the position of Roman Christianity.

    2. The Council of Trent recognized that in this war with the Protestants, there had to be just one leader, and that was the pope, who emerged as more powerful than ever. The council also recognized the need for overwhelming glory, beauty, power, and authority in the Church. The age of the Baroque was born.

Essential Reading:

P. Partner, *Renaissance Rome, 1500–1559: A Portrait of a Society.*

Supplementary Reading:

L. Partridge, *The Art of Renaissance Rome, 1400–1600.*

P. Ramsey, ed., *Rome in the Renaissance: The City and the Myth.*

Questions to Consider:

1. Why is it so important up to the present for the papacy to enjoy the rule of an independent state?

2. The papacy illustrates the belief that high office ennobles some while corrupting others. Can you identify other examples of this phenomenon?

Lecture Eleven—Transcript
Papal Ambition

The tension between conciliarism that had ended the Schism in the Church, and the principle of papal monarchy that had been established during the Middle Ages—and had reached its apogee under Innocent III, who died in 1216—came into close relief with the election of Martin's successor, Eugene IV. These diametrically opposed principles of conciliarism and papal monarchy were focused upon an individual who seemed to lack the diplomatic skills to get himself out of the crisis that to some extent had been suppressed by the need in the Church to reestablish its position in Europe—that situation that had given a little bit of respite to Martin V.

Eugene ran into difficulty almost from the beginning of his career. He was forced to flee Rome briefly because of a popular uprising, and many of the princes of Europe began to use this tension between conciliarism and papal monarchy as an opportunity to reassert their authority over the jurisdiction of the Church. Indeed, one of these princes realized that it would be very effective if, in fact, the Schism could be sustained or reinstated, or if conciliarism could be put in place so that the papacy would remain weak, and the Church could then be brought under the control of secular rulers. This, after all, was the time of the creation of dynastic territorial monarchies, and the independent franchise of the Church within these territorial monarchies always, to a degree, challenged the absolute power of the secular prince to rule as he saw fit.

A council was called in order to depose Eugene, and an anti-pope, Felix V, was elected on the basis of conciliar theory. Once more, it seemed as though the Church would be divided, and there would again be two popes; but this time one ruling according to theory of conciliarism in which he was the elected officer of the entire Church operating collectively, and the idea of papal monarchy represented by Eugene in Rome. Eugene never solved this problem altogether, and the anti-pope, Felix V, continued to rule while Eugene was alive. With his death in 1447, there was elected a most remarkable man, Nicholas V Parentucelli. Nicholas V succeeded in restoring the dignity to the Holy See and, partly because of his own personal qualities, was able to end the Schism that seemed to be growing once more. The anti-pope, Felix V, was convinced to resign, and there was once more a single papacy, a single pope who could rule over all of the Church. The issue of conciliarism didn't really raise its head under his pontificate, largely because of his very irenic quality and his desire to do good.

In many ways, Nicholas was one of the great Renaissance popes, inasmuch as he had spent much time in Florence, and he largely brought the Florentine Renaissance to the Holy City. He also made a decision that would change the nature and nomenclature of the papacy to this day. The Lateran Palace attached to the Cathedral of Rome, the Church of St. John in Laterano, was still uncomfortable. It still was in the process of being rebuilt after having been abandoned during the Babylonian Captivity. But more importantly, it was the Cathedral of Rome; it was associated with the idea of the pope as bishop of Rome. Nicholas realized the authority of the papacy could be much reinforced by more closely connecting it to the memory of St. Peter as the Vicar of Christ on earth. It was Nicholas who moved the headquarters of the Church from St. John Lateran to the Vatican, to that palace that had been built in the Middle Ages next to the Basilica of St. Peter, which recognized the burial place of the first pope and the apostle on whom Christ had decided to build his Church.

The creation of the Vatican, the idea of connecting the papacy with the apostolic succession, and connecting the papacy closely with the idea of Christ's charge to Peter, was that of Nicholas. In many ways, it addressed the conciliar issue head-on without seeming in any way to have addressed it at all. Nicholas was a brilliant man, and he was a good man. These two things together brought a good deal of security and stability to the papacy. He also said when he became pope that he had three ambitions. He wanted to be a good man, which he succeeded very much in doing. He wanted to restore learning, which he succeeded in doing by establishing the Vatican Library and patronizing copyists and scholars who would add very much to the luster of the Church. Finally, he wanted to rebuild Rome, to turn it into an imperial, as well as a papal, city—to reflect this double authority that the pope enjoyed. In this, he was successful as well. To some extent, the modern shape of Rome is just beginning to be seen in that papacy that lasted until 1455.

Nicholas was succeeded by a number of men who in no way met his stature. They were men who added little to the glory of either the papacy or of Rome. Of these, the best known, and to some extent one of the saddest examples, was Pius II. Pius had been a great humanist and scholar, a great diplomat, a man of substantial personal quality. He had also been a Conciliarist. He had been an ideological Conciliarist through most of his career, and indeed had functioned as a secretary to the anti-pope for a while. When he was elected pope, all of those dreams evaporated, and he saw the ambitions of papal monarchy as much more appropriate not just to his new role, but to his ambition. Despite his learning, and despite having overcome a rather reprobate youth—he had written in his youth, in fact, a salacious novel of lust and infidelity, and he had sired a number of illegitimate children, all of whom he dutifully sent home to his father to raise—he had overcome this.

He was now focused on a single issue after his election to the See of St. Peter, and that was to try to overcome the humiliation of the loss of Constantinople to the Turks in 1453. This was, to him, the great Christian tragedy. It was the force that was going to challenge the Church and the rule of western Europe. He was right, and he also knew that it had to be addressed immediately, and by all of the princes of Europe, if it was ever to be successful. He called for a great Crusade of Christian Europe against the Turks to reconquer the city that had been built by Constantine. However, in a sad moment in 1464, as he awaited the arrival of the fleets that would carry the Crusaders to the Bosphorus, he died. The fleets had just begun to appear at that coastal city of Ancona at the time of the pope's death, and they turned around and went home. There was no Crusade, and Constantinople remained the capital of the Turks.

In contrast, his successors had no great policy. They weren't driven by a great ambition to recover the lands of Christendom or to structure the Church in a way that would benefit the faithful and the European mission. Rather, in fact, they saw the Church as an instrument for their own advantage and the advantage of their families. As the papacy ennobled some, it also cast others into a less than bright light. Here, the example is probably Sixtus IV Della Rovere. He was elected in 1471, and he had all of the attributes of becoming a great pope. He was learned; he was very civilized, and he was a great patron of learning. He was a man who should, in fact, have lived up to the greatest opportunity that the papacy offered: to be a model, an example, and a beacon that others could follow.

Instead of that, what he did was use the authority of the papacy to benefit his own family. His nepotism, his desire to make the members of his family the rulers of other people's states—or to give them the great Church livings that would allow them to live in luxury and power forever—undid the great things that he actually did for the city. Sixtus IV, despite his policy of nepotism, was one of the kindest popes to Rome. He built the first bridge across the Tiber since antiquity, the Ponte Sisto. He reestablished the Vatican Library and much enlarged it after Nicholas V's initial foundation. He established the Sistine Choir, which today still is the choir that surrounds the pope for liturgical functions. Of course, he built the Sistine Chapel, which his nephew was to decorate with Michelangelo, and which he decorated on the walls with the greatest of all the Tuscan and Umbrian painters.

However, it was his nepotism that indicated the danger in papal monarchy—the idea of the pope as a prince, as a secular ruler, who had a family that had to be cared for, an opportunity to establish a princely line. These were just too great opportunities to simply pass by, and Sixtus unfortunately fell prey to them. It was he who attempted the assassination of Lorenzo de'Medici in Florence, and he did succeed in killing his brother through the instrument of the Pazzi Conspiracy, because he wanted to give his worthless nephew, Girolamo Riario, a state on the borders of Tuscany. He gave another worthless nephew the archbishopric of Florence, that rich see, to give him authority. All of these elements of nepotism reflected not so much the weakness in character of a man, but the tension and the internal contradiction in an office that was at once spiritual and secular. A priest-king, a priest who had the authority to help the faithful achieve salvation, and a king who had all of the elements of secular rule at his command—Sixtus IV succumbed.

Innocent VIII, his successor in 1484, succumbed in other ways. Innocent was not ambitious for his family in the same way because his family was much more intimate. He had a number of children, all of whom he not only recognized, but all of whom he married into the most powerful families of the Italian Peninsula, including the Medici. He was immensely rich personally; he came from a great Sienese banking family. He had huge resources, so he wasn't interested in dispossessing others, but he was interested in living well. He was a man not of much spiritual development and not of much political ambition. What he wanted to do was to enjoy his family, to live in luxury, and to enjoy the See that God seemed to have given him.

It was with Innocent VIII, to some extent, that the moral position of the papacy began to decline dramatically. Not only here was a pope who had children that he recognized publicly and that everyone knew to be his, but also a pope that seemed to take very little interest in the spiritual wellbeing of the faithful. He was not even a major patron of culture, despite being a pleasant and delightful companion. His one great contribution was his tomb, that of Pollaiuolo, which was one of the few monuments brought from the old basilica of St. Peter into the new, and that still graces the wall of that building to this day.

If Innocent VIII began the moral slide of the papacy into a position of individual development of ambition, and the exercise of pleasure and arbitrary authority for the wellbeing of the pope and his family rather than for the wellbeing of the Church, it was crystallized in Alexander VI Borgia. Alexander VI was a truly remarkable man. He was the richest cardinal, probably, that ever lived. He had been papal vice-chancellor for so long that he got a skim from almost every office in the Church, which allowed him to, in effect, purchase the papacy in 1498. Once he had purchased the papacy, he had very clear plans for it. He also, like Innocent VIII, was not a man who even attempted to cover his personal failings. His long-time mistress, known as the "Queen of Rome," Vannozza Cattanei, lived perfectly openly. Their four children together were not only recognized, but they were often entertained in the papal palace. His daughter, Lucrezia Borgia, actually lived with him in the papal apartments where no woman was supposed to be entertained at all.

Alexander VI was an ambitious man—not for himself, but for his children. He had already achieved his greatest ambition, the Holy See, and he wanted to use it as a platform on which to build a Borgia kingdom out of the states of the Church. In other words, those states that had initially been founded and established in order to protect the independence of the Church from secular rule, Alexander saw as an instrument of secular rule to benefit the Borgia. He was willing to sacrifice ecclesiastical power and spiritual authority in order to achieve these things. His eldest son, Juan, who was to be the initial instrument of this policy, was found murdered, floating in the Tiber, and the assassin was almost certainly his brother, Cesare.

Cesare Borgia had initially been put in the Church in order to become a future pope. Cesare, one of the psychopaths of history, had no interest whatsoever in ecclesiastical living, and he assassinated his brother largely to get out of the Sacred College. Cesare, then, became the captain general of the Church and became the instrument by which a Borgia kingdom would be created. The circumstances, though, were not to allow this to happen. With the death of the pope in 1503, while Cesare himself was ill with malaria, there was a collapse of Borgia power. The Borgias had overreached themselves, and they had tried to turn a spiritual power into a secular machine. There still was not the opportunity to achieve this. The pope did not live long enough, and there were too many forces acting against the Borgia ambition.

In particular, the election of the successor of Alexander VI indicated just why papal policy could not be sustained over long periods of time because of the elective nature of the office. As in any office that is subject to changes in personality and policy, the papacy was often seen as an instrument by which there could be protection for those who had been threatened by previous administrations. Despite a very brief reign of the elderly nephew of Pius III following the death of Alexander VI, the person most feared by the Borgia, their worst enemy—one who had to spend much of the Borgia pontificate in France in exile, hiding from the Borgia wrath—was elected pope. This was the nephew of Sixtus IV, Giuliano Della Rovere, who took the name of Julius II. He took the name of Julius because he wanted to be remembered as a successor of Julius Caesar, and because Alexander VI had, by reputation, chosen the name Alexander so he could be remembered like Alexander the Great.

Julius II had no intention of sustaining Borgia policy. Moreover, he was not guilty of nepotism. His one illegitimate daughter was in no way favored. She was married into the great Orsini feudal family, but the pope did not support her or her husband over much. He was not guilty of family ambition for the Della Rovere, as his uncle had been. But he was ambitious for the papacy and the Church—not so much as a spiritual entity, but as a political entity. Julius II emerges from the succession of St. Peter as the warrior-pope, the pope who preferred the smell of gunpowder to incense, the pope who liked to dress like a Roman emperor, wearing the yellow papal color as a cape around his armor, walking with common soldiers—up to his waist in snow—well into his 60s.

This was a man who saw himself as an emperor and as a prince. He was pope, and he was personally relatively pious. But he also was a person who stressed and privileged the secular role of the papacy as the king element of the priest-king role of the successors of St. Peter. Julius's ambition was to once and for all destroy the power of the great Roman families, which he succeeded in doing, and also to unite the states of the Church behind the papacy so that the states of the Church could be passed down coherently from pope to pope, to protect the independence of the Church—not, I think, from Julius's perspective, to protect the orthodoxy of the Church, the independence of a spiritual leader of a pope, and the papacy from conciliarism—although all of these certainly played a role. It was rather to allow the pope to function as a papal monarch, to be a true king and to rule a state that rivaled the other great states of the Italian Peninsula.

Julius II was very successful during this period of his life in doing this, although he too came into conflict with the other powers that had challenged the Italians for rule of their own nation. The French and the Habsburgs had already entered the field, and Julius found himself playing one against the other in an attempt to ensure that the papacy would not be subject to the rule of the House of Valois or the House of Habsburg. In this he had great foresight, but he was not altogether successful. However, he was successful in reestablishing the authority of the papacy as the great patron of art and culture.

Julius II was a remarkable man. He was not only a soldier who loved battle and warfare, and not only a very skilled administrator, but he was also one of the greatest patrons in the history of the West. He brought Michelangelo to paint the ceiling of his uncle's chapel, the Sistine. He brought Raphael to paint the papal apartments that today are known as the Stanze of Raphael: those rooms that were to be ensured as a papal residence forever, in which the glory, majesty, taste, elegance, and authority of Julius would be forever visible; kept, maintained, and sustained by the greatest painter of his time, Raphael of Urbino.

In 1513, Julius died, his work not completely done, his apartments not finished by Raphael. The ceiling of the Sistine was completed by Michelangelo, but his tomb by that same artist is as yet incomplete. He was succeeded by another pope who saw the advantage of patronage, who saw the advantage of the exercise of artistic and cultural authority as a way of giving grandeur to the papacy, as well as an immortality to the person who served as pope. That was the second son of Lorenzo de'Medici (the Magnificent) of Florence, Giovanni de'Medici, who took the title of Leo X.

Leo was, in so many ways, an attractive man. He was young when he was elected pope, only 37. He was highly educated, extremely cultivated and civilized, elegant company, and one whose ambitions for the papacy were essentially good. He was, however, limited (first of all) by his own personality. When he was elected pope, he skipped from the conclave and said, "Now that God has given us the papacy, let's enjoy it." He did enjoy it, and he enjoyed it in ways from which we benefit today. He enjoyed it because he continued Raphael's work in the Stanze. He enjoyed it because he was a great patron of music, and he expanded the Sistine Choir—and was a patron of composers—to make sure that music would always be a fundamental part of the papal liturgy. He was a person who had Raphael make the great tapestries that are hung to this day for high liturgical events in the Sistine Chapel.

Leo was not a man that we should simply neglect or relegate to the failures of history because something happened during his reign that would ultimately split the Church forever. He was a man who saw only too locally. He saw the world from his perspective and from his experience. When Martin Luther, in 1517, challenged the authority of the papacy and its right to dispense on earth; when Martin focused the discontent of many faithful members of the German Roman confession; when he focused the ambitions and the discontent of the princes of Germany not just against the Church, but also against the Holy Roman Emperor, he did it completely unintentionally.

The Reformation was, to some extent, an unintentional consequence of a set of events that we can really trace back to the Babylonian Captivity, in which the Church was being challenged from within and without; where the whole issue of there being a single route to salvation was assaulted by those heterodox groups that had looked for a way around the problem that the Babylonian Captivity, and in particular the Great Schism, had put in place. It also recognized that other revolution happening in Europe, the creation of those dynastic territorial monarchies.

Those princes that we've already seen playing papal authority against royal or princely authority; those princes who put their own ability to rule their own territory against the traditions of an independent ecclesiastical jurisdiction that had resulted in the French king, in 1438 in the Pragmatic Sanction of Bourges, getting virtual control over the Church, or the Diet of Mainz, the next year, where the imperials largely controlled the German Church. These things were part of a process that, that to a degree, reached completion and was fulfilled by Martin Luther. Luther then crystallized a series of events that happened not just in Rome, but right across the continent. It was Leo X who had the misfortune of serving as a successor to St. Peter when it happened.

Leo completely underestimated the Lutheran revolt. He initially thought it was just another argument among monks, Augustinians against Dominicans. He didn't see that in fact, what was being discussed—not metaphorically, but in the reality of political and religious terms—was an assault on the very idea of papal monarchy and the very concept of a singular Church ruled by a priest-king who was the successor to that Peter on whom Christ built his Church. Leo, not recognizing this, allowed it to fester. Moreover, the political divisions in the German Empire, and the hostility to the ambitions of the Emperor Charles V in particular, allowed German princes to see this as an opportunity to fulfill something that they had often wanted to do: take possession of the property of the Church and of the jurisdiction of canon law and ecclesiastical authority that had always been outside their control, despite the growing authority that they were beginning to wield over ecclesiastical jurisdictions.

Leo was not a successful pope, despite his ability to create beauty, and despite the charm that he exercised on everyone. He also was not very nepotistic. He did, in fact, fight a war in Urbino that took the ruler out of his palace, to be replaced by the nephew of the pope. But that didn't last, and it was a singular event. It was something that he had to do to find a job for his rather worthless nephew, who needed a principality because, after all, he was a Medici as well as being the nephew of the pope. It was after the death of Leo that the crisis truly came—that what was festering in Europe and dividing the continent had been focused very much not just on the Church and on Rome, but also on the Italian Peninsula. The events that had changed Europe so dramatically, that were altering the culture and the dynamic of an entire continent, became focused on the Italian Peninsula because that is where the issue would be determined. To some extent, that is where the ideological division was being discussed.

It was the cousin of Leo X, Clement VII de'Medici, who had to face the crisis. In 1525, the French king, Francis I, was humiliated at the Battle of Pavia by the Holy Roman Emperor, Charles V of Habsburg. The French king was a prisoner in Spain, and Charles seemed to be reigning supreme. Charles, though, after this victory, allowed his army in the Peninsula to languish—an army that was led by a French traitor, the first cousin to the French king who had gone over to the Habsburgs because he had quarreled with Francis's mother over money—again, another administrative and political observation that seems to be recurrent in human history.

The Constable of Bourbon, unable to control this professional army of Spanish veterans and Lutheran German pikemen, followed the army as it ravaged its way through the Peninsula until ultimately, in the spring of 1527, it stood before the gates of Rome. The gates and the wall were breached, and the city was sacked over the next eight months in the most horrific way imaginable. The sack of Rome was one of the most horrific events in all of western European history. It was a terrible moment. It not only destroyed that humanist Renaissance belief in human dignity, but it also destroyed the idea of the pope as the successor of St. Peter who was omnipotent on earth and in heaven. The pope was humiliated. Clement VII was forced to flee from the Vatican Palace to seek some measure of protection in Castel Sant'Angelo. It was from the ramparts of that castle, originally built as the tomb of the Emperor Hadrian, that he watched the city being destroyed by a new barbarian invasion, about which he could do nothing.

The sack of Rome of 1527 was seen by the Lutherans as God's righteous anger. The Antichrist had been chastised. It was seen by Catholics as evidence that God had somehow abandoned Europe. We have to remember that there's a context much broader than Europe. We have to remember that the context of these events must be seen much more broadly than the Italian Peninsula, or even Europe itself.

It was, after all, 1527, just months after the Battle of Mohacs, where the Christian army, led by the King of Hungary, had been slaughtered by Suleiman the Magnificent of the Turks. It was just months before the siege of Vienna of 1529, which seemed to threaten the entirety of Christian Europe at the hands of the infidels, the Turks. It appeared the Apocalypse was at hand, and God was angry with Christianity and with Europe.

Of course, there was no Apocalypse, and indeed this crisis brought forth the ability of the papacy to restructure and redefine itself. In 1534, a new pope was elected—a pope who was a Roman noble. The Farnese pope, Paul III, called the Council of Trent in order to restructure and revitalize the Church. This council was not an act of conciliarism because it was summoned by the pope. In fact, it was almost an act of anti-conciliarism, making the council dependent upon the authority of the pope himself. The council met between 1545 and 1563, and it redefined not just the faith, but specifically addressed the sorts of issues that the Protestants had used to assault the position of Roman Christianity. But from it emerged the idea of papal monarchy in all of its glory.

The Council of Trent recognized that in this war with the Protestants, there had to be just one general and one leader, and that was the pope. Trent not only reformed the Church, but it also gave a new authority to the position of the pope. The pope emerged more powerful than ever, and the Church more glorious than ever because the council also recognized the need for glory, beauty, power, and authority that would overwhelm the senses. The age of the baroque had been born.

Lecture Twelve
Papal Reform

Scope:

The Council of Trent reinforced the idea of papal monarchy, with the pope emerging as a potent example of a priest-king, ruling both as vicar of Christ and as an Italian prince in control of a substantial state. The events of the Protestant Reformation and the Turkish advance had put the Roman Church on the defensive. Thus, the environment of Rome in the later 16th and early 17th centuries was dynamic but conflicted. The decrees of the Council of Trent had resulted in powerful new agencies, such as the Society of Jesus, and a renewed emphasis on Catholic spiritual awareness. Equally, however, the image of an imperial papacy, reflecting the grandeur and authority of both the Church and the ancient Roman *imperium*, promoted ecclesiastical splendor and rich living. Nepotism became endemic, with members of the popes' families enjoying spectacular wealth and power at the expense of the Church, building huge palaces and villas. Rome emerged in the age of the Baroque, then, as a much more beautiful city, but one in which the competing ambitions of holiness and power were in dramatic contrast.

Outline

I. The 25 sessions of the Council of Trent held in the period from 1545 to 1563 had profound effects on the Church, the papacy, and Rome.

   A. A new spirituality was stimulated by the decrees of Trent and by papal and curial emphasis on clerical education, episcopal guidance, and spiritual regeneration.

   B. The council also reaffirmed the principle of papal monarchy, seeing a single ruler—armed with a divine office and unlimited power—as the best response to the Protestant revolt.

   C. As we've seen, there were dangers inherent in the idea of papal monarchy, dangers that the conciliar movement had begun to question. One of the popes who ruled during the Council of Trent, Paul IV Carafa (1476–1559), illustrates how dangerous this reenergized faith could be in concert with omnipotent power.

1. In his younger years, Cardinal Carafa was known for his learning and piety, as demonstrated by his membership in the Oratory of Divine Love. When elected pope, however, Paul became a bigoted tyrant.

2. He instituted the *Index of Prohibited Books* to control what Catholics could read—and know.

3. The Roman Inquisition (established under Paul III in 1542) became a dreaded instrument of control under Paul IV, enforcing a strict adherence to the pope's narrow interpretation of the faith.

4. Paul IV persecuted his former friends and associates and had some of them tried for heresy. By the time of his death, he had filled the prisons of the Inquisition with many whose only crime was a vague suspicion of heterodox belief.

5. On the day of the pope's death, the angry people of Rome rioted and freed the prisoners out of hatred for the pope's tyranny.

II. Other popes, such as Gregory XIII (1572–1585), used their monarchical status to inject a positive element into the restructuring of Roman and ecclesiastical life in order to benefit not just the city and the Church but the community of the faithful and Europeans altogether.

A. Gregory, whose personal piety and probity were beyond reproach, took the advice of Trent seriously, believing that it was the pope's responsibility to reinforce the faith and to bring the faithful into more active and engaged communion with the established authority of ecclesiastical power.

B. To this end, Gregory built and rebuilt churches, particularly those associated with martyrs, which he believed would connect the contemporary Church—beset as it was by the Protestant schism—with the ancient apostolic Church—itself beset by pagan persecution.

C. Gregory also sought to ensure that the intellectual world of Europe was reflected in the authority of the papacy and the institution of the Church itself.

D. Gregory realized the need to stress the act of baptism, of joining the Church. He thus rebuilt the baptistery at St. John Lateran, connecting the site where Constantine was thought to have been baptized to the seat of the pope as bishop of Rome.

E. Gregory is perhaps best remembered for his reform of the Julian calendar to ensure that the liturgical year would be consonant with the solar year. The commission established by Gregory to address this issue unveiled its new calendar in 1582, which is essentially the calendar that we use today.

III. Another pope of the post-Tridentine era that re-created Rome and provided a new focus and energy for the city was Sixtus V (1520–1590).

    A. In his five-year reign, this indomitable personality created much of the Roman landscape we see today. Sixtus also fostered learning by commissioning the construction of a wing to house the ever-expanding Vatican Library. This remarkable work, including the interior decoration, was completed in just 13 months.

    B. Sixtus engaged scholars to discover the locations of ancient obelisks, which symbolized the connection between heaven and Earth of ancient rulers, a union now claimed by the papacy. These obelisks brought to Rome from Egypt by ancient emperors were set up as guideposts around the city, especially near pilgrimage sites.

        1. The only standing obelisk from ancient times, the needle beside the old Basilica of St. Peter, was moved with great difficulty to the huge piazza in front of the new church, a task even Michelangelo thought impossible, and the story of the raising of the obelisk is still popular in Rome today.

        2. Sixtus saw the erection of the obelisks and the restoration of Rome as both a rebuilding of the ancient city by the papacy and as a re-creation of a new kind of imperial symbol.

        3. The restoration was also closely linked to the populace, now reenergized by the forces of antiquity and Humanist knowledge and by the faith through the results of the Council of Trent.

C. Sixtus V also knew that the creation of sacred spaces was important so that the Council of Trent would not be viewed as just a series of decrees but could be seen and felt. The obelisks represented one element of this approach.

   1. Another aspect of this perspective can be seen in the statues of St. Peter and St. Paul mounted on the two surviving Roman columns of Trajan and Marcus Aurelius.

   2. These statutes symbolized the victory of the apostles of the Church and the martyrs of Rome over the emperors but still linked them physically and metaphorically.

D. The re-creation of the chapel in Santa Maria Maggiore that housed the traditional devotional relic of the crib of Christ was another of these acts. The construction of a new and dramatic chapel to house this relic again symbolized the sophistication and sensitivity of Sixtus V.

E. Yet another example is the Scala Santa ("Holy Staircase"), brought to Rome by the mother of Constantine, St. Helena, and by tradition, thought to be the stairs that Christ had walked at the palace of Pontius Pilate to be judged. Sixtus constructed a separate building across the piazza from the Cathedral of St. John Lateran to house these stairs.

F. Sixtus V had all of the genius of a minister of propaganda, and the five years of his pontificate fundamentally changed the nature of the Church. But Sixtus also knew that as the prince of Rome and the king of the Papal States, he had to make contributions to the lives of his subjects.

   1. For example, he rebuilt a large aqueduct to bring water for the first time in more than 1,000 years to some of the highest places in Rome, especially around the Esquiline Hill.

   2. Sixtus also rebuilt the hospital of Santo Spirito, used particularly for pilgrims.

IV. The spiritual regeneration of the Church was apparent in the actions and devotion of Catholics outside the papacy and curia. Three saints, St. Charles Borromeo, St. Philip Neri, and St.

Ignatius of Loyola, made contributions that changed the nature of the Roman Church.

A. San Carlo Borromeo (1538–1584) came to represent both the ideal bishop and a good man.

    1. Despite being the nephew of Pope Pius V and a member of a wealthy Milanese family, he lived simply according to his motto of *humilitas*, or "humility."

    2. St. Charles risked his life by aiding plague victims and refused to give up the religious life, despite pressure from his family. He devoted his life to the Tridentine decrees of clerical education and the improvement of education and faith in general.

    3. Charles was canonized in 1610, less than 30 years after his death; he had become a model bishop, the "poster boy" for a reenergized Church.

B. Another example of reformed piety was St. Philip Neri (1515–1595), known as the Apostle of Rome.

    1. Philip came to Rome from Florence in 1533, cutting himself off from his wealthy family to live a simple life as a tutor for a modest family.

    2. He lived on bread and water and had no possessions, even selling his books when he had finished with them and giving the proceeds to the poor.

    3. In 1548, still a layman, Philip founded a confraternity to aid pilgrims in the city and worked hard to salvage the dissolute lives of young Roman nobles.

    4. In 1551, Philip took priest's orders, and in 1575, Pope Gregory XIII recognized his group as the Congregation of the Oratory. Gregory also gave this congregation a church, which would become the Chiesa Nuova. The congregation gave its name to the musical form *oratorio*.

    5. Although Philip had wished to be a missionary in India, he was convinced "to make Rome his desert" and devoted his life there to the poor, the dissolute, and pilgrims. He died as one of Rome's most honored citizens and was canonized in 1622.

C. New orders were formed as a result of Trent that attempted to fulfill the council's decrees. The Jesuits are perhaps the most famous of these, founded by St. Ignatius of Loyola (1491–1556).

1. Ignatius used his military background as the model for a new kind of religious order based on his book, *The Spiritual Exercises*. The exercises constitute almost military discipline, in which the will is to be made subservient to the needs of the Church and the demands of the papacy.

2. Ignatius built his new order around three functions: teaching, preaching, and conducting missionary activity. His intent was both to win back souls from the Protestants in Europe and to convert newly contacted people in the New World to the Catholic faith.

3. Jesuits gained influence as well by controlling the educational apparatus of the continent. They provided the best schools, became the advisors of kings and princes, and engaged in clandestine activities to try to undermine the Protestants.

4. By the time Loyola was canonized in 1622, the Jesuit order had achieved worldwide influence. It, too, was a reflection of the new Rome and the new Church as a consequence of Trent.

V. Although the spiritual renewal represented by both Counter-Reformation popes and saints changed the perception and character of Rome on one level, the conflicts remained, especially in the ranks of the higher curial officials and even the papacy itself.

A. The pope remained a powerful secular prince, ruling both a large state and an ecclesiastical order. The needs of defense, political and military alliance, and diplomacy compromised the intentions of even the holiest of popes.

1. Members of the pope's family also believed they should have some of the perks associated with princely lineage, such as titles, wealth, and authority.

2. The cardinal-nephews, in particular, enjoyed influence and wealth. Some, such as Scipione Borghese, the cardinal-nephew of Paul V Borghese, used their influence to patronize artists and architects, including Bernini. Others used that wealth for their own benefit.

3. The princely families of Rome to this day—the Borghese, Chigi, Pamphilij, Ludovisi, Barberini—owe their positions to nephews of popes raised by their uncles.

4. Indeed, it was not until the end of the 18th century, with the humiliation of Pope Pius VI Braschi (1717–1799) by Napoleon, that the tradition of establishing a great palace and a princely line at the expense of the Church was brought to an end.

B. Papal Rome was the last independent jurisdiction on the Italian Peninsula to fall to the united kingdom of Victor Emmanuel II in 1870.

1. On September 20, 1870, the armies of Victor Emmanuel broke through the Porta Pia, Michelangelo's last completed work, and joined Rome and what was left of the Papal States to the Italian kingdom.

2. The pope, Pius IX, refused to recognize the authority or the legitimacy of the kingdom of Italy over his former territories. He shut himself up in the Vatican, claiming that good Catholics should not participate in politics.

C. It was not until Mussolini's Lateran Treaty of 1929 that peace was made with the Church. Part of this peace involved the return of secular jurisdiction, as well as ecclesiastical authority, to the pope.

1. Vatican City was created as an independent state to be ruled absolutely by a priest-king.

2. Ironically, this tiny sovereign state exists in the world of the European Union, which can be seen as the re-creation of a new kind of secular empire.

3. The world of the papacy of the Middle Ages and the Renaissance is still very much with us. The memories are long, and the practice remains tense to this very day.

Essential Reading:

N. Courtright, *The Papacy and the Art of Reform in Sixteenth-Century Rome: Gregory XIII's Tower of the Winds in the Vatican.*

J. W. O'Malley, *The First Jesuits.*

Questions to Consider:

1. Why did it take the crisis of the Protestant revolt to generate a movement of fundamental reform in the Roman Church?

2. Can sincere piety and humility coexist with unlimited power?

Lecture Twelve—Transcript
Papal Reform

The 25 sessions of the Council of Trent that were held between 1545 and 1563 had profound effects not just on the Roman Church, but on the city of Rome and the political office of the papacy itself. A new spirituality was stimulated by the decrees of Trent, and papal and curial reform was part of the agenda that was then sent to the very center of Latin Christendom. Indeed, the role of bishops—and the pope, after all, was bishop of Rome—for episcopal guidance, spiritual regeneration, and the other factors that would be taken into account in order to reenergize the Church in the battle with the Protestants, would be part of not just the hopes and visions, but also now part of the pope's brief. There were calls for the reeducation of the clergy to ensure that they actually had sufficient education to not only manage the liturgy, but also to provide models of learning and good living in their communities. They were to be catalysts for spiritual change.

The Council also reaffirmed the idea of papal monarchy, that all of the bishops contributed to the regeneration of the Church, but the pope was the *primus inter pares*, "the chief among the bishops." He was to be the leader that would provide the guidance to ensure the Church not only moved along an appropriate and singular pathway, but also was able to address the assaults of the Protestants in a united manner. However, there were dangers inherent in the very idea of papal monarchy from the beginning, dangers that the conciliar movement had begun to question. These dangers can perhaps be best exemplified by one of the popes that ruled during the Council of Trent, Paul IV Carafa. The reenergized faith and the new power of the papacy could actually be a danger not just to the faithful, but also to the city.

In his younger years, Cardinal Carafa was a learned and pious man. He was a member of a group of clerics and laymen that gathered together in an institution called the Oratory of Divine Love in order to practice personal piety, to be examples for other clerics and laymen to try to achieve some measure of spiritual fulfillment in this world. As pope, he instituted the *Index of Prohibited Books* that determined what Catholics could read and what Catholics could know. Although the Roman Inquisition had been established in 1542 during the pontificate of Paul III, it was Paul IV Carafa that used it as such a dangerous and threatening weapon. It reflected his very narrow interpretation of a faith, and it reflected his own bigoted and narrow perspective of what it meant to be a subject of the pope. He persecuted his former friends, those who had been his pious companions in his youth, and he had some of them tried for heresy.

Indeed, in the most curious example, he hid, as pope, in the bedroom of a dying ecclesiastic so he could hear the Last Rites; just to see at that moment, when he believed that the truth would be revealed, whether this person he suspected of having heterodox beliefs really did. The idea of a pope hiding in a dead man's bedroom in order to hear his last confession reflects the nature and character of Paul IV Carafa. He filled the prisons of the Inquisition with men that he considered of doubtful orthodoxy; those he considered to be dangers to the faith simply by the example of their lives. But these prisons were so full that at the moment of the pope's death, the people of Rome rioted, broke into the prisons of the Inquisition and freed the prisoners. Paul IV was not a popular pope in Rome, and he was an unfortunate example of what happens when bigotry is mixed with absolute divinely sanctioned power.

There were other popes in the period after the Council of Trent that added a different kind of energy, a positive element of the restructuring of Roman and ecclesiastical life in order to benefit not just the city and the Church, but the community of the faithful and of Europeans all together. Here we see Gregory XIII as a wonderful example. Gregory, whose personal piety and probity were beyond question, took the advice of Trent seriously. He believed that it was the pope's responsibility to reinforce the faith in ways that could be broadly understood, and to bring the faithful into more active and engaged communion with the established authority of the ecclesiastical power. To do this, he began building and rebuilding churches, particularly those churches associated with martyrs. Gregory saw the period of persecution in the time of paganism, the time of Diocletian and Nero, to be a reflection of the time in which he saw Catholics being persecuted by the new Protestant powers. He wanted to make this connection between the pagans and the Protestants. A way of doing this would be to indicate that martyrdom is a tradition of the Church that is being sustained.

He also wanted to ensure that the intellectual world of Europe was also reflected in the authority of the papacy and in the institution of the Church itself. He realized that the act of baptism, of joining the Church, was something that should be stressed. Also, the connection between the political and the religious needed to be redefined so that it was less threatening to political individuals, to those who saw the tension between ecclesiastical and secular jurisdictions as one of the dangers of Catholicism. He symbolically rebuilt the baptistery of the Cathedral of Rome, St. John Lateran, because, by tradition, this is the very baptistery that is actually an ancient survival from the villa of the Laterani. It was in this baptistery that Constantine the Great was, by tradition, baptized. The idea of connecting the baptism of Constantine with a place that is also the Cathedral of Rome, the seat of the pope as bishop of Rome, had remarkable effects. It was a brilliant moment of propaganda.

Not only Rome, but time itself was reformed by Gregory, and it is in this way he's best remembered today. It was he who undertook the reform of the calendar to ensure that the liturgical year would be consonant with the solar year. The calendar that was established by Julius Caesar in 45 B.C, the Julian calendar, had by 1570 become wildly out of phase with the solar year. This problem in which the dates of the liturgical events of the Church were off by two weeks almost had to be addressed. This was central to the Church because the early Councils had determined how the dates of important Church festivals, particularly Easter, were to be calculated.

In 1577, Gregory established a Calendar Commission that was to create a new way of determining time so that the solar year and the liturgical year of the Church would be brought back into phase. It worked because the time required for the earth to circle the sun was now the time that was determined by the scientists, thinkers, and theologians of the Calendar Commission. In 1582, the Commission unveiled their new calendar, which is essentially the calendar that we use today, the Gregorian Calendar—the work of one of the popes after the Council of Trent in order to achieve the authority the pope believed he had been given—that is, to bind on earth and in heaven, and time really links the two.

Another pope of the post-Tridentine era that re-created Rome and provided a new focus and energy for the city, that helped define the nature of the papacy through the use of symbols—which was something that Trent strongly encouraged—was Sixtus V. In a reign of just five years, this indomitable personality—this energetic, remarkable, and demanding individual who ruled between 1585 and 1590—really restructured Rome and created, to some extent, the Rome that we see today. He fostered learning, and it was he who built the wing of the library to house the ever-growing Vatican collection, the Apostolic Library. But the wing that he had his architect, Domenico Fontana, build was to separate the huge spaces that had been built for Julius II in the Cortile del Belvedere by the architect Bramante.

In the period of the 16th century and the period that Julius really represented, this large space had been used for theatricals, for bear-baiting and bull-baiting, and for jousts. Now it was to be dominated not just by the palace of the popes, the Apostolic Palace, it was to be dominated on its other side by the Apostolic Library, representing the collective wisdom and knowledge of the Church. The Vatican Library was a symbol as well, and it was built quickly because just the structure and its decoration—these remarkable achievements— were completed in 13 months. When Sixtus V wanted something done, he wanted it done well, and he wanted it done quickly.

This remarkable moment was reinforced outside the Papal Palace, where again the symbolism of Sixtus's imagination could be seen operating almost everywhere. Sixtus knew from his knowledge of classical antiquity that many Roman emperors had brought many Egyptian obelisks, beginning with Augustus, to Rome. Augustus, after the Battle of Actium in 31 B.C. where he defeated the forces of Marc Antony and Cleopatra, symbolized his new rule over Egypt and his own new rule as being the successor of the pharaohs, connecting heaven and earth. That's what the obelisks symbolized. Those obelisks, with their pointed needles, connect heaven and earth and reflect the divine that is in every pharaoh. This was a mantle, with the defeat of Cleopatra, that Augustus claimed.

Sixtus knew that the union between heaven and earth was now in the papacy. He saw this as a symbolic moment that would allow the rule of the pope, of the bishop of Rome, to reconnect with that charge of Christ to Peter. He had his scholars go to the Vatican Library to look up every example they could find of where the obelisks last stood. He then sent teams of workmen, when the ground was wet, with long pieces of metal to drive into the soil until they hit what could be an obelisk. He then excavated, and if an obelisk was found, it was disinterred, and it was set back up in order to provide not just that connection with antiquity—that connection to the rule of the Roman emperors—but also the connection with the pharaohs and the idea of the priest-king, or perhaps the God-king.

The obelisks that began to rise, though, did not see their positions in the ancient world reestablished. They were moved because they were now put in front of the great pilgrimage churches or in front of the centers of Latin Christianity. The obelisk in front of the Cathedral of Rome, St. John Lateran, is the largest and the tallest in Rome. There are also obelisks in Piazza del Popolo, so that when one entered the city through the Flaminian gate, the gate from the north, one would see an obelisk—and similarly, from the three streets that lead to the Piazza del Popolo. There were other obelisks that were set up as well, and one that was moved. It was a challenge to all of the architects of the Vatican as to how to deal with the obelisk of Nero that had once been part of the *spina*, or the "central area," of the racecourse in which, by tradition, St. Peter had been martyred. It was the only obelisk from ancient times still standing—the only one that had not fallen. It was necessary to move it in order to build the new basilica of St. Peter because the new basilica was going to be much, much larger and actually encroach on the space that the old obelisk had sustained.

What to do? It had been suggested to Michelangelo that it could be moved. Michelangelo studied the problem and determined that it was impossible. Sixtus V did not accept the idea of anything being impossible, so he instructed Domenico Fontana to move it. Fontana spent months devising a most remarkable machine that would allow the obelisk, in all of its weight and height, to be set on its side, put on wheels, and moved so that it could be brought into the new huge space in front of the new basilica and once more set up. Fontana was not sure that his scheme would work, and just to be certain—knowing what happened when the pope got angry—he had saddled horses ready so he could escape Rome if the obelisk should fall and shatter.

The story of the obelisk being raised is one of the most popular stories in Rome to this day. As the obelisk, with this great machine, was finally moved in front of the basilica, and as the thousands of sailors, the hundreds of horses, and the winches that were used in order to raise it to a vertical position were put in place, the pope knew the entire population of the city would gather to watch the event. He also knew that all of the sailors would have to pull with exactly the same tension because if one group pulled too hard, then the weight of the obelisk would shift, and it would fall and shatter. Sixtus said that anyone who made any noise during the actual raising of the obelisk would be summarily executed. He thought this would get their attention.

As the obelisk began to rise, and the equipment designed by Fontana—and the system that he had invented in order to do what Michelangelo said was impossible—seemed to be working, it was noted that the ropes began to fray, and they began to smoke because of the tension. Despite the pope's injunction, a sailor from Genoa screamed at the top of his voice: "Put water on the ropes." Instantly, water was thrown on the ropes. The ropes stopped smoking, and the obelisk was raised. Rather than executing him for making the noise, the pope instead said he could have anything that he asked for. The Genoese sailor said he would like to have for himself and his descendants in perpetuity the right to supply the fronds for Palm Sunday in front of St. Peter's, knowing that it would be a very lucrative commission indeed. To this day, it is being sustained.

In other words, the idea of the symbolic moment of re-creating the ancient world with an obelisk that had been set up at the place where Peter was martyred, in the place that associated the power of the emperor with the pleasing of the populace—that is, the racecourse that had been designed by Nero and Caligula—had been once more restored. The idea of *Roma restaurata*, the restoration of Rome, is not just the rebuilding of the ancient city by the papacy in this post-Tridentine period, but now is the re-creation of a new kind of imperial Rome in which the authority of the pope reflects the emperor and St. Peter. It is also closely linked to a reenergized populace—those that were reenergized by the forces of antiquity and humanist knowledge, and those that were reenergized by the faith through the results of the Council of Trent.

Sixtus V knew also that it was important to create those sacred spaces so important to Roman piety so that the Council of Trent would be not just a series of decrees that could be debated, but could be seen and felt. The idea of personal piety became important. The obelisk represented one element. Putting the statues of St. Peter and St. Paul upon the two surviving Roman columns of Trajan and Marcus Aurelius was just as important—symbolizing the victory of the apostles of the Church and the martyrs of Rome over the emperors, but still linking them physically and metaphorically.

The re-creation of the chapel in Santa Maria Majore, which housed the traditional devotional relic of the Crib of Christ, was another of these acts. Again, it symbolized the sophistication and, to some extent, the sensitivity of Sixtus V's personality. This object, which was believed to be the crib in which the Christ child lay, had been an object of popular devotion, and it had its own chapel for many years, since the Middle Ages, in the church of Santa Maria Majore. But a new chapel was built, a huge and dramatic chapel, to house this relic—because the cult of saints, the cult of relics, and the emotional association of the faithful with the traditions of the Church was something that Trent wanted to reinforce and build. Sixtus V had the kind of personality that saw the advantage of this sort of propaganda, and he used it as effectively as possible.

Another example is the Scala Santa. The stairs that were brought to Rome by the mother of Constantine, St. Helena, were by tradition the very stairs that Christ had walked at the palace of Pontius Pilate to be judged. These had existed in St. John Lateran for some time, and they were associated very much with the role of the bishop of Rome. They had been brought, however, by the mother of the Christian Emperor Constantine—so, again, the connection was sophisticated. A separate little building across the piazza from the Cathedral of St. John Lateran was constructed in order to house these stairs. It became a place of popular pilgrimage, as it is to this day. Even now, if you wish to climb those stairs, you have to do so on your knees as an act of popular devotion.

Sixtus V had all of the genius of a minister of propaganda. It worked effectively, and those five years of his pontificate fundamentally changed the nature of the Church. But Sixtus wasn't content with that. He also knew that he was the prince of Rome. He was the king of the Papal States. He was the absolute ruler of his people's secular and terrestrial salvation as well as their religious salvation. He knew that he had to make contributions to them as people living in a complex and difficult city as well. For example, it was he who rebuilt the large aqueduct that would bring water for the first time to some of the highest places in Rome, especially around the Esquiline Hill. Being a man of some strength of character as well as little modesty, he named it after himself; it's the Aqua Felice. His birth name was Felix Peretti; therefore, Aqua Felice is not the "lucky water"; it's the water that Felix, the pope, brought to the people of Rome. That whole area around the baroque parts of the city on the Esquiline and Quirinal Hills, which had not seen fresh water for a thousand years, now could be developed.

Sixtus V Peretti was a remarkable pope. He brought water as well as spiritual fulfillment. He brought water to strengthen the body and the community of the city, and he brought water through the reconstruction of the baptistery of St. John Lateran to strengthen the faith of the religious community. He was a man of symbols, and he was a man who recognized the complexity of his role as a priest-king. The hospital of Santo Spirito was rebuilt, and it was used particularly for pilgrims. He was a man that ensured that the pilgrims would be able to find their way, hence the obelisks; and he was a man that ensured that there would be paved, straight streets. In other words, the idea of Trent was recognized powerfully in the authority of the pope and the ability to build a new Rome, a new city.

Equally, though, Trent was for the religious and spiritual restoration of the city. Three saints, three contemporaries of varying ages, made contributions that changed the nature of the Roman Church. San Carlo Borromeo, St. Charles Borromeo, came to represent both the ideal bishop and a good man. Despite being the nephew of Pope Pius V and a member of one of the greatest and richest Milanese families, he lived very simply according to his motto of *humilitas*, or "humility." He risked his life by aiding plague victims. Despite the pressure of his family, and even his uncle the pope, to give up his religious life, marry, and have children—once his elder brother died and he became the head of the noble family—he refused. He devoted his life to the Tridentine decrees of clerical education and improving education and faith in general. He was canonized in 1610, less than 30 years after his death, and he becomes the idea of the model bishop, the poster boy for a reenergized Church. He remains in many ways, to this day, in the schools that are named after him.

One of his contemporaries was St. Philip Neri, a man from a different background, a middle-class background, born in Florence, but who became the Apostle of Rome. He came to Rome in 1533, but he cut himself off from his wealthy family and his very influential Roman relatives so he could live a simple life. He lived on bread and water, tutoring a modest family while living in a single room in their house. He gave away everything, including the proceeds from the books that he sold after he had finished using them, to the poor. In 1548, still a layman, he founded a confraternity to aid pilgrims in the cities and he worked hard with his lay brothers to try to salvage the dissolute lives of young Roman nobles.

In 1551, he took priest's orders, and in 1575, Pope Gregory XIII recognized his group as a new religious order, the Congregation of the Oratory. Gregory also gave this congregation a church, which would become the Chiesa Nuova. But because of the role that music was to play in the celebration of the liturgy, it took its name from the Italian of oratory, *oratorio*, and it provided the name for a genre of music in which the spiritual words are joined with music in order to create a spiritual moment for both the mind and the imagination. Although Philip Neri had wished to be a missionary and follow the example of Francis Xavier in India, he was told by the Jesuit that he should make Rome his desert, and so he did. He devoted his life to the poor and the dissolute in the city; he devoted his life to pilgrims. He died as one of Rome's most honored citizens, and he was canonized in 1622.

New orders were being formed as a result of Trent—new orders that energized the Church and tried to fulfill its decrees. The Jesuits are perhaps the most famous. St. Ignatius of Loyola used his military background for a new kind of religious order based on the book that he wrote, *The Spiritual Exercises*. *The Spiritual Exercises* really constitute almost military discipline in which the will is to be made subservient to the needs of the Church and the demands of the papacy. He built his new order around three functions: teaching, preaching, and missionary activity. He would use these to win back not just souls from the Protestants in Europe, but to ensure that the peoples contacted as a result of the expanding empires of Spain, Portugal, and France would be converted to the Catholic version of Christianity.

It is largely because of the acts of the Jesuits that this took place in the Americas, and even in parts of the world such as India, where Goa became the activity of St. Francis Xavier. Jesuits began gaining influence as well by controlling the educational apparatus of the continent. They provided the best schools, became the advisors of kings and princes, and they engaged in clandestine activities to try to undermine the Protestants and to save Protestant souls, so they believed. By the time Loyola was canonized in 1622, he had started a movement that would become one of the most influential orders in all of European history. It, too, was a reflection of the new Rome and the new Church as a consequence of Trent.

Although the spiritual renewal represented by the Counter-Reformation popes and saints that we just discussed changed the perception of Rome and the nature of the concept of being a citizen of the Church, there were also elements that still reflected the old tension and conflict that represented both secular and religious power being joined in a single man, the pope, and in a single authority, the Church that ruled both a state and an ecclesiastical order. After all, the needs of defense, of political and military alliance, and of diplomacy compromised the intentions of even the holiest of popes. Friends and members of the pope's family also saw that they were now the relatives of a prince, and they should have some of the perks associated with princely lineage. They should be given titles and wealth. They should establish great lineage, and they should be given some of the Church's authority for their own private use.

The Cardinal-Nephews in particular represented this. Those who were the real nephews or the adopted nephews of popes used their influence with the Holy See to enrich themselves and their families. Some, like the cardinal-nephew of Paul V Borghese, Scipione Borghese, a cardinal, did well by patronizing Bernini and creating one of the great art collections of the 17th century. Others that were perhaps less inclined to the production of beauty used that wealth for their own benefit. When we see the princely families of Rome to this day—the Borghese, Chigi, Pamphilij, Ludovisi, Barberini—we're seeing the families of the nephews of popes that had been raised to that lineage as a consequence of their uncle's activity. It was only with the humiliation of Pope Pius VI Braschi, who died in 1799, by Napoleon that this confusion finally ended.

Papal Rome was the last independent jurisdiction on the Italian Peninsula to fall to the kingdom of a united Italy. In 1870, on the 20th of September, the armies of Victor Emmanuel II broke through Michelangelo's last completed work, the Porta Pia, and joined Rome and what was left of the Papal States to the Italian kingdom. The pope, Pius IX, refused to recognize the authority or the legitimacy of the kingdom of Italy over his former territories. Therefore, *Pio Nono*, as he's known in Italian, Pius IX, became *Pio* no-no—who became the prisoner of the Vatican, who shut himself up and said that good Catholics should not participate in politics.

It was not until Mussolini's Lateran Treaty of 1929 that peace was made with the Church. Part of this peace, though, was the return of secular jurisdiction, as well as ecclesiastical authority, of the person of the pope. The creation of the Vatican City, an independent state ruled by another priest-king, absolutely and theocratically, as the Vatican is ruled today. The great irony, of course, is that this is taking place as we speak in a world of the European union, in which the European union can be seen to be the re-creation of a new kind of secular empire. The world of the papacy of the Middle Ages and the Renaissance is still very much with us. The memories are long, and the practice remains tense to this very day.

Timeline

313 .... Edict of Milan: Constantine declares Christianity to be the official religion of the Roman Empire.

476 .... Deposition of the last Roman emperor.

552 .... The Byzantine exarchate established at Ravenna.

c. 750 .... The Donation of Constantine forged.

800 .... Charlemagne crowned as the first Holy Roman Emperor.

1016 .... Pisa and Genoa combined drive the Saracens from Sardinia.

1052 .... Genoa is organized as a self-governing commune.

1077 .... Pope Gregory VII humiliates Emperor Henry IV at Canossa; Pisa given authority over Corsica.

1095 .... Preaching of the First Crusade by Pope Urban II at Clermont.

1137 .... Pisa shatters its maritime rival, Amalfi.

1167 .... Siena establishes an independent communal government of nobles.

1190 .... Death of Frederick I Barbarossa, under whom the division between Guelf and Ghibelline was crystallized.

1195 .... Pisa officially organized as a free, self-governing commune.

1204	Europeans in the Fourth Crusade establish the Latin Empire at Constantinople.
1241	Pisa defeats the Genoese fleet.
1260	The Sienese defeat Florence at the Battle of Montaperti.
1264	Obizzo d'Este seizes control of Ferrara.
1266	Charles of Anjou establishes the French Angevin dynasty in Naples.
1282	The Sicilian Vespers: Sicily revolts against the crown of Naples and attaches itself to the royal House of Aragon.
1284	Genoa conclusively defeats Pisa at Meloria.
1287	Siena institutes a communal government called The Nine.
1293	Florentine Ordinances of Justice promulgated.
1297	Closing of the Great Council in Venice (*Serrata*).
1298	Genoa, under Admiral Doria, defeats the Venetians at sea at Curzola.
1309	Pope Clement V takes up permanent residence in Avignon: beginning of the Babylonian Captivity.
1311	The Peace of Constance, a treaty between the Holy Roman Emperor and the Lombard cities; the Visconti establish hereditary control of Milan as *signori*.

1315	Council of Ten established in Venice.
1327	Emperor Louis IV captures Pisa.
1328	Luigi Gonzaga seizes control of Mantua.
1339	Simon Boccanegra elected as the first doge of Genoa.
1343	Walter of Brienne expelled from Florence; the *Monte* is established.
1345	Bankruptcy of Bardi and Peruzzi banks.
1348	The Black Death appears in Italy, killing significant portions of the population.
1355	Beheading of Venetian doge Marin Falier for treason; fall of The Nine in Siena.
1371	Revolt of the Sienese woolworkers.
1377	The papacy returns to Rome from Avignon.
1378	The Great Schism begins; Ciompi revolt in Florence.
1380–1381	War of Chioggia; Venice defeats Genoa and begins a policy of expansion onto the mainland.
1382	Joanna I of Anjou dies without heirs, resulting in competing French and papal interests in the throne of Naples.
1385	Giangaleazzo Visconti consolidates power in Milan.
1402	Giangaleazzo Visconti, duke of Milan, dies, removing the threat to

Florence for control of all north-central Italy.

1405	Venice conquers Padua.
1406	Florence conquers Pisa.
1408	Creation of the Bank of St. George in Genoa.
1409	Council of Pisa.
1412	Galeazzo Maria Visconti murdered.
1414	Council of Constance: Pope Martin V elected to end the Great Schism.
1420	Martin V officially returns to Rome.
1425	*Monte delle doti* (state dower fund) established in Florence.
1434	Cosimo de'Medici returns from exile to take control of Florence.
1442	Naples falls to an Aragonese siege under Alfonso, king of Aragon and Sicily.
1444	Federigo da Montefeltro becomes the duke of Urbino.
1447	Francesco Sforza assumes control in Milan.
1453	Fall of Constantinople to the Turks.
1454	The Peace of Lodi.
1455	The formation of the Italian League by Francesco Sforza and Cosimo de'Medici.
1474	Ercole I of Ferrara marries Eleonora of Aragon, daughter of Alfonso the Magnanimous.
1475	Fall of Caffa to the Turks.

1478	Pazzi conspiracy: death of Giuliano de'Medici.
1479	The dynastic union of Spain under Ferdinand of Aragon and Isabella of Castile.
1480	Turks capture the Italian city of Otranto, holding it for a year.
1488	Guidobaldo da Montefeltro of Urbino marries Elisabetta Gonzaga of Mantua.
1490	Francesco il Gonzago of Mantua marries Isabella d'Este.
1491	Lodovico il Moro of Milan marries Beatrice d'Este.
1494	Charles VIII of France invades Italy; the Medici are driven from Florence.
1495	Savonarola's constitution proclaimed in Florence; Charles VIII captures Naples.
1495	Creation of the League of Venice.
1496	Restoration of the Aragonese dynasty in Naples under Frederick III.
1497–1498	Vasco da Gama circumnavigates the Cape of Good Hope.
1498	Savonarola is executed.
1499	France, under Louis XII, captures Milan.
1500	Pandolfo Petrucci consolidates his power as Il Magnifico, tyrant of Siena.
1503	Naples is placed under a Spanish viceroy.

1505	The Treaty of Blois establishes Spanish sovereignty in Naples.
1509	Florentines starve Pisa into submission; the League of Cambrai defeats Venice at Agnadello.
1511	The Holy League formed by Pope Julius II.
1512	The Medici resume power in Florence; France defeats the combined papal/Spanish powers at Ravenna.
1515	Francis I of France wins the Battle of Marignano.
1516	The Treaty of Noyon acknowledges French sovereignty over Milan; Charles V becomes king of Spain.
1517	Martin Luther initiates the Protestant revolts; Turks consolidate control of Persia, Syria, and Egypt.
1519	Charles V elected Holy Roman Emperor.
1521	Pope Leo X excommunicates Martin Luther; Sultan Selim I of Turkey captures Belgrade and Rhodes.
1522	The Spaniards sack Genoa.
1524	France captures Milan.
1525	Battle of Pavia: Francis I of France is imprisoned by the emperor's forces.
1527	Sack of Rome; Medici expelled from Florence.
1527	Habsburgs driven from Genoa by Andrea Doria.

1529	Charles V crowned Holy Roman Emperor at Bologna; Treaty of Cambrai, in which France renounces all claims to Italian territories.
1530	The end of the Florentine Republic.
1537	Cosimo I de'Medici (later, grand duke of Tuscany) assumes control in Florence.
1545	Council of Trent called by Paul III.
1552	Spaniards expelled from Siena.
1555	Siena capitulates to Florence.
1559	Treaty of Cateau-Cambrésis establishing the shape of the European state system under the victorious Habsburgs.
1565	Siege of Malta.
1569	Cosimo I elevated as grand duke of Tuscany.
1570	Ottoman conquest of Cyprus.
1571	Christians defeat the Turks at the Battle of Lepanto, halting Turkish expansion in the west.

Popes Following the Great Schism

Papal Name	Baptismal Name
Martin V (1417–1431)	Oddone Colonna
Eugene IV (1431–1447)	Gabriello Condulmaro
Nicholas V (1447–1455)	Tommaso Parentucelli
Calixtus III (1455–1458)	Alfonso de Borgia
Pius II (1458–1464)	Enea Silvio de Piccolimini
Paul II (1464–1471)	Pietro Barbo
Sixtus IV (1471–1484)	Francesco della Rovere
Innocent VIII (1484–1492)	Giovanni Battista Cibò
Alexander VI (1492–1503)	Rodrigo Borgia
Pius III (1503)	Francesco Todeschini Piccolomini
Julius II (1503–1513)	Giuliano della Rovere
Leo X (1513–1521)	Giovanni de'Medici
Adrian VI (1522–1523)	Adrian Dedel
Clement VII (1523–1534)	Giulio de'Medici
Paul III (1534–1549)	Alessandro Farnese
Julius III (1550–1555)	Giammaria Ciocchi del Monte

Holy Roman Emperors from 1046 to 1576

Emperor	Dynasty
Henry IV (1046–1056)	Salian (Frankish)
Henry V (1111–1125)	Salian (Frankish)
Lothair III (1133–1137)	Supplinburger
Frederick I Barbarossa (1155–1190)	Hohenstaufen (Staufen)
Henry VI (1191–1197)	Hohenstaufen (Staufen)
Otto IV of Brunswick (1209–1215)	House of Welf
Frederick II (1220–1250)	Hohenstaufen (Staufen)
Henry VII (1312–1313)	House of Luxembourg
Louis IV the Bavarian (1328–1347)	House of Wittelsbach

Emperor	Dynasty
Charles IV (1355–1378)	House of Luxembourg
Sigismund (1410–1437)	House of Luxembourg
Frederick III (1452–1493)	House of Habsburg
Maximilian I (1508–1519) (emperor-elect)	House of Habsburg
Charles V (1530–1556) (emperor-elect, 1519–1530)	House of Habsburg
Ferdinand I (1556–1564) (emperor-elect)	House of Habsburg
Maximilian II (1564–1576) (emperor-elect)	House of Habsburg

Glossary

accoppiatori: The committee charged with determining which citizens were eligible for election to public office in Florence.

Arsenal, the: The state-controlled munitions and shipbuilding factory in Venice.

Babylonian Captivity (1305–1377): The residence of the popes in Avignon.

botteghe: The workshops of artisans and artists.

Byzantine exarchate: A province of the Byzantine emperor.

campanilismo: The belief that all that matters is the territory from which the bell tower—*campanile*—of one's local church is visible.

cantucci: Tuscan almond biscotti or biscuits.

capitano del popolo: The official head of the common people in Italian cities.

certosa: Literally, in Italian, "charterhouse," a Carthusian monastery.

ciambello: A sweet, cake-like bread traditionally made at festivals.

città marinara: Literally "a maritime city" in Italian.

cittadini originari: Wealthy, influential citizens who did not qualify for admission to the Great Council of Venice after the Serrata of 1297 but who still enjoyed certain legal privileges and whose genealogies were maintained in the Silver Book.

commenda: A mercantile contract lasting for just one voyage in which the risk and profits of the voyage are shared among several investors.

conciliarism: The principle that general church councils were superior to popes and exercised authority over them.

condottiere: A mercenary captain.

Council of Ten: A powerful committee of 10 men established in 1315 with responsibility for state security in Venice.

Council of Trent (1545–1563): Called by Pope Paul III Farnese to address the reform of the church in the face of the Protestant Reformation.

Donation of Constantine: A forged document in which Constantine, the first Christian emperor, purported to give the rule of the Western empire to the papacy in 337.

Edict of Milan (313): Constantine's recognition of Christianity as the official religion of the Roman Empire.

episcopal see: The territory and authority of a bishop.

gattopardismo: A term from Giuseppi di Lampadusa's novel *The Leopard* (in Italian, *Il Gattopardo*), which states that for everything to remain the same, everything must seem to change.

Ghibelline: A supporter of the authority of the Holy Roman Emperor.

Golden Book: The official genealogy of the Venetian nobility.

grandi: Old mercantile families who adopted the traditions of the feudal nobility.

Great Schism (1378–1417): The period of the divided papacy, during which there were two, and after 1409, three competing popes.

Guelf: A supporter of papal power.

Holy See: The jurisdiction of the pope as bishop of Rome.

latifundia: The vast agricultural estates held by landlords.

monte **(plural: *monti*)**: The name given to the parties or factions instituted in Siena in the second half of the 14th century.

Monte, **the**: The single fund into which the public debt of Florence was consolidated after 1343.

parlamento: A gathering of the adult male heads of households called to decide constitutional questions.

Peace of Lodi (1454): This treaty recognized the spheres of influence of the five great states of Italy—Venice, Milan, Florence, the papacy, and Naples.

plenitudo potestatis: Literally, in Latin, "the fullness of power," referring to the absolute authority of the pope to determine both political and theological policy.

podestà: A military leader, usually a foreigner, hired to oversee the military security of a state.

Regno: Italian for "kingdom"; usually refers to the Kingdom of Naples.

Risorgimento: Literally, in Italian, a "resurgence"; the Italian unification movement in the 19th century.

Rota: The highest canon law judicial body in Rome.

scuole: Religious confraternities in Venice.

Serrata: Closure of the Great Council in Venice in 1297.

signori: In Italian, "lords"; territorial rulers who exercised authority in a state.

terraferma: The portion of the Venetian Republic on the Italian mainland.

trulli: Curious rounded habitations indigenous to Puglia, made out of whitewashed limestone and topped with cone-shaped, grey stone roofs.

Veneto: The modern region of Italy with its capital at Venice.

Via Francigena: The overland route taken by pilgrims and merchants in the Middle Ages from France to Rome.

vin santo: A sweet, fortified Tuscan wine reminiscent of sherry.

Biographical Notes

Frederick II, Barbarossa (1194–1250). Frederick of Hohenstaufen was born in Sicily, the son of the Holy Roman Emperor Henry VI and Constance, daughter of King Roger of Sicily and queen of Sicily in her own right. Frederick was crowned king in 1198; his mother acted as his regent first, followed by the pope. Frederick's claims to the imperial throne were contested by the German princes, but after military victory, he was crowned king of the Romans by the pope in 1215 and, in 1220 in Rome, Holy Roman Emperor. Most of his life was spent in Italy or on crusade, because he had married the heiress of the Latin Kingdom of Jerusalem. Frederick negotiated his claims to rule with the Muslims in control of the city, resulting in his coronation as king of Jerusalem in 1229.

In Italy, the Lombard League, led by one of Frederick's sons, revolted against imperial authority but was defeated by Frederick in 1237; he then made another son, Conrad, king of Jerusalem, his heir. He continued his war against the cities of Lombardy, further angering an already exasperated pope. Pope Gregory IX excommunicated the emperor, driving him to attack the Papal States and set his sights on Rome. The war between the imperial (Ghibelline) power of Frederick and the papal (Guelf) power of Gregory continued after the pope's death. Gregory's successor, Innocent IV, although initially less hostile to Frederick, soon renewed the war, excommunicating him once more and declaring him deposed as Holy Roman Emperor in 1245. Frederick's position in Italy, however, remained strong until he was defeated at Parma in 1248 by the Guelf faction, and his camp was taken. Later, his son Enzo was captured by the Bolognese and locked in prison for the rest of his life. Still, the Ghibellines were able to recapture much lost territory and Frederick was able to return to southern Italy, where he died in 1250, leaving as his heirs Conrad, Holy Roman Emperor and king of Sicily, and Manfred, prince of Taranto.

Charles of Anjou (1227–1285; king of Sicily, 1262–1282; and king of Naples, 1282–1285). Charles was born the posthumous son of King Louis VIII of France. After an adventurous youth as a Crusader, he was offered the throne of Sicily by Pope Urban IV as a consequence of the usurpation of that dignity by Manfred of Sicily in

1258, whose Hohenstaufen dynasty threatened the authority of the papacy in Italy. King Manfred invaded the papal dominions, forcing the pope to flee; Charles arrived in Rome in 1265 and was crowned king of Sicily in 1266. Manfred, in the interim, was losing the initiative in his war against the Church. At Benevento, Charles defeated and killed him, thereby becoming undisputed king of Sicily. Conradin, the young Hohenstaufen king earlier deposed by Manfred, collected another imperial army and marched south. He was defeated by Charles, captured, and beheaded in Naples (1268).

Charles's policies in Naples and his foreign ambitions galvanized the Ghibelline opposition, which identified Peter of Aragon as its champion. Peter had a claim to Naples through his marriage to Manfred's daughter and the Hohenstaufen heiress, Constance. The result was the Revolt of the Sicilian Vespers, which broke out in Palermo but soon spread across the island. The French were massacred, and Charles fled to Calabria. Peter of Aragon landed in Sicily and was proclaimed king, beginning the Aragonese dynasty. The French king and the pope continued to support Charles, and Charles's intent was the reconquest of Naples; however, in 1285, he died without restoring the Angevins to Sicily.

Andrea Doria (1468–1560). Born into a noble Genoese family, Andrea Doria lived the life of a soldier of fortune in his youth as a consequence of his father's early death. He served in the papal guards, then joined the armies of Naples before entering the order of the Knights of St. John of Jerusalem. Having committed himself to the French cause in Italy, he was able to return to Genoa, which was under French control at the time. His military and naval skills recommended him to the Genoese, who commissioned him to lead their navy. In addition, he used his personal wealth to acquire galleys for a private fleet, which he used effectively to subdue the Muslim pirates in the Mediterranean.

The internal discord in Genoa resulted in Doria's crews recognizing his leadership rather than obeying the unstable republic; consequently, he took his galleys and entered the service of Francis I of France as an admiral. It was Doria who rescued the survivors of the French army after its defeat at Pavia (1525). Nevertheless, in 1528, Francis I reneged on his agreement to pay Doria for his service, driving him to switch allegiance to the emperor Charles V. With imperial support, he reentered Genoa, abolished the ancient republic, and established an aristocratic republic, in which the nobles ruled without the plebeians. Charles V rewarded Doria further by appointing him grand admiral of the imperial fleets, an office he used effectively against the Turks. Near the end of his life, he retired to his palace, dying in Genoa in 1560.

Ercole I d'Este (1431–1505, r.1471–1505). The son of Niccolo III d'Este of Ferrara, Ercole enjoyed an excellent Humanist education at the court of Alfonso the Magnanimous of Naples. He would later marry Alfonso's granddaughter, Eleonora. With his brother Borso's death in 1471, Ercole became duke and began his celebrated patronage of music, literature, and building. His interest in music, particularly the new Netherlandish style, made him one of Italy's most important patrons, and his support of Boiardo and Ariosto resulted in the establishment of the Italian epic tradition for which Ferrara is justly renowned. Ercole died in 1505 and was succeeded by his son, Alfonso.

Isabella d'Este (1474–1539). Born in 1474 to the duke of Ferrara, Ercole I, and his wife, Eleanora of Aragon, Isabella d'Este and her sister, Beatrice, were raised in the court culture of Ferrara, surrounded by poets, painters, and intellectuals. They each received a Humanist education, uncommon for women of the period, and Isabella was known to be a talented dancer, singer, and musician, who also excelled at hunting and riding. In 1490, Isabella married solider and marquess Francesco Gonzaga (1466–1519) at the age of 16. As marchioness, she had a great impact both on court life and in the political sphere. She was an avid reader and collector of art, books, tapestries, and antiquities. She was a patron of Leonardo da' Vinci, Titian, and Perugino and brought to Mantua great intellectuals of the period, including Pietro Bembo and Castiglione. Isabella was also a skilled ruler and gained a reputation for justice, diplomacy, and tenacity when governing Mantua for her husband during his absences on military campaigns, when he was briefly imprisoned in Venice, and again after his death.

Ferdinand of Aragon and Naples (1452–1516). With the marriage of Ferdinand, king of Sicily (1468–1516), Castile and Leon (1474–1504), Aragon (1479–1516), and Naples (1504–1516), to Isabella of Castile in 1469, Spain was united. Their rule focused on strengthening royal authority and curbing noble power. Because of their efforts to maintain the purity of the Christian faith (through the establishment of the Inquisition in 1478 and the expulsion of the Jews in 1492), they were given the title of "Catholic monarchs" by Pope Alexander VI in 1494. From 1479 to 1516, Ferdinand was involved on some level in almost every international conflict and negotiation, including a struggle with France for control of Italy during the Italian Wars (1494–1559).

Lodovico III Gonzaga (1412–1478, r. 1444–1478). Lodovico was the son of Marquis Gianfrancesco Gonzaga of Mantua and inherited the title in 1444. He sustained the imperial allegiance of the city by marrying the niece of the emperor. His skills as a *condottiere* prince and the reputation of his mercenary army were such that he fought for the dukes of Milan, the Republic of Venice, and the king of Naples. The Peace of Lodi (1454) not only ended many of Lodovico's commissions as *condottiere* but required him to yield some of the territory he had incorporated into his state. After 1466, however, he recovered his influence by enjoying almost continuous employment by the dukes of Milan.

Despite his military calling, Lodovico was a great patron of culture. Andrea Mantegna was his court painter, and the family of the marquis has been lovingly represented in the *Camera degli Sposi* (*Camera Picta*) of Mantegna in the ducal palace. Lodovico also patronized the great Florentine architect and theorist Leon Battista Alberti, whose church of Sant'Andrea was built at the marquis' request to house the relic of the sacred blood of Christ collected by St. Longinus.

Lodovico died in 1478 and was succeeded by his son Federigo I (d. 1484) as marquis of Mantua.

Joanna I of Naples (1328–1382, r. 1343–1382). The daughter of Charles of Calabria of the Neapolitan House of Anjou, Joanna was married as a child to her cousin Andrew, a prince of the Hungarian branch of the Angevins. The intent of King Robert of Naples, Joanna's grandfather, was that on his death, the crown of Naples should be shared between Andrew and Joanna. With the support of the pope, whose fief Naples was, Joanna resisted, and in 1344, she was crowned as sole ruler in Rome; the following year, Joanna had her husband killed.

Joanna then married Louis of Taranto, who ruled jointly with her from 1353 until his death in 1362 and with whom she repelled an invasion from Louis of Hungary, who wished to restore his branch of the family's claims to Naples and avenge the murder of Andrew. Despite another marriage after Louis of Taranto's death, Joanna had no living direct heirs. She supported the papacy in Avignon during the Great Schism and adopted as her heir Louis of Anjou. However, the Roman pope, Urban VI, was unwilling to see a French king on his southern frontier; thus, he declared Joanna deposed and granted the crown to Charles of Durazzo, her nephew by marriage, whose claim was equally supported by the Hungarian Angevins, Joanna's enemies. Charles captured Naples and Joanna in 1381 and ordered the queen to be strangled with a silken cord in 1382.

Joanna II of Naples (1371–1435, r. 1414–1435). The daughter of Charles III, Joanna II succeeded to the throne in 1414. She was known for her dissolute life, which was reflected in her assuming, as a widow of 45, a 26-year-old lover, to whom she granted considerable authority. Pressured by the feudal baronage of Naples to remarry after her accession as a means of controlling her favorite, Joanna chose James de Bourbon, a relation of the king of France. Against Joanna's wishes, he had himself declared king and ordered the murder of his wife's lover and her imprisonment. But his own insensitivity to the Neapolitan feudatories and his highhanded actions prompted the nobles and people to revolt, driving James from his throne and Naples in 1418.

Joanna chose another lover, Giovanni Caracciolo, whose influence proved equally disastrous. He advised her not to agree to the requests from Pope Martin V—the feudal overlord of Naples—for money and soldiers. Martin declared Joanna deposed and offered the crown to Louis of Anjou. When Louis invaded the *regno*, Joanna countered by inviting the help of King Alfonso V of Aragon, whom she would adopt as her heir. In 1421, Alfonso entered Naples, but he ordered the imprisonment of the queen's favorite, Caracciolo, and Alfonso moved against Joanna herself, intent on taking the crown before her death. Joanna and Caracciolo escaped and sought refuge with Louis of Anjou. Joanna reversed her offer to Alfonso and adopted her former enemy, Louis, as her heir.

Alfonso left Naples to return to Aragon, and Louis and Joanna, supported by the Genoese, were able to recapture Naples from the

Aragonese in 1424. Chaos returned when another revolt broke out in 1432 after Caracciolo broke with Joanna, only to be murdered, an event that gave rise to general unrest. Louis of Anjou died while fighting the rebels in 1434, and Joanna adopted his son, Rene of Anjou, as her heir. Joanna II died in 1435.

Cosimo de'Medici, il Vecchio (1389–1464). Cosimo, the son of the wealthiest banker in Italy, Giovanni di Averrado de' Medici, was a follower of Humanism, a patron of the arts, and the founder of the Platonic Academy in Florence. He used his wealth to commission works by such artists as Lorenzo Ghiberti and Benozzo Gozzoli; to subsidize the search for Classical texts by Humanists; to rebuild San Lorenzo and the convent of the Badia at Fiesole; and to construct the Palazzo Medici. His political contributions are equally impressive. By 1433, the Medici were the most prominent and influential family in Florence. As a result, they had many opponents, including the Albizzi and Peruzzi families, who collaborated to run Cosimo out of town. In 1434, Cosimo returned to Florence with the help of the Popular Party and effectively "ruled" Florence until his death in 1464. Although never officially elected into Florentine government, Cosimo used his connections to ensure the promotion of his policies and the election of his supporters. In 1454, Cosimo helped to negotiate the Peace of Lodi with Milan, which established a balance of power in Italy.

Lorenzo "il Magnifico" de'Medici (1449–1492). Son of Piero de'Medici and grandson of Cosimo, Lorenzo took control of Florence at the age of 20 following his father's death. He was an active member of the Platonic Academy, a patron of the arts, and a beloved citizen of Florence. He was trained in the Humanist tradition and surrounded by the leading intellectuals and artists of the day, including Pico della Mirandola, Angelo Poliziano, Marsilio Ficino, Michelangelo, and Botticelli. Politically, he was very astute and successfully strengthened and held together the republic during his rule (1469–1492). In 1478, he survived an attempt on his life by his detractors, the Pazzi family, in a plot that involved Pope Sixtus IV. This incident sparked a war between Naples and the papacy, which was ended through Lorenzo's efforts.

Piero de'Medici (Il Sfortunato) (1471–1503). The eldest son of Lorenzo the Magnificent, Piero de' Medici ("the Unfortunate") succeeded his father in 1492 as ruler of Florence but lacked his father's diplomacy and ability to rule effectively. During the French invasion of 1494, the Medici were expelled from Florence by their fellow citizens. All of Piero's attempts to regain his position in Florence failed, and he drowned while serving in the French army at the Battle of Garigliano.

Guidobaldo da Montefeltro (1472–1508). Guidobaldo was the son of Federigo da Montefeltro and Battista Sforza, duke and duchess of Urbino. He followed his father to become duke in 1482, serving until his death in 1508. Like his parents, Guidobaldo and his wife, Elisabetta Gonzaga, supported the arts and culture of Urbino. The unique court culture established there attracted young men from all over Europe and encouraged the participation of women. The great painter Raphael was raised in the court culture of Urbino during Guidolbaldo's reign, and Baldassare Castiglione served under him. Castiglione's *The Book of the Courtier* is set in Urbino and relates a discussion among members of Italy's leading families at the palace of Guidobaldo and Elisabetta. Guidobaldo is the absent character in this work, confined to bed, with Elisabetta acting as host.

Pandolfo Petrucci (1425–1512). Born into a noble Sienese family, Petrucci suffered exile with his faction, the *noveschi*, until they were triumphantly returned in 1487. He married the daughter of the powerful and rich noble Niccolo Borghese, and Pandolfo benefited from his influential brother's offices on the latter's death in 1497. By this time, he was, in effect, master of Siena, using his power to reward his supporters and punish any dissidents, including his father-in-law, whom he had murdered. His clever foreign policy managed to keep Siena away from the ambitions of Cesare Borgia and the Florentines, although at some cost to Sienese territorial claims. Near the end of his life, Petrucci retired to the small town of San Quirico, leaving the rule of Siena to his sons. It was there he died in 1512.

Francesco Sforza (1401–1466). As a *condottiere* employed by the duke of Milan, Francesco Sforza led a number of successful campaigns on Rome. Hoping to retain some of these captured lands for himself, he attempted to persuade Duke Filippo Maria Visconti to provide him with an independent principality in Lombardy as a dowry for marrying his daughter. The duke refused and Sforza turned against him, joining the Florentine and Venetian alliance. When the duke died in 1447, Sforza set in motion his plan to seize power. After defeating the Venetian army at Caravaggio, he conquered Milan in 1450, taking the title of duke. He persuaded Cosimo de'Medici to withdraw from the Venetian alliance to form a new Milanese-Florentine alliance, a move that brought the wars to an end with the signing of the Peace of Lodi in 1454.

Lodovico "il Moro" Sforza (1451/52–1508). Known as "il Moro" for his swarthy complexion, Ludovico Sforza, son of Francesco, served as the duke of Milan from 1494–1499. To protect Milan, he entered into an alliance with Charles VIII before the 1494 invasion of Italy but, by 1495, had turned against the French. He was expelled from Milan in 1499 by Louis XII, who had a hereditary claim to the duchy. Overall, Ludovico was not a particularly competent ruler, showing much more interest in the social and cultural pursuits of his court. During his short marriage to Beatrice d'Este (who died in childbirth in 1497), the Milanese court flourished with the arrival of Leonardo da Vinci as military engineer and court painter.

Giangaleazzo Visconti (d.1402). After murdering his uncle Bernabo, Visconti seized power in Milan in 1385 and, 10 years later, was recognized as duke by the emperor. During his reign, Visconti united the territories of Milan, supported the armament and silk industries, built hospitals and the Milan cathedral, and tried to enrich the culture of his city. He also led numerous campaigns to expand his territories and purchased or conquered cities around Milan, such as Pisa. Successfully taking over much of Lombardy, he set his sights on Umbria and Tuscany, including Florence, the only city that refused to surrender to Visconti. With his sudden death in 1402, Florence was saved and his efforts to carve out a northern Italian kingdom were dissolved; however, Italy was sent into chaos as struggles to regain conquered territories developed.

Bibliography

Asbridge, T. *The First Crusade: A New History: The Roots of Conflict Between Christianity and Islam.* Oxford: Oxford University Press, 2005. An excellent new analysis of the First Crusade and its implications.

Aston, Margaret, ed. *The Panorama of the Renaissance: The Renaissance in the Perspective of History.* New York: Harry N. Abrams, 1996. A beautifully illustrated, comprehensive survey of Renaissance Europe.

Atiya, Aziz S. *Crusade, Commerce and Culture.* Bloomington: Indiana University Press, 1962. A discussion of the interrelation between the Crusades and commercial and cultural contact with non-Christian communities around the Mediterranean.

Bartlett, Kenneth R. *The Civilization of the Italian Renaissance.* Sources in Modern History. Lexington, MA: D.C. Heath, 1992. A collection of primary-source readings with introductions discussing many aspects of Italian Renaissance civilization.

Barzini, Luigi. *The Italians.* New York: Touchstone, 1996. A wonderful, insightful, and ironic assessment of Italian history and character.

Becker, Marvin B. *Medieval Italy: Constraints and Creativity.* Bloomington: Indiana University Press, 1981. A history of Italy in the Middle Ages looking at the conditions that permitted the development of the Renaissance.

Bellonci, M. *A Prince of Mantua: The Life and Times of Vincenzo Gonzaga.* Translated by Stuart Hood. New York: Harcourt Brace, 1956. A popular biography by a gifted Italian writer.

Bentley, Jerry H. *Politics and Culture in Renaissance Naples.* Princeton, NJ: Princeton University Press, 1987. The best modern study of culture and politics in the kingdom around the time of Alfonso the Magnanimous.

Bertelli, Sergio. *Italian Renaissance Courts.* London: Sidgwick and Jackson, 1986. An illustrated survey of the court culture of the Italian Renaissance.

Black, Chris F., et al. *Cultural Atlas of the Renaissance.* New York: Prentice Hall, 1993. A comprehensive survey of major centers in the

European Renaissance from the point of view of their cultural achievement.

Bloomquist, T., and M. Mazzaoui. *The Other Tuscany: Essays in the History of Lucca, Pisa and Siena During the Thirteenth, Fourteenth and Fifteenth Centuries*. Michigan: Medieval Institute Publications, 1994. A collection of essays on the city-states of Tuscany, excluding Florence.

Blumenthal, U. *The Investiture Controversy*. Philadelphia: University of Pennsylvania Press, 1991. A comprehensive overview of the causes of the struggle between empire and papacy.

Boorstin, Daniel. J. *The Discoverers: A History of Man's Search to Know His World and Himself*. New York: Random House, 1983. An investigation of how new knowledge drives cultural and intellectual innovation.

Bowsky, William. *The Finance of the Commune of Siena, 1287–1355*. Oxford: Oxford University Press, 1970. A somewhat specialized study of how the mercantile government of The Nine addressed the problems of public finance.

———. *A Medieval Italian Commune: Siena under the Nine, 1287–1355*. Berkeley: University of California Press, 1981. Still the best study of the complex history of Siena during its most successful years.

Bradford, Ernle. *The Great Siege: Malta, 1565*. Hertfordshire, UK: Wordsworth Military Library, 1999. A gripping and well-researched popular narrative of the great siege of Malta by the Turks.

Brown, Alison. *The Medici in Florence: The Exercise and Language of Power*. Florence: Olschki, 1992. A study of the various instruments the Medici used to maintain their grip on power.

Brown, Patricia Fortini. *Art and Life in Renaissance Venice*. Princeton, NJ: Princeton University Press, 1998. A study of the relationship between art and society in the Republic of Venice during the period of the Renaissance.

Brucker, Gene A. *Renaissance Florence*. Berkeley: University of California Press, 1983. Still the best short, comprehensive survey of Florentine history during the period of the Renaissance.

Burckhardt, Jacob. *The Civilization of the Renaissance in Italy*. Vol. I: *The State as a Work of Art, The Development of the Individual,*

The Revival of Antiquity. New York: Harper & Row Publishers, 1975. See below.

————. *The Civilization of the Renaissance in Italy*. Vol. II: *The Discovery of the World and of Man, Society and Festivals, Morality and Religion*. New York: Harper & Row Publishers, 1975. Together, these two volumes are the foundation of Renaissance studies. First printed in 1860, they introduced the model of cultural history in the study of Renaissance Italy.

Burke, Peter. *The Italian Renaissance: Culture and Society in Italy*. Princeton, NJ: Princeton University Press, 1986. A dynamic survey of the relationship between Italian Renaissance culture and the society that produced it.

Chamberlin, E. R. *The Count of Virtue: Giangaleazzo Visconti*. London: Eyre and Spottiswoode, 1965. A popular biography of the first duke of Milan.

Chambers, D. S. *The Imperial Age of Venice, 1380–1580*. London: Thames and Hudson, 1970. An excellent illustrated survey of Venetian politics, society, and culture during the Renaissance.

Cochrane, Eric, ed. *The Late Italian Renaissance, 1525–1630*. J. R. Hale, general ed. London: Macmillan and Co., 1970. A comprehensive collection of essays studying various aspects of late Renaissance Italy.

————. *Historians and Historiography in the Italian Renaissance*. Chicago: University of Chicago Press, 1981. An invaluable survey of historical writing during the Italian Renaissance.

Cole, Alison. *Virtue and Magnificence: Art of the Italian Renaissance Courts*. New York: Harry N. Abrams, 1995. A series of studies of Italian court patronage during the Renaissance—beautifully illustrated.

Courtright, N. *The Papacy and the Art of Reform*. Cambridge: Cambridge University Press, 2003. A study of Gregory XIII's political, religious, artistic, and calendar reforms by investigating the decorative program of the Tower of the Four Winds in the Vatican.

Croce, Benedetto. *A History of the Kingdom of Naples*. Chicago: University of Chicago Press, 1970. A short and accessible guide to the history of the kingdom by one of Italy's most famous historians.

Dennistoun, James. *Memoirs of the Dukes of Urbino*. New York: John Lane Company, 1909. A modern English translation of Della Casa's celebrated 16th-century treatise on manners.

Epstein, Steven A. *Genoa and the Genoese, 958–1528.* Chapel Hill, NC: University of North Carolina Press, 2001. The best general survey available of Genoese history from the Middle Ages through the Renaissance.

Finlay, Robert. *Politics in Renaissance Venice*. New Brunswick, NJ: Rutgers University Press, 1980. An excellent study of the complexities of political life in the Renaissance republic.

Finley, M. I., et al. *A History of Sicily*. New York: Viking, 1987. A short but excellent treatment of the complex history of the island.

——— and Denis Mack Smith. *The History of Sicily*. New York: Viking, 1987. A comprehensive but condensed study of the complex history of Sicily written by masters of Italian historical research.

Fleet, Kate. *Europe and Islamic Trade in the Early Ottoman State: The Merchants of Genoa and Turkey*. Cambridge: Cambridge University Press, 1999. Written from both Turkish and Italian sources, this book illustrates how the Turks took advantage of economic policy as well as military power in the expansion of the Ottoman Empire.

Gardner, Edmund G. *Dukes and Poets in Ferrara: A Study in Poetry, Religion and Politics of the Fifteenth and Sixteenth Centuries*. London: Constable, 1904. An old but nevertheless important study of the Este court; available in reprint.

Goldthwaite, Richard A. *The Building of Renaissance Florence: An Economic and Social History*. Baltimore: Johns Hopkins University Press, 1980. A study of palace construction in Florence during the period of the Renaissance.

———. *Wealth and the Demand for Art in Italy, 1300–1600*. Baltimore: John Hopkins University Press, 1993. An economic investigation of art as a commodity in the Italian Renaissance.

Gundersheimer, Werner L. *Ferrara: The Style of a Renaissance Despotism*. Princeton, NJ: Princeton University Press, 1973. A thorough analysis of the rule of the Este family in Ferrara.

Hale, J. R. *Florence and the Medici: The Pattern of Control*. New York: Thames and Hudson, 1977. A nicely illustrated, accessible history of the Medici family in the context of their control of the city of Florence.

Hanlon, Gregory. *Early Modern Italy, 1550–1800*. London: Macmillan, 2000. An excellent, broad survey of Italian history from the late Renaissance until the time of Napoleon.

Hay, Denys, and John Law. *Italy in the Age of the Renaissance, 1380–1530*. Longman History of Italy. Essex: Longman Group UK Limited, 1989. A broad survey of peninsular history throughout the entire sweep of the Renaissance.

Heywood, William. *A History of Pisa in the Eleventh and Twelfth Centuries*. Cambridge: Cambridge University Press, 1921. Now dated but still useful as a history of the commune during its formative years.

Hibbert, Christopher. *The House of Medici: Its Rise and Fall*. New York: HarperCollins, 1982. A popular discussion of the Medici family.

Hook, Judith. *Lorenzo de'Medici: An Historical Biography*. London: Hamish Hamilton, 1984. The best modern biography of Lorenzo, il Magnifico.

———. *Siena: A City and Its History*. London: Hamish Hamilton, 1979. An excellent, accessible introduction to the city's history.

Kent, Dale. *The Rise of the Medici: Faction in Florence, 1426–1434*. Oxford: Oxford University Press, 1978. A specialist analysis of how Cosimo de'Medici and his faction achieved power in Florence in 1434.

Kirk, Thomas Allison. *Genoa and the Sea: Policy and Power in an Early Modern Maritime Republic, 1559–1684*. Baltimore: Johns Hopkins University Press, 2005. A scholarly and detailed analysis of the Genoese century.

Konstan, A., and T. Bryan. *Lepanto, 1571: The Greatest Naval Battle of the Renaissance*. London: Osprey, 2003. A short history of the sea battle in which the Turkish advance was finally stopped.

Lampedusa, Giuseppe di. *The Leopard*. Translated by Archibald Colquhoun. Pantheon Modern Classics. New York: Wm. Collins Sons and Random House, 1960. A great Italian novel of the Risorgimento, written with sensitivity and insight about the nature of southern Italian society, history, and life.

Lane, Frederic. *Andrea Barbarigo, Merchant of Venice, 1418–1449*. New Haven: Yale University Press, 1976. A study of one Venetian merchant's career as a reflection of the interpenetration of politics and mercantile activity.

Larner, John. *Italy in the Age of Dante and Petrarch, 1216–1380*. Vol. 2. New York: Longman Group Limited, 1980. Perhaps the best survey available of late medieval and early Renaissance Italy.

————. *The Lords of Romagna: Romagnol Society and the Origins of the Signorie*. Ithaca, NY: Cornell University Press, 1965. A study of the petty despotisms of the province of the Romagna and the Papal States during the late Middle Ages and early Renaissance.

Lopez, Robert S., and Irving W. Raymond, trans. *Medieval Trade in the Mediterranean World*. New York: Columbia University Press, 1990. An economic history of long-distance trade in the Mediterranean.

Lubkin, Gregory. *A Renaissance Court: Milan under Galeazzo Maria Sforza*. Berkeley: University of California Press, 1994. A detailed, comprehensive study of the court of Milan during the short rule of one of its less attractive dukes.

Machiavelli, Niccolo. *The Prince*. Translated and edited by Robert M. Adams. New York: Norton, 1977. The celebrated short text that has engaged political thinkers from the time of its first printing in 1532.

Mallett, Michael. *The Borgias: The Rise and Fall of a Renaissance Dynasty*. Chicago: Academy Chicago Publishers, 1987. A popular history of this infamous family, elegantly written by an excellent professional historian.

Martines, Lauro. *April Blood: Florence and the Plot Against the Medici*. Oxford: Oxford University Press, 2003. A compelling relation of the Pazzi conspiracy of 1478 that resulted in the death of Giuliano de'Medici.

————. *Power and Imagination: City-States in Renaissance Italy*. New York: Alfred A. Knopf, 1979. A survey of the states of Italy during the Renaissance.

Mollat, Guillaume. *The Popes at Avignon, 1305–1378*. London, Thomas Nelson & Sons, 1963. Still the standard history of the Babylonian Captivity.

©2007 The Teaching Company.

Najemy, John M. *Corporatism and Consensus in Florentine Electoral Politics, 1280–1400*. Chapel Hill, NC: University of North Carolina Press, 1982. A specialist's study of guild and factional interaction during the early years of the Florentine Republic.

Norwich, John Julius. *A History of Venice*. New York: Alfred A. Knopf, 1982. A wonderful survey of Venice from its beginning until the end of the republic.

———, ed. *The Italian World*. London: Thames and Hudson, 1983. A beautifully illustrated history of Italy through its art and society.

O'Malley, J.W. *The First Jesuits*. Cambridge: Harvard University Press, 1993. A history of the Society of Jesus (Jesuits) from its foundation by St. Ignatius in 1540 until 1565, written by a member of the order.

Origo, Iris. *The Merchant of Prato*. Harmondsworth, Middlesex: Penguin Books, 1963. An engaging, detailed, popular narrative of the life of a 14th-century Tuscan merchant derived from his own correspondence.

Partner, Peter. *Renaissance Rome, 1500–1559: A Portrait of a Society*. Berkeley: University of California Press, 1976. The most accessible study of the city and the papacy in the first half of the 16th century.

Partridge, Loren. *The Art of Renaissance Rome, 1400–1600*. New York: Harry N. Abrams, 1996. A beautifully illustrated and important study of the development of a distinctive Roman Renaissance culture.

Phillips, Mark. *The Memoirs of Marco Parenti: A Life in Medici Florence*. Princeton, NJ: Princeton University Press, 1987. A narrative of an individual patrician's life during the period of Piero and Lorenzo de'Medici.

Polizzotto, Lorenzo. *The Elect Nation: The Savonarolan Movement in Florence, 1494–1545*. Oxford: Clarendon Press, 1994. The best study of Savonarola and his influence in Florence and the continuation of his theocratic ideas in the city until their suppression by Cosimo I.

Portoghesi, Paolo. *Rome of the Renaissance*. London: Phaidon, 1972. A beautifully illustrated study of Renaissance architecture in Rome.

Prescott, O. *The Lords of Italy*. New York: Harper & Row, 1972. A popular but engaging study of medieval Italian rulers.

Queller, D. *The Fourth Crusade: The Conquest of Constantinople.* Philadelphia: University of Pennsylvania Press, 1999. Still the best discussion of the Latin conquest of Constantinople.

Ramsey, P., ed. *Rome in the Renaissance: The City and the Myth.* Binghamton, NY: Medieval Renaissance Texts and Studies, 1982. An excellent collection of essays about many aspects of Renaissance Rome.

Riley-Smith, J. *The Oxford Illustrated History of the Crusades.* Oxford: Oxford University Press, 2001. The best illustrated history of the Crusades in English.

Sapori, Armando. *The Italian Merchant in the Middle Ages.* Translated by Patricia Ann Kennen. New York: Norton, 1970. A necessary study by a leading Italian economic historian of mercantile activity in the medieval Mediterranean.

Simon, Kate. *A Renaissance Tapestry: The Gonzaga of Mantua.* New York: Harper & Row, 1988. An accessible survey of the Gonzaga rulers of Mantua during the Renaissance.

Stephens, J. N. *The Fall of the Florentine Republic, 1512–1530.* Oxford: Clarendon Press, 1983. A specialist study of Florence from the return of the Medici until the suppression of the last republic.

Stinger, Charles. L. *The Renaissance in Rome.* Bloomington: Indiana University Press, 1998. The best comprehensive survey of Rome during the Renaissance.

Tabacco, Giovanni. *The Struggle for Power in Medieval Italy: Structures of Political Rule.* Cambridge: Cambridge University Press, 1989. Still a central analysis of medieval Italy, written by a leading Italian historian.

Trease. G. *The Condottieri: Soldiers of Fortune in Italy's History.* New York: Holt, Rinehart & Winston, 1971. A rich and interesting popular history of Italian mercenary captains.

Tuohy, Thomas. *Herculean Ferrara: Ercole d'Este, 1471–1505, and the Invention of a Ducal Capital.* Cambridge: Cambridge University Press, 1996. A study of the extensive civic patronage of Ercole d'Este in Ferrara from archival sources (the earthquake of 1570 destroyed most of his construction).

Vespansiano da Bisticci. *The Vespasiano Memoirs: Lives of Illustrious Men of the XVth Century.* Renaissance Society of America Reprint Texts 7. Translated by William George and Emily Waters.

Introduction by Myron P. Gilmore. Toronto: University of Toronto Press in association with the Renaissance Society of America, 1997. A wonderful collection of biographies of the clients of the 15th-century Florentine bookseller Vespansiano da Bisticci.

Waley, Daniel. *Siena and the Sienese in the Thirteenth Century.* Cambridge: Cambridge University Press, 1991. A scholarly but still accessible general history of Siena during its most celebrated period.

Weinstein, Donald. *Savonarola and Florence: Prophesy and Patriotism in the Renaissance.* Princeton, NJ: Princeton University Press, 1970. An important discussion of Savonarola and the role his prophetic sermons played in the millenarian traditions and Humanistic vision of Florence.

Welch, Evelyn. *Art and Society in Italy, 1350–1500.* Oxford History of Art. Oxford: Oxford University Press, 1997. An excellent, illustrated survey of the relationship between art and social structure during the Renaissance.

White, Jonathan. *Italy: The Enduring Culture.* New York: Continuum, 2000. An analysis of the continuities and discontinuities in Italian culture from Dante to the present.

Notes